BISON
BOOKS

RACHEL FISHER MILLS
Courtesy of Oregon Historical
Society, Portland, Oregon

TABITHA BROWN
Courtesy of Pacific University
Forest Grove, Oregon

Covered Wagon Women

Diaries & Letters from the Western Trails 1840–1849

Volume 1

edited & compiled by
KENNETH L. HOLMES

Introduction to the Bison Books Edition
by Anne M. Butler

University of Nebraska Press
Lincoln and London

⊖ The paper in this book meets the minimum requirements of American
National Standard for Information Sciences—Permanence of Paper for
Printed Library Materials, ANSI Z39.48-1984.

First Bison Books printing: 1995

Library of Congress Cataloging-in-Publication Data
Covered wagon women: diaries & letters from the western trails, 1840–1849
/ edited and compiled by Kenneth L. Holmes; introduction to the Bison
Books edition by Anne M. Butler.
p.   cm.
Originally published: Glendale, Calif.: A. H. Clark Co., 1983.
"Reprinted from volume one . . . of the original eleven-volume edition"—
T.p. verso.
"Volume I."
Includes index.
ISBN 0-8032-7277-4 (pa: alk. paper)
1. Women pioneers—West (U.S.)—Biography.   2. West (U.S.)—His-
tory.   3. West (U.S.)—Biography.   4. Overland journeys to the Pacific.
5. Frontier and pioneer life—West (U.S.)   I. Holmes, Kenneth L.
F591.C79   1996
978—dc20
95-21200   CIP

Reprinted from volume one (1983) of the original eleven-volume edition
titled *Covered Wagon Women: Diaries and Letters from the Western Trails,
1840–1890,* published by the Arthur H. Clark Company, Glendale, California.

Dedicated to
CLIFFORD MERRILL DRURY
whose three-volume series,
First White Women Over the Rockies,
laid the foundation for much
of what follows here.

INTRODUCTION TO THE BISON BOOKS EDITION
Anne M. Butler

O that I had time and talent
to describe this curious country.
—Elizabeth Dixon Smith

Happily, the concept of a women's West no longer surprises us. Women were shaped by the West, but they did their own share of shaping, leaving a female signature on land and lives. It took Americans several decades to acknowledge this historical reality. The recognition came slowly, but we have moved beyond an earlier perception of the West as an arena reserved for male exploits. While once historians described the West as the exclusive territory of trappers, cowboys, miners, and soldiers, all of whom sprang from Anglo stock, the region is now recognized as far more gendered in its history. Women like Elizabeth Dixon Smith, the articulate and observant pilgrim quoted above, have identity and voice in the annals of western history.

Scholarly and popular publications alike have pushed back the confining parameters of western history to reveal a rich panorama of social, economic, and political forces that molded women's lives. Noted historians have turned out revealing and important works about women in the West. Yet, even as the scholarly investigation of western women has expanded, so the discussion over the nature of the experience has intensified. The more we know, the harder it seems to be to pinpoint the meaning of life for pioneer women in the American West. Did migrant women look to the West with quivering fear or joyful anticipation? What changes threaded through family interactions as a result of the struggle to relocate in the West? Were men and women affected differently by these incredible journeys? Did the pioneer experience exacerbate conditions of oppression for American women, or did it release women from cultural and economic limitations? Did the arrival of white women add to the mounting racial conflicts in the West, or did women reach across cultural divisions and perceive gender commonalities? Did pioneer wives and mothers encourage general female independence, or did they intensify the oppression of all women through their own cultural and habitual sexism and racism? Clearly, the response of Anglo women to the pioneer era remains a thorny issue for historians.

Much of the scholarly literature rests on the premise that the time period, which included a growth in American manufactures, a flood of new immigrants, and an explosion in domestic migration and western land grabbing, also saw the rise of a powerful social philosophy, ultimately known as the cult of true womanhood.[1] In the mid-1800s, as the nation resonated with a vigorous spirit that encouraged individualism and personal achievement, a counter message cast a long shadow across the lives of women. While men partook of coarse national impulses, women were valued in the private sphere, inside the American home. The message women got effectively shut them out of opportunities for rigorous education, professional advancement, political involvement, and economic independence. This exclusion occurred simultaneously with the championing of education, advancement, involvement, and independence all along the ladder of America's masculine hierarchy.

Thus, the privacy of the home came to circumscribe the legitimate arena for womanly attention. Within the domain of the home, women could cultivate traits designed to make them pure, passive, and pious. In a rough-and-tumble era of American history, women, denied access to public avenues of power, became exclusively responsible for creating a family sanctuary. With this charge to be the moral guardians of the family, society dictated that a woman's fulfillment centered on domesticity, childbearing, and the reflected glory of her husband.

Although the notion seems incredibly simplistic, almost amusing, it assumed a power unto itself. It infiltrated all aspects of womanhood—physical, intellectual, and spiritual—producing inflexible rules of female conduct. With a hefty assist from ministers, physicians, journalists, and a wide range of self-appointed "authorities," the cult of true womanhood emerged as the single definition of the female experience.

At odds with this rigorous standard were the public values of the day, the institution of slavery and the specific lives of thousands of women—poor immigrants, factory workers, women of color—for whom the code had neither practical nor appealing application. Such women ignored the cult's dicta, intent on actively salvaging as much of their own culture as possible within the context of an ever stronger white Protestant America. However, the cult of domesticity and passivity touched the hearts and minds of many women, especially of the hard-working white lower-middle class, who yearned for a life that would allow them the designation of "lady."

This powerful ideology of acceptable womanhood provides the lens through which scholars have examined a range of womanly activities across the spectrum of U.S. history. Grounded in eastern intellectual and social forces, the cult of true womanhood invites western applications, since, with its rigid female limitations, it contrasts so dramatically with burgeoning frontier society. Perhaps nowhere in the nation, between 1830 and 1900, were power strategies, self-aggrandizement, and personal advancement played out with cruder force than in the American West. The more recent bonding of a feminine eastern ideology with the masculine frontier West has shifted the historian's lens over time, illuminating new shadings and angles within western women's experiences and providing a rich literature for consideration.

In 1979, John Mack Faragher, in *Women and Men on the Overland Trail,* ventured into the murky waters of spousal relationships, using the overland trail as the framework for his investigation. Faragher predicted his important study on the assertion that an uneven power structure between men and women guided family relationships.[2] Faragher's female migrants found little in the travel west that altered or mitigated their difficult role in marriage. In Faragher's view, rather than a liberating adventure, the trip to the West meant more and harder work for women. He argued that overland migrations did not bring about significant changes in gender roles and expectations, but solidified existing power divisions between men and women. Faragher's women arrived in the West overworked and still constrained by the values that enclosed their lives in the East. Nonetheless, in the overland trek, wives shared a commonality of purpose with husbands, a bond that explained why marriages survived. Although Faragher later somewhat adjusted his historical lens concerning *Women and Men on the Overland Trail,* nothing alters the fact that he introduced provocative ideas to western women's history.[3]

A collection of reminiscences gathered from white women who lived in nineteenth-century Kansas served as the foundation for Joanna L. Stratton's 1981 work, *Pioneer Women: Voices from the Kansas Frontier.* This book directed popular attention to pioneer women as historical informants. Stratton offered irrefutable evidence that ordinary women stored a solid portion of the national experience within their personal histories.[4] Although the book highlighted the diversity of women's lives, it tended to accept at face value the collective distant memory. Stratton stepped back from a healthy skepticism that would have conceded the slippery nature of human recollection. In the end, Stratton's gentle management of the reminiscences left an impression of only the heroic and the brave. Valid assessments of many individuals, these noble labels did not envelop women's lives with the larger historical context.

In 1982, Lillian Schlissel, in *Women's Diaries of the Westward Journey,* placed new templates over the overland trail by looking to the perspective of women. Schlissel, drawing on an impressive array of contemporary letters and diaries, saw critical communication gaps and different life plans separating the spheres of women and men in the nineteenth century.[5] Although husbands and wives spoke the same language, used the same vocabulary, they did not necessarily share parallel responses to the surrounding new world. Their personal goals diverged; their personal fears differed. For men, the economic prize at the end of the trip diminished the dangers of the road. For women, the overland trip, with its many hazards, intensified ordinary concerns about family safety and survival. Thus, Schlissel explained the reluctance of many women migrants. This study reversed long-cherished notions of westward migration as a happy outing in which both men and women viewed the "conquest of the West" as the proverbial chance of a lifetime. Lillian Schlissel forcefully showed the importance of viewing historical events through women's eyes as well as men's, because separate gender visions lead to separate interpretations. She distinguished between the man's zest for an exciting way to change his life and the woman's concern for maintaining family during the trying time of transition. Not merely a tale of adventure versus stability, Schlissel's book revealed that the overall lack of alternative lives for married women, their obligation and desire to support husbands, and their commitment to family unity led pioneer wives to embark on a trip that often seemed overwhelming to the spirit. Schlissel demonstrated that the inclusion of women in the historical account produces a fuller, richer sense of the past, even as we labor to untangle the conflicting threads.

Sandra Myres's 1982 book, *Westering Women and the Frontier Experience, 1800–1915,* continued the debate over women's roles in the West. However, Myres elevated the West to the primary focus of her research, with women as one set of regional players. According to Myres, the West offered special prospects for those of both sexes with the gumption to grab a western brass ring. She conjectured that a geographic move might not have liberated women economically and politically, but their lives changed in substantive ways in the West. Myres pointed to western women in new public roles as political leaders, educators, entrepreneurs. In addition, she argued that, on the farm and in the home, western women expanded the parameters of their authority. Myres believed a clear difference existed between the image of womanhood and the lives of women.[6]

Still, the long arm of the cult of true womanhood reached deep into western scholarship. The connections between eastern domesticity and western experience refused to yield to easy resolution. Glenda Riley, in a series of major publications, further honed the discussion, suggesting that the West beckoned to women, but with fewer chances to change than for men. Marital status, employment opportunities, social rank, race and ethnicity, western location—all impinged on a woman's ability to enter a new field of endeavor. Nonetheless, Riley perceived a distinct female frontier, with its "own mode[s] of operation, culture[s], and value system[s]."[7] In *Frontierswomen: The Iowa Experience* and *The Female Frontier,* Riley challenged scholars to rethink the variety of glib assertions they held about western women.[8] But above all, the title of her 1992 book, *A Place to Grow,* summed up Riley's perception of the female world of the West.[9] With each new book, Riley called for expanding research models to include ethnicity, race, and class. She, perhaps more than any other scholar, argued for a female historical kaleidoscope that would delicately rearrange the endless patterns of the "real West" for women.

Clearly, the scholars mentioned here converge, overlap, and differ in their views of women in the West. All have participated in making women central to understanding the West across time. Some mesh together more comfortably than others. Sandra Myres eschewed the work of John Mack Faragher, while Lillian Schlissel questioned Myres's *Westering Women and the Frontier Experience.*[10] Susan Armitage critiqued Glenda Riley's *Female Frontier,* and Antonia Castenada chided almost everyone who wrote about western women.[11] By the

1990s, the debate about women in the West once again shifted and reassembled; scholars distanced themselves from an exclusive focus on the Anglo pioneer wife and mother.[12]

But what accounts for this interpretive uncertainty? Is one group of scholars right and another wrong? What information guides us when confronted by conflicting interpretations? For example, the letters and diaries gathered into this volume represent the writings and reflections of thirteen different Anglo women who turned their faces to the American West in the 1840s. How can we make sense of their words and understand their historical import? Where do they fit in a changing research model that has branched beyond a one-culture, one-race definition of the West? How can we integrate the writings of thirteen white women into a scholarly debate that increasingly takes on the hues of many cultures? Why should a baker's dozen from among perhaps a half million migrants compel our attention?

Extraordinary national changes pulsated through the United States just as these thirteen women moved from the East to the West. The very wagon trains in which they traveled gave visual affirmation to these women of their own participation in a dramatic national undertaking. These women, who trod through the routines of everyday life, must have felt some place in the larger context of the history of their time.

In the 1840s, the decade covered by volume 1 of *Covered Wagon Women: Diaries and Letters from the Western Trails,* America's expansionist zest gripped the nation. The United States stood on the cusp of the major diplomatic thrusts that delineated its contiguous boundaries. For all its political rhetoric and florid editorials, expansionism, in practical terms, depended on Anglo- and European-stock pioneers to secure the new western territories. Pioneer migrations, when multiplied by the thousands, translated into the dramatic upheaval and relocation of American families. Through the shifting and the moving, easterners, almost without realizing it, transformed themselves into westerners. When the wagon dust settled, the recently arrived citizens of the West had created a new and unpredictable political constituency for the federal government.

Women composed one element of that constituency and within their gender, many groupings. Despite their exclusion from the legal procedures of government, women still lived as Americans with ideas and convictions about the democratic process. Although pioneer women seldom expounded on political philosophy in their personal writings, it would be folly to assume them uninformed in matters of government. Actually, they often demonstrated a bonding to governmental principles and a sense of national identity. Such is found in Louisiana Strentzel's poignant comment about the caravan's mourning the death of former President James K. Polk. In Oregon, Tabitha Brown carefully monitored the impact of local politics on school construction. Keturah Belknap understood the diplomatic nuances in Joe Meek's trip to Washington, D.C. Each reflected her sense of American citizenship.

If these women of the halcyon days of Manifest Destiny took a small part in the open discussion of politics, they showed no such reticence in the realm of economics. In a nation given to exaggerated economic swings, few Americans could have missed the grueling financial hardships that existed between 1839 and 1843, a seemingly endless extension of the Panic of 1837. America's roller-coaster economy, complete with bank closures, specie suspension, and unsound financial management, taught average families more about monetary risk than they wanted to know.

With family survival wedded to successful farming, women had to know about agricultural practices and market prices. Western women could not afford the luxury of economic ignorance and they did not expect to be marginal voices in the management of family finances. Letter writer Phoebe Stanton cut through the overly optimistic account of her husband, Alfred, to give their eastern relatives a more accurate assessment of their financial status. Twenty-four-year-old Anna Maria King wrote of crops and costs, planting and harvesting, as only a shrewd farmer could do. The widowed Elizabeth Dixon Smith grasped the dynamics of poverty and the strain of feeding seven children. She understood how the principles of supply and demand correlated with sending hungry young sons to the mines for work. An anonymous woman filled her letter with the economic woes of those who tried their chances with urban employment.

In addition, these women wrote back to friends and family who might follow, giving explicit information on the expenses of migration. This practical advice—western woman to eastern woman—in part explains the phases to the overland migrations, which changed and eased with each passing year. The later travelers benefited from the trials of the earliest migrants. They learned how to plan for the trip, what to expect, what to avoid. They heeded the warnings that came from a Betsy Bayley or Donner Party survivor Virginia E. B. Reed, who succinctly directed, "Take no cutoffs."

In the social climate of the 1840s, most Americans felt the growing chill of sectionalism and the rising tide of civil disaffection. Few lived ignorant of the political fights over black slavery or the growing spirit of social reform. Social reorganization joined with political divisiveness and economic seesawing to fuel the American experience.

The women migrants captured the tone and time of these currents. Sometimes they voiced the desires of those seeking spiritual renewal; sometimes they echoed the powerful racism of the nineteenth century. Even as Rachel Fisher dismissed the Sioux as "beggarly," she revealed much about their economic and social condition in 1847. Teenager Sallie Hester, undoubtedly influenced by the murmurs of those around her, called the Pawnee "dangerous and hostile," but most of her diary glowed with the adventure and beauty of her trip. Tamsen Donner, destined to die high in the Sierra Mountains, expressed no fear of the Indians, for perhaps she sensed the real danger lay not with people but with the brutal elements. Mormon midwife Patty Sessions recorded a more engaging encounter with Indians, as well as some piercingly important comments about religious practice among early Mormon women. All carried eastern social values onto an alien terrain and into other cultures. They drew on these values, for good and ill, to sustain themselves in an experience they expected often not to survive.

Nonetheless, women migrants vigorously engaged the region into which they moved. Their letters and diaries show them to have been sharp observers of the land and the people on it. Although often sick and frightened, the women could be lyrical about the stunning beauty around them. Like Elizabeth Dixon Smith, they sensed the grandeur of the West, but circumstances, work, and duty pressed them on.

Almost without exception, once the long overland migration ground to a halt, women wrote effusively of the potential of new locations. Letters and diaries formerly weighted with anxiety and suffering reversed tone and took on celebratory themes, even as families struggled for economic stability. Relieved of the burdens of trail routines, fear of family danger, and exhaustion of travel, women turned toward making a western life for themselves, their husbands, and their children. Surely, in that undertaking they reached back into their earlier lives and thought to reconstruct a previous time. Yet, when they looked inward, these women found intellectual, physical, and spiritual transformation.

Perhaps not wittingly, western women migrants, as they wrote on a broad range of topics, revealed the ways in which they accommodated and resisted the constraints of gender. In the process, each defined her personal sense of womanhood and found her western place. Accordingly, these women fashioned their roles within their own community, built onto the scaffolding of cross-cultural interactions, added to the patterns of regional experience, and enhanced the course of national events.

The voices here are few, the writings brief, the personalities clear. Complete answers to all the questions posed at the outset of this essay are not to be found in the pages of this volume. Yet, each sentence and notation transcends its literal rendering and links these women to the political, social, and economic forces of the era. The depth and the range of these documents give voice to thousands of nameless, silent pioneer women who left no letters and diaries. Thus, these few women enlarge the layered context of a history that seeks to encompass the many aspects of race, class, and gender in the American West.

The content of *Covered Wagon Women: Diaries and Letters from the Western Trails* represents far more than the fragmented legacy of a small group of little-known white women. Each pioneer woman included here contributed her mite of glass to the stunning patterns found in the female kaleidoscope of the American West. Readers can return to these thirteen migrants again and again, looking for new markers that point to western women as fully engaged participants in the shaping of American history.

NOTES

1. The definitive work on this philosophy is Barbara Welter, "The Cult of True Woman-hood, 1820–1860," *American Quarterly* 18 (summer 1966): 151–74.

2. John Mack Faragher, *Women and Men on the Overland Trail* (New Haven: Yale University Press, 1979), 1–15, 179–87.

3. John Mack Faragher, "Twenty Years of Western Women's History," *Montana The Magazine of Western History* (spring 1991): 71–73.

4. Joanna L. Stratton, *Pioneer Women, Voices from the Kansas Frontier* (New York: Simon & Schuster, Touchstone Books, 1981). See for example, 33–44, 205–22, 234–52.

5. Lillian Schlissel, *Women's Diaries of the Westward Journey* (New York: Shocken Books, 1982), 10–16.

6. Sandra L. Myres, *Westering Women and the Frontier Experience, 1800–1915* (Albuquerque: University of New Mexico Press, 1982), 267–70.

7. Glenda Riley, *The Female Frontier: A Comparative View of Women on the Prairie and the Plains* (Lawrence: University Press of Kansas, 1988), 11.

8. Glenda Riley, *Frontierswomen: The Iowa Experience* (Ames: Iowa State University Press, 1981; Iowa Heritage Collection reprint edition, 1994); *The Female Frontier: A Comparative View of Women on the Prairie and the Plains* (Lawrence: University Press of Kansas, 1988).

9. Glenda Riley, *A Place to Grow: Women in the American West* (Arlington Heights, Illinois: Harlan Davidson, 1992).

10. Sandra L. Myres review of John Mack Faragher, *Women and Men on the Overland Trail* in *American Historical Review* 85:1 (February 1980): 210–11; Lillian Schlissel, review of Sandra L. Myres, *Westering Women and the Frontier Experience* in *American Historical Review* 88:4 (October 1983): 1079–80.

11. Susan Armitage, review of Glenda Riley, *The Female Frontier: A Comparative View of Women on the Prairie and the Plains* in *Western Historical Quarterly* 20:2 (May 1989): 220; Antonia Castenada, "Women of Color and the Rewriting of Western History: The Discourse, Politics, and Decolonization of History," *Pacific Historical Review* 61 (November 1992): 501–33.

12. For example: Susan Armitage and Elizabeth Jameson, *The Women's West* (Norman: University of Oklahoma Press, 1987); Sarah Deutsch, *No Separate Refuge: Culture, Class, and Gender on an Anglo-Hispanic Froniter in the American Southwest, 1880–1940* (New York: Oxford University Press, 1987); Vicki Ruiz, *Cannery Women, Cannery Lives: Mexican Women, Unionization and the California Food Processing Industry, 1930–1950* (Albuquerque: University of New Mexico Press, 1987); Vicki Ruiz, Lillian Schlissel, and Janice Monk, *Western Women: Their Land, Their Lives* (Albuquerque: University of New Mexico Press, 1988); Peggy Pascoe, *Relations of Rescue: The Search for Female Moral Authority in the American West, 1874–1939* (New York: Oxford University Press, 1990); Sarah Deutsch, Virginia Scharff, Glenda Riley, and John Mack Faragher, "Historical Commentary: The Contributions and Challenges of Western Women's History," *Montana* (spring 1991): 57–73; Benson Tong, *Unsubmissive Women: Chinese Prostitutes in Nineteenth-Century San Francisco* (Norman: University of Oklahoma Press, 1994).

Contents

Illustrations

Introduction

The chief figure of the American West, the figure of the ages, is not the long-haired, fringed-legging man riding a raw-boned pony, but the gaunt and sad-faced woman sitting on the front seat of the wagon, following her lord where he might lead her, her face hidden in the same ragged sunbonnet which had crossed the Appalachians and Missouri long before. That was America, my brethren! There was the seed of America's wealth. There was the great romance of America – the woman in the sunbonnet; and not, after all, the hero with the rifle across his saddle horn. Who has written her story? Who has painted her picture?

Emerson Hough, *The Passing of the Frontier.*[1]

Who indeed?

She has done it! The woman in the sunbonnet has told her own story. She has painted word pictures of the road she traveled with her family. The words were written right in the wagon on the way west. Sometimes it was in the form of a letter written to the folks back home and sent off from Fort Laramie or Fort Boise, or from the end of the trail in Oregon or California or Utah or some other western locale.

That is what this series is all about. It is a collection of contemporary diaries and letters describing the day by day events of the overland journey – and an occasional odyssey back the other way.

With the publication of volume one of this series we have been able to lay our hands on well over one hundred of these poignant primary records, written

---

[1] (New Haven, Conn., 1920), 93-94.

for the most part by what we might think of as ordinary women telling of an extraordinary experience. It is not our plan to publish items readily available in published form. We have sought out unpublished manuscripts or rare printed journals. Some were published privately for a small number of readers, perhaps relatives, but they are of such universal interest that they are included here.

Most of the writers were housewives and mothers. About ten per cent were teenage girls – fulfilling a mandate of friends back home who at a going-away party presented them with a blank diary as a gift in which to record the great adventure. Most of the writers had the care of children – often large families with as many as six or eight of them.

An occasional diarist was pregnant. Some said not a word about the matter. Note the words of Amelia Knight, who kept a detailed journal of her overland trip in 1853,[2] capping it off with the following final entry written near Milwaukie, Oregon, now a suburb of Portland:

SATURDAY, SEPT. 17 – In camp yet. Still raining. *Noon*. It has cleared off and we are all ready for a start again for some place we don't know where. *Evening*. Came 6 miles and have encamped in a fence corner by a Mr. Lambert's about 7 miles from Milwaukie. Turn our stock out to tolerably good feed.

A few days later my eighth child was born. After this we picked up and ferried across the Columbia River, utilizing a skiff, canoes and flatboat. It took 3 days. Here husband traded 2 yoke of oxen for a half section of land with ½ acre planted to potatoes, a small log cabin and lean-to with no windows. This is the journey's end.

No other diary entry of the 1840's can compare in

[2] Ft. Vancouver Hist. Soc., *Clark Co. Hist.*, VI (1965), 55.

this matter of giving birth with that of Susan Magoffin, wife of a United States military officer, at Bent's Fort while on a journey over the Santa Fe Trail in 1846:[3]

> The mysteries of a new world have been shown to me since last Thursday! In a few short months I should have been a happy mother and made the heart of a father glad, but the ruling hand of a mighty Providence has interposed and by an abortion deprived us of the hope, the fond hope of mortals! . . .
>
> *Friday morning 31st of July.* My pains commenced and continued till 12 o'c. at night, when after much agony and severest of pains, which were relieved a little at times by medicine given by Dctr. Mesure, *all was over.* I sunk off into a kind of lethargy, in *mi alma's* arms. Since that time I have been in my bed till yesterday a little while, and a part of today.
>
> My situation was very different from that of an Indian woman in the room below me. She gave birth to a fine healthy baby, about the same time, *and in half an hour after she went to the River and bathed herself and it,* and this she has continued each day since. Never could I have believed such a thing if I had not been there. . .

The presence of a male doctor was unusual in mid-nineteenth century. Usually the person attending such a birth would have been a midwife. These women were largely unnamed, but one might say that the midwife was often the most important person to have nearby on frontier occasions, and especially on the overland journeys.

One of the midwives is fairly well known. She was the Mormon woman, Patty Bartlett Sessions. Leonard J. Arrington describes her journal as "particularly poignant during the Winter Quarters period."[4] Its

---

[3] Stella M. Drumm, Ed., *Down the Santa Fé Trail and Into Mexico: The Diary of Susan Shelby Magoffin, 1846-1847* (New Haven, Conn., 1926), 67-68. Normally one would think that the Magoffin diary would appear in the present collection. It was judged that it is easily available to readers. Certainly one of the great diaries, it was republished by Yale University Press, 1962.

poignancy is not limited to that time but is also that way during the overland journey from the Winter Quarters to Salt Lake City. She had already become known as "Mother Sessions" long before, and on the westward way she continued to minister to women in child-birth. She also did work, both women's work and men's work, as she mended clothing and wagon covers and also made repairs on the wagon. (Her husband was along but she mentions him not once.)[5] It is with great good fortune that we have been permitted by the Historical Department of the Mormon Church to include the overland part of her daily journal in this volume.

Not only does the prevalence of births attract the attention of the student of overland travel, but the prevalence of death, constant and prevailing.

Picture 25-year-old Rachel Fisher on the way to Oregon in 1847. Read her letters that are printed in this, our first volume. The first, sent back from Fort Laramie, told of the death of her husband, John, on June 6, as she saw him "breathe the last breath of Earthly life without a single grown." Her second letter, written March 18, 1848, from "Tuality County," Oregon, told of the death of her little girl, Angeline, on August 12, 1847. The bodies were both buried along the trail. She arrived in the Oregon country as a young widow with none of her close family left alive. What she did not tell, but it can be gleaned from family records, was that before she had left home in Salem,

4 "Persons for All Seasons: Women in Mormon History," *Brigham Young Univ. Studies*, XX, no. 1, (Fall 1979), 44.

5 Maureen Ursenbach Beecher, "Women's Work on the Mormon Frontier," *Utah Hist. Qtly*, XXXXIX, no. 3 (Summer 1981), 279-81.

Iowa, the young couple had already lost three other children to various diseases.

Walter Prescott Webb, in his classic book, *The Great Plains*, told of a government report that estimated that "each mile of the two-thousand-mile journey cost seventeen lives – a total of thirty-four thousand lives." [6] Any such figure is at best a good guess; but nevertheless the number of deaths was staggering. Of course, the number of deaths in families living back east or in the newly settled western lands makes us stop to think as we seek to relive nineteenth century America.

Most of these women expressed little or no concern about the new wave of the future, women's rights, being enunciated at that time by Amelia Bloomer and a few others. However, four of them – at least – after the 1840's wore the new costume invented by that emancipator of women, and named for her, "bloomers."

It is our purpose to let them tell their own story in their own words, with as little scholarly trimming as possible. There will naturally be some square brackets, but not squads of them marching line by line across the page. We will not place an omnipotent and omnipresent *sic* wherever a word is mis-spelled. It will be assumed that the intent has been to transcribe each word or phrase as accurately as possible. The number of mis-spellings with which we have to deal would sometimes require that there would be hundreds of *sics* in the text. Perhaps the reader can imagine ONE GIGANTIC *SIC* at the end of each volume. If you thought that William Clark of the Lewis and Clark expedition was the most ingenious speller in American history, be prepared for a nice surprise. He was no more in-

---

[6] (Boston, 1931), 149.

ventive a speller than some of our women diarists and
letter writers.

Some of these records have already been published
by some relatives or by some pioneer historical society.
The publishers of these accounts seemed to think that
it was in poor taste to print mother's or grandmother's
writings as she wrote them, mis-spelled, mis-punctu-
ated, or mis-capitalized – or only capitalized in the
strangest places. We disagree with this approach. Nor
will our transcriptions be "edited for readability" as
some such documents have been published in more
scholarly modern productions.[7] Such a method is not
for this publication. The manner of writing, including
spelling, punctuation, and capitalization or lack of it,
is an important statement by the writer. It tells something important about her and about the society in
which she lived and moved and had her being. We believe with Theodore C. Blegen that scholars and their
editors have often shown "inverted provincialism," in
"correcting" the literature of our folk culture.[8] Here
we will be faithful to the writer's own expressions,
crude though they may seem to some readers. Incident-
ally, some of the best literary style is found to have
been written by the hands of the worst spellers. Isn't it
lovely that one woman insisted upon calling her diary
her "Journal of Travails," a Freudian slip of special
meaning to her?

In some cases, however, we do not have the original

---

[7] See John Mack Faragher's review of *Ho for California!: Women's Overland Diaries from the Huntington Library,* edited by Sandra L. Myres (San
Marino, Calif., 1980), in *Western Hist. Qtly,* XIII, no. 1 (January 1982),
69-70. Faragher's book, *Women and Men on the Overland Trail* (New
Haven, 1979), is also helpful.

[8] Theodore C. Blegen, *Grass Roots History* (Port Washington, N.Y., 1947),
3-13.

but instead a hand-written copy or a typescript made by a relative or by some other student of western history. It may not be a completely accurate transcript, but, as the original is no longer available, we use the copy as the best transcript available. In other cases the original was printed by some religious or secular periodical or newspaper, or in book form. If the hand-written original is no longer available, we use the printed copy as the best record at hand, but it has to be second or third best. It is no less important for the record.

The only gestures we have made for the sake of the reader have been as follows:

1. We have added space where phrases or sentences ended and no punctuation was to be found in the original – just enough so that the words, phrases, clauses, and sentences do not run together.

2. We have put the daily journals into diary format even though the original may have been written continuously line by line because of the original writer's shortage of paper.

Many geographic references are mentioned over and over again in the various accounts. The final volume in the set will include a gazeteer, in addition to the index and bibliography, to aid the reader.

Most of the women were white Anglo-Saxon Protestants. Some of them were very devout, wishing over and over that they did not have to travel on the Sabbath. Others never menioned religion in any way – not the Sabbath, nor anything else of a "spiritual" nature. There were also the Mormons, the most prolific diary-writers of all, and some of them saturated their daily entries with religious terminology, while other Mormon women hardly mentioned their faith.

The main triad of daily concerns – concerns that came up over and over again in the journals – were feed and forage for cattle and horses, fuel for fires, and water. Just to use one diary to illustrate this we will take that of Elizabeth Dixon Smith (1847), which is printed later in this first volume. It is one of the great human historical records of all time. Here are some quotes, variations of countless such statements that appear in her diary and many, many others:

> July 4 – "midling feed   found old trunks of cedar to burn."
> July 10 – "encamped on a creek   found feed and willows."
> July 15 – "found wo[o]d and water but no feed to night."
> July 16 – "found feed   layed by to paster our cattle."
> July 30 – "sage still to cook with."
> August 4– "layed by to let our cattle feed and rest."
> August 15 – "Encamped without feed, water or supper."

Then there were the problems of the care of the children, how and where to wash the clothes, the breakdown of a wagon, the straying of animals, and the crossing of countless small streams or washes which were more often met than the occasional river. However, there were drownings in the great rivers, too.

The variety of interests on the part of the writers is manifeset in their diaries: One teen-ager kept a detailed record of every animal seen or heard-of along the way. Several writers were enamored of the variety of plants and went into great detail describing them. Geologists might be jealous of the way some of these unlettered women told of the marvels of geology along the trails. Then there were the grave counters, those who told in detail of the graves seen continually along the way and what was inscribed on the crude markers.

Some went into detail about sickness in their families and among the other emigrants. Others kept a graphic record of Indians seen along the way, fear and prejudice being expressed in some cases, admiration and concern in others.

There are diaries and letters that tell of journeying along all of the major cross-country trails, and some minor ones as well, joining western localities. The first volume, which deals with the 1840's, principally documents the two great overland trails over South Pass, to Oregon, to California, and to Utah. However, there is also an intriguing letter written by Louisiana Strentzel delineating her journey with her family over what was called the Gila Trail into southern California.

Some of the travelers told of variations of the regular routes – experimental short-cuts, if you will – some of these being a shorter and easier way, but others tedious, round-about routes that resulted in long periods of being lost, hungry, and sick.

The key to the trans-continental movement of wagons was that there were great natural roads that, once discovered, could be followed easily by the emigrants. Aubrey L. Haines, in his *Historic Sites Along the Oregon Trail,* suggests that the trail "was hardly a thoroughfare in the modern sense, but more of a 'travel corridor.' " [9]

There is a well-worn anecdote about a tenderfoot and an old-timer and a conversation they had about the way west:

"The Indians must have patronized the railroads well," observed the tenderfoot, "since their trail passes by all the stations."

---

[9] (Gerald, Mo., 1981), ix.

"Law, no," said the old-timer, "they wa'n't no rail-road them days, but when they come to build it, they follered the trail the hull way."

This little folktale illustrates one of the most interesting sagas of the history of the American continent, the story of the development of our historic highways, and later railroads, then highways once more.

Here are the steps in the history of a trail: (1) the great game animals (buffalo, elk, deer); (2) the Indians; (3) non-Indian explorers; (4) the trappers; (5) settlers with wagons; (6) railroads; (7) modern motor highways.

When living in northern Idaho in the late 1940's this author talked to several ancient 90-year-olds about what the land was like when they came. One of these men told me that the Indian grassland trails, made with horses and dragged travoises, were worn to look as if a massive rake had been dragged along the ground leaving parallel and intertwining single horse trails. That is what the great cross-country trails looked like through the mid-continent grasslands.

An early railroad time-table told the history of the Overland Trail in this way:

> No engineer examined its course, determined its grades and curves, marked its fords, built bridges, or surveyed its mountain passes. Selected originally by the instinct that guides wild animals in their choice of easy grades, it developed naturally from a trapper's pathway into an emigrant road, and later into a trade route.[10]

On leaving the Missouri Valley, the wagons passed

---

[10] Much of the material on these pages was written up by the author in the Lewiston, Idaho, *Tribune,* Feb. 17, 1952, "White Man Late Arrival On Idaho Travel Routes."

through tall grasses of the lower plains; then, as the altitude increased, the tall grasses gave way to the short grasses, especially buffalo grass, of the high plains. Here the grass was short but very nutritious. Over much of the way the grass was tightly sodded and made traveling easy. In fact, it was easier for the wagons over the grasslands than it often was in the east on the dusty and muddy roads of civilization before the modern use of macadam. Then the wagons moved across the gentle mountain passes and through the mesquite and desert grass country of what is now southern Idaho and the great basin.[11]

Another thing to keep in mind is that the overland trails were not narrow lines to be followed, but were what Archer B. Hulbert called "ganglia of trails often spreading out miles in width."[12] Occasionally there were narrow places to travel through or over or down, and then there developed ruts that are still visible in some places. Hulbert, who played an important role in the movement of the 1920's to survey the great trails, added, "new tracks were broken out in different seasons in the same year; in different years other courses were followed; in most places these trails consisted of parallel tracks rods in width, sometimes miles in width. . . This helps one to understand, although many miles apart, how rival towns may claim to have been located on an old trail; often both claims are perfectly correct."[13]

---

[11] United States Department of Agriculture, Wash., D.C., *Grass, The Yearbook of Agriculture, 1948*. Many good maps and references in this classic.

[12] "Western Trails: Work of the Stewart Commission," *The Frontier, A Magazine of the Northwest,* IX(no. 1 (November 1928), 52-54.

[13] *Ibid.,* 53.

Our women, through their contemporary on-the-spot records, will help us to see what the way west was actually like as their wagons creaked their way over the "travel corridors."

Decisions have had to be made about how much to include of the preliminary records telling of life before the journey began somewhere in the east or the middle west – also about how much of the story of life after the arrival at the western destination. In these cases we have tended to be inclusive rather than exclusive, feeling that both the prologue and the epilogue are often as revealing as the story of the journey itself. This was not the case, however, with several about which we judged the prelude or aftermath was either too long, or that it was not as significant as it might be, or that we would have to conserve space, making room for other overland journeys, our principal goal.

The main sources of the overland records have been the historical societies and libraries throughout the United States, university and college libraries, and public libraries, state and local. The western state historical societies and state libraries have supplied a major share of the manuscripts. The Bancroft Library, Berkeley, and the Huntington Library at San Marino, California, have been unfailingly helpful, as has the staff at Yale University's Beinecke Rare Book and Manuscript Library. More than any other institution, however, the Oregon Historical Society in Portland has been the richest treasure trove of materials and very wise in advice and help. Special mention should also be made of the kindness of the library staff at the Western Oregon State College (the new name for Oregon College of Education at Monmouth), where the editor has taught for many years. Our library has an especially fine collection of western materials, and the author has virtually lived in the collection over several years.

Perhaps the distinctive feature of this collection of diaries and letters, however, is the number of documents from private family collections. We have used several methods for finding them. We have written letters-to-the-editor columns of newspapers and have had response from persons in large and small communities and on the farm. We have telephoned KGO, the giant talk radio station in San Francisco and have been allowed to describe at length the project and have had an amazing response. Quite a numer of otherwise unknown journals and letters have been discovered in this way. The KGO announcers have been unfailingly helpful in this part of the venture. Then we have talked, both publicly and privately, to groups and individuals. Through a conversation with a friend one prime journal, from as close as three blocks from our home here in Monmouth, was located.

All of this has convinced us that there are still many documentary sources, treasures of this sort, all over our region and throughout the country. There are families and individuals who have in their possession, stowed away in some dresser or desk drawer, a diary or a letter written by great-grandmother while traveling overland. In the introductions to the individual items throughout this publication we will be very specific about how we found them. And we hope that the publication of this project will put us on the scent of even more trail records.

This work is a follow-up on that of Dr. Clifford Merrill Drury of Pasadena, California. This former

pastor of Pacific Northwest Presbyterian churches and
professor at San Francisco Theological Seminary at
San Anselmo, California, is now retired. Over the years
he became a specialist and authority on the work of
the American Board of Foreign Missions emissaries
to the Indians of the Pacific Northwest during the
1830's and afterwards. In 1963 the Arthur H. Clark
Company published in three volumes Drury's *First
White Women Over the Rockies,* with the sub-title,
*Diaries, Letters, and Biographical Sketches of the Six
Women of the Oregon Mission who made the Overland
Journey in 1836 and 1838.* In a sense the work we are
beginning here is a continuation of the above volumes.

The 1840's were marked by a modest growth of non-
Indian population in the Oregon Country. The Federal
Census of 1850, taken in the summer, revealed a count
of 13,294,[14] the population equivalent of a small town
or a middle-sized college today. California had a population, not counting Indians, of less than 8,000 in 1846.
Then came the gold rush, and 115,000 persons, mostly
male, were added to California's population.[15] Utah's
population in 1850 was 11,380.[16]

The best analysis of the numbers crossing the Plains
to Oregon, California, and Utah from 1840 through
1860 is found in John D. Unruh, Jr., *The Plains Across,*
a thoroughgoing study of the overland movement, published in 1979.[17] Unruh's tables on pages 119 and 120

[14] Lloyd D. Black, "Middle Willamette Valley Population Growth," Oregon
Hist. Qtly., XLIII, no. 1 (March 1942), 39-54.

[15] David Lavender, *California, A Bicentennial History* (New York, 1976),
15.

[16] Richard D. Poll, General Ed., *Utah's History* (Provo, 1978), 668.

[17] Unruh's book was published by the University of Illinois Press, Urbana.
Tragically, the young author did not live to see the publication of this
important book.

are especially helpful, giving the latest, and probably the most reliable estimates of the numbers of emigrants over the great overland trail and its subsidiaries year by year. His figures of pre-gold rush overlanders as 11,512 for Oregon, 2,735 for California, and 4,600 for Utah, a total of 18,847, show how relatively meager was the number of travelers before 1849. Then his estimate for 1849 indicates that only 450 went to Oregon that year, 1,500 to Utah, and a booming 25,000 to California. This is the tip off as to why we have, so far, no women's journals for Oregon in 1849. But we only have two for California for 1849 – why? Simply because there was a vast predominance of men on the gold rush trail for that year.

When we look at the number of women who wrote overland diaries and letters for the decade of the 1840's in our first volume, it does not loom large. So far we have seven women who traveled to Oregon and wrote about it and four to California. There are undoubtedly more that we have not been able to locate.

The number of diaries and letters burgeoned out for the 1850's with by far the largest number coming from the years 1852 and 1853. They dwindled off for the rest of the decade, and then there were a few yearly for the rest of the century. In later years there were a number of diaries of shorter journeys within the far and Rocky Mountain west. Other states became the destination: Colorado, Idaho, Montana, Nevada, Arizona. Many of the diaries that come from the post-1850's decades are quite interesting, often paralleling the railroad tracks on the transcontinental journey with much waving of hands and smiling between railroad passengers and wagoneers.

Thus the women tell their own story, right as it was happening, or immediately afterwards. "Immediacy" is the key word. These are primary documents of the first order. No fond recollections written years later can compare.

Theodore T. Geer, Governor of Oregon from 1899 to 1903, grandson of Joseph C. Geer, who married one of our diarists, Elizabeth Dixon Smith, tells in his book, *Fifty Years in Oregon,*[18] of attending a Fourth of July celebration of the Sons and Daughters of Oregon Pioneers in Salem a few years before publishing his 1912 book. The orator of the occasion dwelt upon the virtues of the "Pilgrim Fathers," "paying them a red-hot tribute for their many privations." After this speech the presiding officer gave others a chance to speak, and a well-known pioneer lawyer uttered the following matchless words:

Mr. President, I was very much interested in the eulogy the orator of the day paid to the Pilgrim Fathers, all of which was no doubt deserved; but I want to say a word for the Pilgrim Mothers. All my life, Mr. President, I have heard speakers sing the praises of the Pilgrim Fathers for the great hardships they underwent. It has always been the Pilgrim Fathers this and the Pilgrim Fathers that, and I think the time has come when we should give due credit to the Pilgrim Mothers, for they not only endured all the hardships of the Pilgrim Fathers, but, in addition, endured the Pilgrim Fathers besides.

KENNETH L. HOLMES

Monmouth, Oregon, 1982

---

[18] (New York, 1912), 15.

Routes of the Covered Wagon Women

The approximate routes of the major overland trails used by the women in volume I are shown by a dotted line. Sources of information:

Conkling, Roscoe P. *The Butterfield Overland Mail, 1857–1869:* Vol. 3 (Atlas). Glendale, Cal: 1947.

Hafen, L. R., and R. L. Layton. "Fur Country of the Far West (map)," *Mountain Men and the Fur Trade of the Far West,* I. Glendale, Cal: 1965.

Haines, Aubrey L. *Historic Sites along the Oregon Trail.* Gerald, Mont: 1981.

Hunt, Thomas H. *Ghost Trails to California.* Palo Alto, Cal: 1974.

"Map of Pioneer Trails, 1541–1867." Van Nuys, Cal: 1972.

Morgan, Dale L. *Rand McNally's Pioneer Atlas of the American West.* Chicago: 1956.

"Historical Map of the United States." Washington: National Geographic Society, June, 1953.

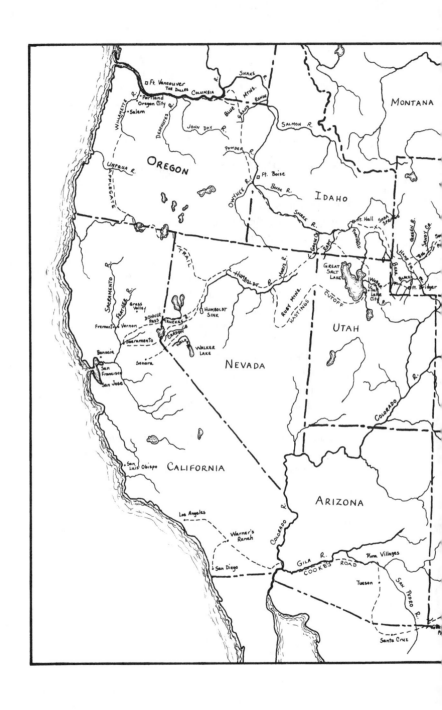

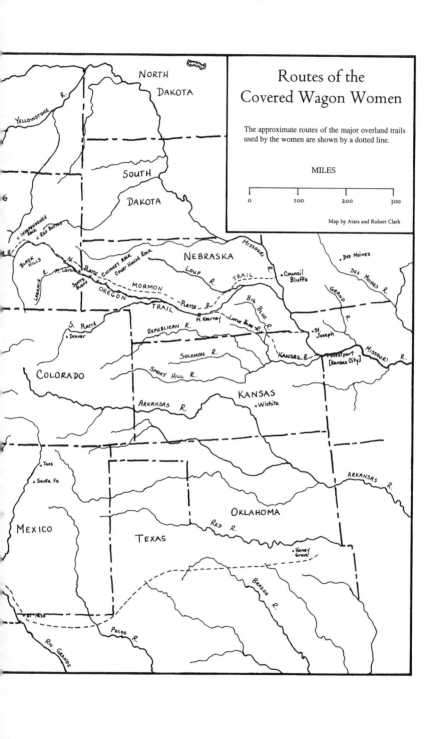

Routes of the
Covered Wagon Women

The approximate routes of the major overland trails used by the women are shown by a dotted line.

MILES

0   100   200   300

Map by Atara and Robert Clark

NORTH DAKOTA

SOUTH DAKOTA

NEBRASKA

KANSAS

COLORADO

OKLAHOMA

TEXAS

MEXICO

Yellowstone R.

Independence Rock
Red Buttes
Black Hills
Laramie R.
Ft. Laramie
Scotts Bluff
Platte R.
Chimney Rock
Court House Rock
OREGON TRAIL
MORMON TRAIL
Platte R.

Loup R.

Missouri R.

Des Moines
Des Moines R.
Council Bluffs
Grand R.

S. Platte
Denver
Republican R.
Ft. Kearney
Little Blue R.
Big Blue R.
St. Joseph
Solomon R.
Smoky Hill R.
Kansas R.
Westport (Kansas City)
Missouri R.

ARKANSAS R.
Wichita

Taos
Santa Fe

ARKANSAS R.

Red R.
Honey Grove
Brazos R.

El Paso
Pecos R.
Rio Grande

Across the Plains in 1845 ❦ Betsey Bayley

INTRODUCTION

Her maiden name had been Elizabeth Munson, nick-named "Betsey." She and Daniel Dodge Bayley were married in Madison County, Ohio, on February 14, 1824. She was born in Hartford, Connecticut, on February 29, 1804 [1] a leap-year baby. Daniel was a native of Grafton County, New Hampshire, born July 8, 1801.[2] He was listed in the 1850 Federal Census of Oregon as a farmer. There are other sources that designate him as a shoemaker and a merchant. He served as postmaster both of Chehalem, and of Garibaldi, Oregon, the latter town which he is supposed to have named for the great Italian patriot, who was a Bayley hero.[3]

When the Bayleys crossed the Plains in 1845, there were seven children. They, too, were listed in the 1850 census as Timothy, 20 years; Caroline, 18; Mianda, 16; Bishop Asbury, 11; Zernai, 9; Iola, 7, and Delphine, 4 years old. All of the children were born in Springfield, Clark County, Ohio, except the last-named who was born in Missouri.[4]

The Bayley family had moved from Ohio to the area of Savannah, Missouri, near St. Joseph, in 1841. Even at that time they had ideas of farming much farther west, looking

---

[1] Myron A. Munson, *The Munson Record,* 2 vols. (New Haven, 1895), I:503-07.

[2] Donna M. Wojcik, *The Brazen Overlanders of 1845* (Portland, 1976), p. 384.

[3] Lewis A. McArthur, *Oregon Geographic Names,* 4th Ed. (Portland, 1974), pp. 147, 302-03.

[4] Elsie Youngberg, *Oregon Territory, 1850 Census* (Lebanon, Oregon, 1970), p. 301; Wojcik, *op. cit.,* pp. 384-85.

forward to taking the long trek to Oregon sometime in the
future. Daniel proceeded to prepare the wood and to plan
for the construction of two wagons of light, tough wood.
A granddaughter told many years later of the family tradition about his preparations: "He had seasoned this
wood two years, boiled in oil, chosen every piece himself,
and like the great Temple of Solomon there was no un-
worthy piece found therein. Strong and tough but light.
The yokes for his oxen were light too. Every ounce considered on such a trip." [5]

In the organization of the "Savannah Oregon Emigrating
Society" Daniel Bayley acted as chairman at the April 28,
1845, meeting at the encampment at Missouri Bottom.
There he was chosen as a member of the "executive
council." This was a well-organized company, with a well-
thought-out constitution. There are several extant versions
of this document, but the most interesting one is that which
was published in the Weston, Missouri, *Journal,* on March
15, 1845.[6]

Betsey Bayley's reminiscent letter written in 1849 is a
record of their journey to Oregon and of conditions after
arriving there. It is especially good in recording the story
of the days they wandered on the east side of the Cascade
range, having been led astray by the ex-mountain man
Stephen Meek.

There is one fascinating episode that took place on the
overland journey that is described in Betsey Bayley's letter:

At Fort Hall the Indians came to our camp and said they wanted
to trade. They trade horses for wives. Mr. Bayley joked with

[5] "Calbreath Document," in author's possession. Copied from original
loaned by Mrs. Evelene Calbreath, Portland, Oregon.

[6] *Quarterly of the Oregon Hist. Soc.,* IV, no. 3 (Sept. 1903), "Oregon
Material Taken from a File of an Independence (Mo.) and Weston (Mo.)
Paper for 1844 and 1845," pp. 278-90; also XXV, no. 4 (Dec. 1924), Fred
Lockley, "The McNemees and Tetherows with the Migration of 1845, Organi-
zation Documents of That Migration," pp. 353-77.

them, and asked a young Indian how many horses he would give for Caroline. The Indian said "three." Mr. Bayley said, "give me six horses and you can have her," all in a joke. The next day he came after her, and had the six horses, and seemed determined to have her. He followed our wagons for several days, and we were glad to get rid of him without any trouble.

This is an example of one of those tales that manage to grow with telling over a long period of time. It became a part of Oregon folklore. The numbers of horses grew from three and six to thirty and sixty, and the trade is supposed to have actually taken place with the dubious climax that the men of the expedition raided the Indian camp later and rescued the girl.[7] This contemporary document is a corrective for the tall tale of later years.

By selling one wagon and a yoke of oxen at The Dalles, the Bayleys were able to continue down the Columbia to the Willamette River and to the area where Portland had just been founded and named in 1844. Daniel Bayley there heard of a man named Sidney Smith who was seeking new settlers to take up land in his neighborhood in the fertile Chehalem Valley, where Smith had already pioneered as a settler. It must have been quite a surprise to this bachelor to have a family with seven children to move in on him in his log cabin, but that is what happened. Naturally this brought Sidney Smith and the Bayley girls into such proximity that the next step was predictable. In 1846 17-year-old Mianda became his wife.

Another contemporary document that is strangely poetic in its legal language is the official description of the Bayley claim in the Chehalem Valley in the Oregon Provisional Government land records:

Daniel F. Bayley claims 640 acres of land in Yam Hill County situated as follows, To Wit: Commencing at a tree marked on

7 "Kidnaped by Indians, A Pioneer's Story," Portland *Oregonian,* May 20, 1911.

the West bank of the North Fork of the Yam Hill river, being
the northerly corner of Frederick Pauls claim. Thence northerly
along said north fork crossing the same at the mouth of a small
creek two miles – Thence westerly half a mile to a tree marked:
Thence southerly two miles to a tree marked on David Pauls
north line: Thence along said line to the place of beginning,
which he holds by personal occupancy. Dated Oregon City, 4th
June 1846.[8]

Notice that the wife is not even mentioned in this trans-
action by which the family settled on a donation claim a
full square mile in extent as was allowed by the Oregon
Provisional Government. In reality the husband would have
been able only to obtain one-half a square mile without
having Betsey as a wife.

Betsey Bayley lived ten years in Oregon. She died on
her 31st wedding anniversary, February 14, 1855.[9]

As with all pioneer families, death was a near neighbor.
A little more than a year later the following story appeared
in the pioneer newspaper, the *Oregon Statesman* of Salem,
in its issue of May 20, 1856:

SUICIDE. – Tim Bailey, [a common misspelling] of Yamhill, a young man, and son of Daniel D. Bailey, of Chehalem, in
that county, recently committed suicide by taking poison. We are
told that five or six years ago he had about $6,000, and said he
was going to live on that as long as it lasted, and when it was
gone kill himself. He spent it, drinking pretty freely, and with
the last bought the poison with which he put an end to his
existence.[10]

One happy aspect of the Bayley story that got the attention of the public over many years was the longevity of
the five sisters who came over the Oregon Trail in 1845.
All lived long rich lives, and this was duly noted in the
newspapers of the day. On June 3, 1899, and again on

8 Oregon State Arch., Provisional Land Records, Vol. 2, p. 44.
9 Wojcik, *op. cit.*, p. 384.   10 Page 3, column 2.

May 20, 1911, the Portland *Oregonian* published extensive stories about the five Bayley sisters, all "Pioneers of
Oregon."

It is an anacronism that the letter as it is reproduced
here is taken from a handwritten copy of a newspaper story
in the Sabina, Ohio *News,* and reprinted in the *Oregonian.*
All searching through the files of the latter newspaper has
so-far been fruitless. The original has not been located.
The manuscript copy is in the library of the Oregon Historical Society, Portland.

THE LETTER OF BETSEY BAYLEY

Chehalem Valley, Yamhill County, Oregon
                                        Sep 20, 1849
Mrs. Lucy P. Griffith, South Charleston, Ohio
    My Dear Sister:

It is a long time since I have seen or heard from
you, and I don't know whether I am writing to the
dead or the living. There is a vast distance between
us; the Rocky mountains separate us. We left Missouri
in the year 1845, and started on our pilgrimage to
Oregon territory. The fore part of our journey was
pleasant. The company we started in consisted of sixty-
four wagons. We had splendid times until we took
what is called "Meek's cut off". You have no doubt
heard of the terrible suffering the people endured on
that road. We followed this road until is was impossible to go further. We camped at a spring which we
gave the name of "The Lost Hollow," because there
was very little water there. We had men out in every
direction in search of water. They traveled forty or
fifty miles in search of water, but found none. You

cannot imagine how we all felt. Go back we could not,
and we knew not what was before us. Our provisions
were failing us. There was sorrow and dismay depicted
on every countenance. We were like mariners lost at
sea, and in this mountainous wilderness we had to remain for five days. At last we concluded to take a north-
westerly direction, and soon the joyful news sounded
through the caravan that the advance guard had come
to water. The mountains looked like volcanoes and the
appearance that one day there had been an awful thun-
dering of volcanoes and a burning world. The valleys
were all covered with a white crust and looked like
salaratus. Some of the company used it to raise their
bread. After we got in the right direction people began
to get sick; the water drank was wholesome. I think
the health of my family was preserved by accident.
At the Lost Hollow I filled all the vessels that would
hold water, and among the number was a tar keg, so
when the good water failed we were supplied from the
tar keg; anyhow, we never got sick. I saw a great many
curiosities on the journey; the buffalo and hot springs
where water boiled up hot enough to scald hogs, the
natural clay houses, a great many Indians of different
tribes. Some of these go stark; this tribe they call the
Digger Indians; their food consists of bugs, crickets,
ants and worms. In winter they live in the ground and
in summer they wander from place to place. We had
no difficulty with the Indians but once. At Fort Hall
the Indians came to our camp and said they wanted
to trade. They trade horses for wives. Mr. Bayley
joked with them, and asked a young Indian how many
horses he would give for Caroline. The Indian said
"three". Mr. Bayley said, "give me six horses and you

can have her", all in a joke. The next day he came
after her, and had the six horses, and seemed determined to have her. He followed our wagons for several days, and we were glad to get rid of him without
any trouble. The Indians never joke, and Mr. Bayley
took good care ever after not to joke with them.

We left Missouri on the 22d of April and arrived
in Chehalem Valley on the 13th of December, all well
and hearty, and have been so ever since. Oregon is the
healthiest country I ever lived in; there is no prevailing disease, and many people come here for health.
The climate is mild and pleasant, and the air pure and
bracing. I have kept fresh meat for three weeks, good
and fresh without salt. Chehalem Valley is a most
beautiful place. It is surrounded with hills, mountains
and beautiful groves. We live in full view of Mount
Hood, the top of which is covered with eternal snow.
The country abounds in almost all kinds of vegetation.
It is one of the best wheat countries in the world. You
can sow wheat any time of the year, and you are sure
of a good crop. Vegetables do well; cabbage will grow
all winter. I have seen heads of cabbage branch out
from an old stalk that was three years old. The country produces almost all kinds of fruit – whortleberries,
blackberries, thimbleberries, strawberries, etc. The
first year we came here strawberries bloomed all winter, but in 1847 we had a hard winter; the snow laid
on the ground for three weeks, but I did not think
this a hard winter, compared with Missouri or Ohio.
In this country it scarcely ever snows, and if any snow
falls at all it melts quickly. Men can work in thin shirt
sleeves all winter. Oregon is settling very rapidly.
People are flocking here from all parts of the world.

The population of Oregon at present is about 9000. Every thing was prosperous until the breaking out of the gold fever in California, when the men, most of them left plow and ax in search of the glittering dust. Two millions of dollars have been brought in less than a year and a half, and somebody coming every day. We live in a very pleasant part of the country, and are now doing better than at any time during our lives. We have a farm of 160 acres under fence, and a fine young orchard coming on, and I hope to reap the benefit thereof and have a long life of happiness under the "vine and fig tree" of my own planting, for happiness consists in a contented mind. It took us seven months and twenty-one days to reach Oregon from Missouri. This was a long time to live in a wagon, and it seems, now that we are here, that I am in a foreign land but in my imagination I often visit the old cottage where we have spent many happy days together with our dear parents, and I shall never forget the good instructions received from the lips of one of the dearest of mothers, and often pray that we may be as good as she was. Give my love to your little ones, and to my brothers and sisters. If you receive this write me. I remain yours, in the bonds of love and sisterly affection, Betsey Bayley.

A Letter from the Luckiamute Valley

⸸ Anna Maria King

INTRODUCTION

The Luckiamute River of Oregon flows into the Willamette from the west not far south of the Monmouth-Independence area where the editor of this set of books has lived for many years. The Luckiamute pronounced LUCKY-ah-mute, with accent on the first syllable) flows through the beautiful Kings Valley,[1] named for Nahum King, whose two sons were involved in the life of Anna Maria King, the writer of this choice letter. Although the typed and printed versions were signed both by Stephen and Maria, it is clear from internal evidence that the letter was written by the wife. Her name appears in various other records as Maria, Mariah, and Marie. She seems to have signed it both as Maria and Mariah. She also used two spellings for her first name, Anne and Anna.

The letter is dated 1846, but it tells of the cross-country journey of the pioneers of 1845. The copy we have used was mimeographed by the Works Progress Administration County and Local Historical Records Survey of Oregon sometime during the presidency of Franklin Delano Roosevelt. In the introduction a field worker tells that it came from a typewritten copy of a newspaper story that had been found in the pocket of Solomon King at the time of his death on March 13, 1913. A notation indicates that Maria was the wife of Solomon King, yet the names signed

---

[1] The possessive apostrophe is never used in the spelling of "Kings Valley."

at the end of the missile were Stephen and Mariah King. How could that be?

The answer is clear. At the time of the overland journey she was the wife of the older brother, Stephen King. Solomon, a younger brother, was 12 years old.

But Stephen King died on November 28, 1852. On April 23, 1853, there appeared the following "Administrator's Notice" in the *Oregon Statesman* newspaper of the territorial capital, Salem.

> Notice is hereby given that letters of Administration have been granted by the Probate Court of Benton county to the undersigned on the estate of Stephen King, deceased, late of said county, bearing date April 4th, A. D. 1853. All persons having claims against said estate are requested to present the same for payment, legally authenticated, and all persons indebted to said estate are requested to make immediate payment.
>
> ANNE MARIA KING, Ad'r.
> Benton Co. O. T. [Oregon Territory] April 13, '53.

A year after Stephen's death, Maria married his younger brother, Solomon, on November 20, 1853. Solomon was then 20 years old.

Maria had been born Anna Maria Allen. According to the United States Census for 1870, her native state had been Massachusetts.[2] How she met the King family of Ohio we do not know at present.

The end of her long life, which took place on September 30, 1905, was announced in the Corvallis, Oregon, *Gazette* on October 3rd of that year:

> Saturday night occured the death of Mrs. Sol King at the age of 83 years, 6 month and 4 days. Services were held yesterday morning at the family home northwest of this city and were conducted by Rev. M. S. Bush. Interment was made in Odd Fellows Cemetery.

---

[2] H. I. Hiday, *Oregon, 1870 U. S. Census, Benton County.*

The Solomon Kings seem to have lived in Kings Valley
until 1872, when Solomon set up a livery stable in Corvallis,
and they moved to that city. In 1876 he was elected sheriff
of Benton County, a position he held for five terms, ten
years. By the 1880's the Kings were residing on a 1200 acre
farm one mile west of downtown Corvallis, not far from
where the campus of Oregon State University now stands.
They had quite an elegant residence. They raised short-horn
cattle, ran a dairy and did general farming. There were
five children from the union of Maria and Solomon.[3]

This was another family that, in crossing over the Oregon
Trail, were led astray in what is now eastern Oregon by
Stephen Meek. She spells is "Meiks."

THE LETTER OF ANNA MARIA KING

Luckiamute Valley, Oregon
April 1, 1846

Dear Mother, Brothers and Sisters:

After travelling six months we arrived at Lynntin
on the Willamette, November the 1st. We had beautiful weather all the way, no rain of any account. We
got along finely until we came to Fort Boisien with
3 or 4[00] miles of Lynnton when along came a man
by the name of Meiks, who said he could take us a
new route across the Cascade mountains to the Willamette river in 20 days, so a large company of a hundred and fifty or two hundred wagons left the old road
to follow the new road and traveled for 2 months over
sand, rocks, hills and anything else but good roads.
Two thirds of the immigrants ran out of provisions

[3] David D. Fagan, *History of Benton County, Oregon* (Portland, 1885),
pp. 519-20; *Portrait and Biographical Record of the Willamette Valley*
(Chicago, 1903), pp. 1087-88.

and had to live on beef, but as it happened we had
plenty of flour and bacon to last us through. But worse
than all this, sickness and death attended us the rest
of the way. I wrote to you at Fort Larim that the
whooping cough and measles went through our camp,
and after we took the new route a slow, lingering fever
prevailed. Out of Chamber L. Norton's,[1] John's [2] and
our family, none escaped except Solomon and myself.
But listen to the deaths: Sally Chambers,[3] John King
and his wife, their little daughter Electa and their
babe, a son 9 months old, and Dulancy C. Norton's [4]
sister are gone. Mr. A. Fuller [5] lost his wife and daughter Tabitha. Eight of our two families have gone to
their long home. Stephen was taken with the fever at
Fort Boisen; he had not been well since we left Ohio,
but was now taken worse. He was sick for three months,
we did not expect him to live for a long time, was afraid
he had consumption, but he is now well and hearty,
getting fatter every day, and he weighs as much as he
did when he came over the mountains, and as for my-

---

[1] He is listed in the 1850 Oregon Federal Census as Lucius Norton, 31,
a farmer from Ohio. His wife was Hopestel, also mispelled as "Hopestill."
Donna M. Wojcik, *The Brazen Overlanders* (Portland, 1976), p. 468, lists
him as Lucius Varolus Norton. Our subsequent footnotes refer to Wojcik's
book, with all the references from her "Roster of Emigrants" of 1845,"
pp. 381-514.

[2] John and Susan King died on October 26, 1845, of drowning in the
Columbia River as a result of a rafting accident, Wojcik, p. 445. Also
drowned were their little daughter, Electa, and their baby son, age 9 years,
according to Anna Maria.

[3] Sally Chambers was the daughter of the Nahum Kings. She was the
wife of Rowland (Rolland) Chambers, Wojcik, p. 396. Wojcik says Sally
died in the Malheur Mountains of Oregon.

[4] So far the relationship of Dulancy C. Norton and his sister are not known.

[5] Wojcik, p. 419, lists him as Arnold Wesley Fuller, whose wife died on
April 28, 1845, at the emigrant camp in Kansas Territory. Nothing seems
to be known about the daughter, Tabitha, who died on the way west.

self I was never heartier in my life since I left Missouri. I have not had even one sick day. The rest of our party are getting well and hardy now, I believe.

Those that went the old road got through six weeks before us, with no sickness at all. Upwards of fifty died on the new route.

The Indians did not disturb us any, except stealing our horses. We have made our claim on the Luckiamute, a western branch of the Willamette, now a day's ride from the ocean and 100 miles south of the Columbia river. It is a beautiful country as far as I have seen. Every person eighteen years old holds a section by making improvements and living on it five years. They sow wheat here from October till June, and the best wheat I ever saw and plenty of it at 75 cents and $1.00 per bushel; potatoes 25 c. peas $1.00 per bushel, corn 50 c, beef 6 c and 8 c, pork 10 c. sugar 12½ c. molasses 50 c. tea 75 c sheeting from 16 to 25 c. calico from 10 c to 50 c. and salt is 1 c a pound, and other things accordingly. Mills are plenty, no trouble about getting grinding. The water is all soft as it is in Massachusetts. Soda springs are common and fresh water springs without number. It is now the 1st of April and not a particle of snow has fallen in the valley neither have I seen a bit of ice a half inch thick this winter but it rains nearly all winter but this does not hinder them from plowing and sowing wheat. We have the most frost in the spring. They don't make garden until the last of April or the 1st of May, but it comes good when it does come. There are thousands of strawberries, gooseberries, blackberries, whortleberries, currants and other wild fruits but no nuts except filberts and a few chestnuts. The timber is principally fir and oak.

You perhaps wish to know how I like the country.
I like it well. It is an easy place to make a living. You
can raise as many cattle as you please and not cost you
a cent, for the grass is green the whole winter and
cattle are as fat as if they had been stall fed the whole
year round. Wheat is raised without trouble and will
fetch anything, the same as cash. A wagon from $100
to 150, 100 dollars for a yoke of oxen, $50 for a cow.
And work will fetch anything you want at from $1
to $1.50 a day, a dollar a hundred for making rails,
and so on. And although I was much apposed to coming as anyone could be, if I were back there and know
what I know now, I should be perfectly willing to
come.

The land you get is sufficient to pay for your trouble
and if you were here and John and Warren each of
them and yourself had a claim, I should like to live
there. We have all got claims joining, What winter
states will do for us I cannot tell. You know more about
that than I do. The Indians appear to be very friendly,
like to have the Bostons come, as they call them. You
think it is a long road and so it is, but the worst is over
when you get started. Be sure and have plenty of flour,
that is the main object; start with at least 175 or 200
pounds, and 75 pounds of bacon to the person, fetch
no more beds than you want to use, start with clothing
a plenty to last you one year after you get here if you
have nothing to buy with, after that you will raise
a plenty to buy with start with at least four or five
yoke of cattle to the wagon, young cattle four or five
years old are the best, fetch what coffee, sugar and
such things you like, if you should be sick you need
them. I write to you as if I expected you to come. I

need not do that as I know of   although I wish you were here.

I can't help but believe you would be suited not that it will do my dear mother any good to see her children well fixed to get a living. That is if Congress ever does anything for Oregon. It is not like any other new country – a farm to pay for – it is already paid for when you get here. You don't know how I want to see you, and if I am never to see you let me hear from you as often as possible. I want to know how you are all getting along and what you are doing. Give my love and respects to all.

We have had two weddings in our family. Rolland Chambers and Livisa King [6] and Amos King [7] to Melinda Fuller. Young men have to pay five dollars a year if they don't live on their claim. The people all look hale and hearty here. We are all looking for Moses Moon and Herman Hallock this fall.

Write the first opportunity, and every one. It has been so long since I have heard from you.

From your affectionate Children
Stephen and Mariah King.

---

[6] This was the second King girl who was married to Rolland Chambers. Lovisa King was the sister of his first wife, Sally (Sarah). Wojcik, p. 419.

[7] Amos King was the son of Nahum and Serepta King. Melinda Fuller was the daughter of Arnold and Sarah Fuller. Wojcik, p. 419.

A Brimfield Heroine   Tabitha Brown

INTRODUCTION

In the legislative chambers of the Oregon State Capitol in Salem there are inscribed 158 names of citizens prominent in Oregon's early development. Of these, six are women.

Two Indian women are there: Sacajawea of the Lewis and Clark party; and Marie Dorion, wife of the guide of the Astorians. Narcissa Whitman, the missionary, is there, as is Frances Fuller Victor, writer of a number of volumes on early Pacific Northwest history. The other two provide documents for our story of diaries and letters. Abigail Scott Duniway, the leading women's suffrage advocate for the region, was one of them. She wrote an important transcontinental diary in 1852.

The sixth woman thus memorialized in the Capitol was Tabitha Brown, the writer of the "Brimfield Heroine" letter here published. It first appeared in the Palmer, Ohio, *Journal,* thus titled, on February 18, 1882. The Brimfield, Massachusetts, Public Library provided us a copy of the *Journal* article. It was reprinted in *Congregational Work* in June, 1903. The "Brimfield Heroine" article became known to western readers and scholars when it was published in the *Quarterly* of the Oregon Historical Society in its Volume V, June, 1904, issue. This last edition of the letter is the one usually used for subsequent study.

However, there appeared in the same periodical in December, 1942, a notice that the diary of Tabitha Brown had been donated to Pacific University.[1] Search in the li-

brary of that school turned up not a diary, but a typewritten
copy of the letter — really as two letters, and this is the
copy we have used here; for the printed copies all differ
from the original in a number of ways and even differ from
each other in minute details.

Tabitha Brown (May 1, 1780 - May 4, 1858) traveled
west with a wagon train during the summer of 1846. She
was a widow of 66 years. She had been born in Brimfield,
Massachusetts, the daughter of Dr. and Mrs. Joseph Mof-
fat. She had been married to an Episcopal clergyman, the
Rev. Clark Brown, who had died after a short but distinguished career in 1817. The death took place in William
and Mary Parish, in rural Maryland, just across the bor-
der from Mount Vernon, Virginia.[2]

Tabitha taught school for a period after her husband's
death. Eventually she and her family moved to St. Charles,
near St. Louis, Missouri, where we find them living in 1824.

Her oldest son, Orus Brown, traveled west over the
Oregon Trail with two friends in 1843. He spent some
months in present Washington County, Oregon, and returned over the trail to Missouri in 1845 to urge his relatives to go with him to Oregon.[3] So it was that in April,
1846, they began their journey. "Grandma" Tabitha Brown
went along too, as did their father's retired sea-captain
brother, John Brown, 77 years old.[4] Orus and Lavina Brown

---

[1] *Oregon Hist. Qtly.*, XLIII (Dec. 1942), p. 373. The donor was A. N.
Bush of Salem, "whose wife was a great-granddaughter of Tabitha Brown."

[2] Two books summarize the biographies of Clark and Tabitha Brown. Both
were written by Ella Brown Spooner: *Clark and Tabitha Brown* (New York,
1957), and *Tabitha Brown's Western Adventures* (New York, 1958). Ella
Brown Spooner had already written and published *The Brown Family
History* (Laurel, Montana, 1929).

[3] See also "Virgil K. Pringle–1846," written by Ella Pringle Young, in
Book of Remembrance of Marion County, Oregon, Pioneers, 1840-1860
(Portland, 1927), pp. 77-79.

[4] Captain Brown was undoubtedly the oldest traveler over the Oregon
trail up to the date of his journey. He was lionized by the early settlers
in Salem, where he settled, gave orations at patriotic meetings, such as

took a family of eight children on their journey.[5] Tabitha's daughter, Pherne, went along too, as the wife of Virgil Pringle. The Pringles, who were to become pioneers of Salem, Oregon, took along their family of five children.[6]

Fortunately Virgil Pringle kept a systematic daily diary of the trip, which complements Tabitha's letters. This is also in the Pacific University Library, as are some lovely paintings of prairie flowers done along the way by Pherne.[7]

One noteworthy aspect of the Brown family's journey was that they followed what became known as the Applegate Trail through southern Oregon into the Willamette Valley, so that her letter and Virgil's diary become major documents in the history of that approach to the Pacific Northwest. The route has been called the Scott-Applegate Trail because it was explored in early 1846 by a party under the leadership of one Levi Scott, aided by the two Applegate brothers, Lindsay and Jesse.[8] This party trav-

---

Washington's Birthday, February 22, 1847. (Oregon City *Spectator*, II, no. 5, April 1, 1847). His obituary appeared in the March 9, 1848, issue of the *Spectator* (III, no. 3): "At Salem . . . suddenly, but not unexpectedly, Capt. John Brown departed this life, on the morning of the 19th ult. Aged 79 years and 4 months. Time dealt kindly with Capt. Brown; but it is 'alloted unto all men to die.'"

[5] The children who came overland with the Orus Browns are listed in the 1850 Federal Census as follows, with their ages: Alvin, 21; Andrew, 19; Theresa, 16; Caroline, 15; Lerila, 12; Rosalie, 11; Virgil, 9; and Lucy, 7. Their birthplace was Missouri.

[6] The Pringle children listed in the 1850 census who traveled overland were: O. M., 18 (Male); Alfred, 16; Crilla L., 14 (Female); Emma, 12. They, too, were all born in Missouri.

[7] Virgil Pringle's diary was published in the Oregon Pioneer Association *Transactions* for 1920, pp. 281-300. It was reprinted in Dale Morgan, *Overland in 1846*, 2 volumes (Georgetown, Calif., 1963), pp. 159-88. Morgan did not know of the Pacific University copy. Ella Brown Spooner published two of Pherne Pringle's paintings in black and white between pages 60 and 61 of *Tabitha Brown's Western Adventures*.

[8] Lindsay Applegate, "Notes and Reminiscences of Laying Out and Establishing the Old Emigrant Road into Southern Oregon in the year 1846," *Quarterly* of the Oregon Hist. Soc., XXII, no. 1 (March 1921), pp. 12-45.

eled by horseback from west to east and met the westward
bound Browns and their friends near the American Falls
in present-day south Idaho. This meeting took place, according to Virgil Pringle's diary, on Sunday, August 9,
1846. So it was that the Brown wagon train sought to
follow during the following weeks that southern route into
Oregon under less than ideal circumstances. They traversed
two other later states of the Union, Nevada and California,
as they entered the promised land, losing wagon after
wagon. The whole experience sparked a major battle of
words in the early Oregon newspaper, the *Spectator* of
Oregon City, about what had happened and who was to
blame.[9]

Tabitha covers this part of the story very well. These
two letters, as well as others written by her from Oregon,
describe the region as a veritable mecca for the settlers.
She told in detail of the role she played in the initiation of
education in the new territory, including the founding of
Pacific University, the Congregational college in Forest
Grove, Oregon. Her school for the children of depleted
families who had traveled the Oregon Trail was the fore-
runner of the college. That is why she is so clearly memorialized in the modern Oregon State Capitol.

It is with the gracious permission of the library of Pacific
University that the following record of Tabitha Brown's
overland travel is printed.

TABITHA BROWN: LETTER I

> Forest Grove, West Tualatin Plains
> Washington Co. Oregon Territory
> August, 1854

_____

[9] Oregon City *Spectator*, I, no. 26, December 10, 1846, p. 2; II, no. 1,
February 4, 1847, p. 2; II, no. 3, February 18, 1847, p. 2.

My Dear Brother and Sister:

It is impossible for me to express to you the unspeakable pleasure and happiness your letter of the 29th of June gave me yesterday evening. Not hearing from you for so great a length of time. I had concluded myself to be the last one of my Father's family, remaining here a Pilgrim in the wide world, to complete the work that God intended me to do.

Oh! that I could be present with you and Margaret, and relate in the hearing of your children the numerous viccissitudes and dangers I have encountered by land and sea since I last parted from you and Margaret in Brimfield. It would fill a volume of many pages, but I will give a few items from the time I left Missouri in April of 1846 for Oregon. I expected all three of my children to accompany me, but Manthano [1] was detained by sickness and his wife was unwilling to leave her parents. I provided for myself a good ox-wagon team, a good supply of what was requisite for the comfort of myself, Captain Brown, and my driver, for Uncle John insisted on coming and crossed the plains on horseback. Orus Brown, with wife and eight children; Virgil Pringle, Pherne's husband, with five children, fitted out their separate families and joined a train of forty more for Oregon in high expectations of gaining the wished-for land of promise.

The novelty of our journey, with a few exceptions, was pleasing and prosperous until after we passed Fort Hall; then we were within 800 miles of Oregon City. If we had kept the old road down the Columbia River

---

[1] Manthano Brown (1802-1876) was the second son of Clark and Tabitha Brown. He and his family stayed in Missouri, where they farmed. Ella Brown Spooner, *Clark and Tabitha Brown* (New York, 1957), pp. 116-19.

– but three of four trains of emigrants were decoyed off by a rascally fellow who came out from the settlement in Oregon, assuring us that he had found a *near cut-off;* that if we would follow him we would be in the settlement long before those who had gone down the Columbia. This was in August. The idea of shortening a long journey caused us to yield to his advice. Our sufferings from that time no tongue can tell. (He left a pilot with us who proved to be an excellent man; otherwise we never would have seen Oregon.) He said he would clear the road before us; that we should have no trouble in rolling our wagons after him; he robbed us of what he could by lying; and left us to the depredations of Indians, wild beasts, and starvation – but God was with us. We had sixty miles desert without grass or water, mountains to climb, cattle giving out, wagons breaking, emigrants sick and dying, hostile Indians to guard against by night and by day to keep from being killed, or having our horses and cattle arrowed or stolen. We were carried south of Oregon hundreds of miles into Utah Territory and California; fell in with the Clammette and Rogue River Indians; lost nearly all our cattle; passed the Umpqua mountains (twelve miles through) I rode through in three days at the risk of my life, having lost my wagon, and all I had but the horse I was on.

Our family was the first that started into the Canyon, so we got through much better than those who came after, but of hundreds of wagons but one came through without breaking. The Canyon was strewn with dead cattle, broken wagons, beds, clothing, and everything but provisions of which we were nearly destitute. Some people were in Canyon two and three weeks before they could get through; some died without any warning from fatigue and starvation; others ate the flesh of the cattle that were lying dead by the wayside.

After struggling through mud, rocks and water up to our horses sides in crossing this twelve-mile mountain, we opened into the beautiful Umpqua Valley, inhabited only by Indians and wild beasts. We had still another mountain to cross – the Calapooia – besides many miles to travel through mud, snow, rain and hail. Winter had set in; we were yet a long distance from any white settlement. The word was *Fly,* everyone who can, from starvation; all not compelled to stay by the few cattle to recruit them for further travelling. Mr. Pringle and Pherne insisted on my going ahead with their Uncle John and try to save our own lives. They were obliged to stay back for a few days to recruit their few worn out cattle. They divided their last bit of bacon, of which I had three slices, a tea-cupful of tea; the last division of all we had – no bread. We saddled our horses and set off, not knowing that we should ever see each other again. Captain Brown was too old and feeble to render any assistance or protection to me. I was obliged to ride ahead as a pilot, hoping to overtake four or five wagons that left camp the day before. Near sunset came up with two families that left camp that morning. They had nothing to eat, and their cattle had given out. We camped in an oak grove together for the night; in the morning I divided my last morsel with them, and left them to take care of themselves. I hurried Captain Brown to ride fast so as to overtake the wagons ahead. We passed through beautiful valleys, and over high hills; saw but two Indians at a distance through the

day. In the afterpart of the day Capt. Brown com-
plained of sickness, and could only walk his horse at
a distance behind me; he had a swimming in his head
and a pain in his stomach. About two or three hours
by sun he became delirious, and fell from his horse.
I was afraid to jump down from my horse to assist him
as it was one that a woman had never ridden before;
he tried to raise upon his feet, but could not. I rode
close to him, and set the end of his lignum-vitae cane
that I had in my hand hard into the ground by him
to pull up by; I then urged him to walk a little. He
tottered along a few yards, and gave out. I then saw
a little sunken spot a few steps from me; I led his horse
down into it; with much difficulty I got him once more
raised on his horse. I then requested him to hold fast
by the saddle and the horse's mane, and I would lead
by the bridle. Two miles ahead was another mountain
to climb over. As I reached the foot of it he was able
to take the bridle into his own hand, and we passed
safely over into a large valley – a wide, extensive, solitary place, and no wagons in sight!

The sun was now setting, the wind was blowing, and
the rain was drifting, upon the side of distant mountains – poor Me! I crossed the plain to where these
mountain spurs met Ravines, betwixt the points. Here
the shades of night were gathering fast, and I could
see the wagon track no further. I alighted from my
horse, flung off my saddle and saddle bags, and tied
him fast with a las[so] rope to a tree. The Captain
asked what I was going to do. My answer was, I am
going to camp for the night. He gave a groan, and fell
to the ground. I gathered my wagon sheet, that I had
put under my saddle; flung it over a firm projecting

limb of a tree, and made me a fine tent. I then stripped the Captain's horse, and tied him; placed saddles, blankets, bridles, etc. under the tent; then helped up the bewildered old gentleman, and introduced him to his new lodgings upon the naked ground. His senses were gone; I covered him as well as I could with blankets, and then seated myself upon my feet behind him, expecting he would be a corpse by morning. Pause for a moment and consider my situation – worse than alone; in a strange wilderness; without food, without fire; cold and shivering; wolves fighting and howling all around me; darkness of night forbade the stars to shine upon me; solitary – all was solitary as death – but the same kind Providence that ever has been was watching over me still. I committed my all to Him and felt no fear. As soon as light had dawned, I pulled down my tent, saddled the horses; found the Captain so as to stand upon his feet – just at this moment one of the emigrants that I was trying to overtake came to me – he was in search of venison – half a mile ahead were the wagons I was trying to catch up with. We were soon there, and ate plentifully of fresh venison. Within 8 or 10 feet of where my tent was set fresh tracks of two Indians were plain to be seen, but I did not know they were there. They killed and robbed a Mr. Newton but a short distance off, but would not kill his wife because she was a (Clushman?)[2] woman. The Indians killed another man on our cut-off; the

---

[2] The word, "Clushman" appears here in parentheses with a question mark after it. Whether the question mark appeared in Tabitha Brown's original or was added by the transcriber, there is no way to know. The word was spelled several ways, more often "Kloochman," meaning "woman" in Chinook Jargon, the inter-tribal trade language of the Pacific Northwest Indians. See footnote 5 below.

rest of the emigrants escaped with their lives. We then
travelled on, and in a few days came to the foot of the
Calapooia Mountain, Here we were obliged to wait
for more emigrants to help cut a road through; here
my children and grandchildren came up with us – a
joyful meeting. They had been near starving. Mr.
Pringle tried to shoot a wolf, but he was too weak
and trembling to hold his rifle steady. They all cried
because they had nothing to eat. Just at this time their
son came to them with a supply, and they all cried
again.

Winter set in. We were many days in crossing the
Calapooia Mts. having to go ahead only a mile or two
each day. The road had to be cut and opened for us,
and the mountain was covered with snow. With much
difficulty we crossed over to the head waters of the
Willamette; followed the River down a few days; and
gave up the idea of reaching the settlement until spring
returned. Provisions gave out. Mr. Pringle set off on
horseback for the settlements for relief, not knowing
how long he should be gone, or whether he would get
through at all. In a week or so our scanty provisions
gave out; we were once more in a state of starvation;
much crying, and many tears were shed through the
day by all but one; she had passed through many trials,
sufficient to convince her that tears could avail nothing
in our extremity. Through all my sufferings in crossing the Plains, I had not once sought relief by the shed-
ding of tears, nor thought we should not live to reach
the settlements. The same Faith and hope that I had
ever in the blessings of kind Providence strengthened
in proportion to the trials I had to encounter. As the

only alternative or last resort for the present time, Mr.
Pringle's son Clark shot down one of his father's best
work oxen and dressed it; we had then something to
eat, poor bones to pick, without bread or salt.

I must now digress a little. The year of '43 Orus
Brown came to Oregon to look at the country; in '45
returned. When within four or five hundred miles of
the United States frontier, he and three other men with
him were taken by the Pawnee Indians, and robbed.
They got away from them and subsisted on berries and
rose-buds until they reached the frontier settlements.
Very likely you saw the publication of Dr. White,[3]
Orus Brown, Chapman and one other taken by the
Pawnees in 1845. In '46, when we started for Oregon,
Orus was appointed pilot, having crossed the Plains
twice before. His company was six days ahead of ours,
so he had gone down the old emigrant route, and
reached the settlements in September. In six or eight
weeks he had heard of the suffering emigrants at the
south; he set off with four pack-horses and provisions
for our relief. He met Mr. Pringle; turned him about;
a few days and nights, and they were at our Camp.
We had all retired to rest in our tents, hoping to forget
our troubles until daylight should remind us of our
sad fate. In the gloomy stillness of the night, hoofbeats
of horses were heard rushing to our tents – directly a
halloo – it was the well-known voice of Orus Brown
and Virgil Pringle; who can realize the joy? Orus,
by his persuasive perseverance, encouraged us to one
more effort to reach the Settlement. Five miles from

---

[3] Miss A. J. Allen, *Ten Years in Oregon: The Travels and Adventures
of Dr. Elijah White and Lady* (Ithaca, N.Y., 1850).

where we were campt fell in with a company of half-breed French and Indians with pack-horses. We hired six of them and pushed ahead. Again our provisions were becoming short; we were once more on allowance until we reached the first settlers; then our hardest struggles were ended. On Christmas Day at 2 P. M. I entered the house of a Methodist minister, the first I had set foot in for nine months. He requested me to take the whole charge of his house and family through the winter — his wife was as ignorant and useless as a Heathan Goddess. My services compensated for my own board and Captain Brown's through the winter. For two or three weeks of my journey down the Willamette I'd something in the end of my glove finger which I supposed to be a button. On examination at my new home in Salem I found it to be a six and one-fourth cent piece;[4] this was the whole of my cash capital to commence business in Oregon. With it I purchased three needles; traded off some of my old clothes to the squaws for Buckskin; worked it into gloves for the Oregon *Ladies* and *Gentlemen;* which cleared me upwards of $30.00 extra of boarding.

Now my dear relatives, I think you would like to rest awhile. I should like to be present to hear the comments that will naturally be passed by the listening circle at the rehearsal and adventures of the Oregon Pioneer. I think I hear you and Margaret say: "I should like to see that Oregon Pioneer; I wonder if she is anything like what she used to be."

---

[4] This was one-half of a "bit." The bit was one-eighth of a Spanish dollar coin. So it is that we still use the terms, "two bits," "four bits," "six bits." These were little pie-shaped cut-up parts of the original coin, or they were smaller coins, as in this case. Tabitha Brown's little 6¼ cent piece was not much money.

Yes – Niker hias scocum Tillscum, Close Tumtum.
     me very brave   woman, good   heart.
    Cumtux   Chemuke   Wawwwaw?
  Understand   Indian   talk? [5]

                              Tabitha Brown

LETTER II

[No salutation.]

May '47 I left Salem, which is now our seat of Government, for Oregon City, 30 miles down the Willamette in an open boat, in company with my Methodist minister and family. From thence down the Columbia River to the Pacific Ocean. Here I spent the summer at Clatsop Plains, a settlement south of the Bay. At that time there were but ten families residing there. I boarded with a Mr. Gray and Lady missionary from Ballstown, N. Y., a very genteel family; and spent the summer in visiting and bathing in the ocean. The surf of two oceans has rolled over me – Atlantic and Pacific. In October I started in an open boat up the river for Salem again; wind and tide against us; was 13 days reaching Oregon City. Here I was within 20 miles of Tualatin Plains – Orus Brown's location. It would never do for a mother to pass by. Luckily I

---

[5] This was her attempt to render a message in the Chinook Jargon, the short-hand inter-tribal trade language of the Pacific Northwest tribes from Oregon to Alaska. It became a constant of the early white man's slang in in every day talk, so much so that J. K. Gill, the Portland bookstore, for many years published a *Gill's Dictionary of the Chinook Jargon.* The last edition bought by this author at the Gill store a number of years ago was the eighteenth, published in 1960, and compiled by John Gill. A helpful reference on this subject is Edward Harper Thomas, *Chinook: A History and Dictionary* (Portland, 1970).

found a man with an empty wagon going out, who lived neighbor to Orus. I gave two dollars for my passage, calculating to spend two weeks only with O. and family, and reach Salem before the winter rains set in. Went to a Presbyterian meeting on Sunday; after the meeting Orus gave me an introduction to Mr. and Mrs. Clark, missionaries from N. Y. who came here in 1840. They invited me home with them to spend a few days. Winter set in; they pressed me hard to spend the winter with them. I accepted their invitation. Our intimacy ever since has been more like mother and children than strangers. They are about the same age as my own children, and look to me for advice and counsel equally as much. They even think they have the greatest claim, for they insist upon my spending the balance of my days with them, but my children would think their claim more binding than Mr. Clark's if I were not able to do for myself. My children, and the grandchildren who are settled for themselves, are all doing well, and are what in the States would be considered wealthy. Orus owns one section of the best of land in the center of this plain; nearly one half under improvement; a two-story frame white house; his farm well stocked with horses, cattle and hogs, and clear of debt. Pherne's husband has the same five miles from this Plain. He has other town property in Salem. His daughter Virginia married a Mr. Smith from Rochester, N. Y. His two oldest sons are married; all doing well within one hour's ride of him. Alvin Brown, Orus' Eldest son I am staying with for a short time. He has one of the handsomest and most valuable half-sections in the country, joining his father; well stocked and well fenced. He has a small house and intends putting up a large one next season. He is clear of debt and a worthy young man.

Back to my narrative once more. In October, 1847, news from the suffering emigrants told of much sickness and death on the Plains, and many poor orphan children left to an un-feeling world to be cared for by strangers. I said to Mr. Clark; why has Providence frowned on me and left me poor in this world? Had He blessed me with riches as He has many others, I know right well what I should do. "What would you do?" was the question. "I should establish myself in a comfortable house, and receive all poor children and be a mother to them." He fixed his keen eye upon me, and asked if I was candid in what I'd said. "Yes, I am." "If so I will try with you, and see what we can do." Mr. Clark was to take the agency, and try to get assistance to establish a school, for the first in the Plain; I should go into the old log meeting-house, and receive all the children; rich and poor. Those whose parents were able to pay $1.00 a week, including board, tuition, washing, and all. I agreed to labor one year for nothing; Mr. Clark and others agreed to assist me as far as they were able in furnishing provisions, provided there was not a sufficiency of cash coming in to sustain the poor. The time fixed upon was March, '48. In April I rode up to Salem to visit my children. Captain Brown died at my grand-daughter Smith's whilst I was at Mr. Pringle's. I did not see him till after he was dead. He was delighted with Oregon; became very fleshy; spent his time with people from eastern cities, and felt himself at home. He enjoyed life too well; was too advanced in life to nerve himself for so many exciting attentions bestowed upon him, by reason of his age and gentlemanly deportment, in whatever company he fell in with. It was a novelty to see a man eighty-one years old in Oregon in '47. He sunk under it without any disease whatever, got up one morning in health, was taken with shortness of breath, and died in one hour after. He experienced religion in Missouri, and joined the Methodists as there was no Presbyterian church nearer than forty miles.

Again to my journal. The last Saturday night in April I arrived at the Plains again; found all things in readiness for me to go into the Old Meeting-House and cluck up my chickens the next Monday morning. The neighbors had collected together what broken knives and forks, tin pans and dishes they could part with for the Oregon Pioneer to commence housekeeping. A well educated lady from the east, a missionary's wife, was the teacher. My family increased rapidly. In the summer they put me up a house – I had now thirty boarders of all sexes and ages, from 4 years old to 21. I managed them, did almost all of my own work, but the washing, which was always done by the scholars. In the spring of '49 we called for trustees; had eight appointed; they voted me the whole charge of the boarding house free of rent; established the price of board at $2.00 a week, and whatever I made over and above my expenses was my own. In '51 I had forty in my family, at $2.50 a week; mixed with my own hands 3423 pounds of flour in less than five months.

Mr. Clark, for the establishment of the school, gave over to the trustees one-fourth section of land for a Town plot. A large, handsome building is upon the spot we selected at the first starting. It has been under Town incorporation for two years; and at the last session [of the legislature] a Charter was granted in connection for a University to be called the Pacific University, with a limitation of $50,000. The President and Professor are already here from Vermont. The teacher and his wife in the Academy are from New York. You must excuse my troubling you with such a lengthy narrative; I have endeavored to give general outlines of what I had no expectation that a single relative of my own would ever know of me; what I had done, where I had gone, or what had become of me, until I received your letters.

[No signature to this letter.]

The Donner Party Letters
Tamsen E. Donner ⸭ Virginia E. B. Reed

INTRODUCTION

On March 26 and April 2, 1846, there appeared an advertisement in the *Sangamo Journal* of Springfield, Illinois, with the headline: "WESTWARD, *HO!* FOR OREGON AND CALIFORNIA!" The ad had been placed by "G. Donner and others" and called for young men who might want to "go to California without costing them anything." They were to be hired by "gentlemen" who would leave Sangamon County the first of April.[1] Not one word was said about women, but it is with two of the women of the party that we are especially concerned because of letters they wrote back home telling of their experiences.

The Donner Party seems early on to have been called the Donner-Reed Party because George Donner and James Reed were the principal organizers of the enterprise. The letters published here were written by two women, one from each of these families.

Tamsen Donner's letters have to do with the early part of the overland journey. She was Mrs. George Donner,[2] and, if anyone can be called the heroine of the awful trag-

---

[1] Quoted in full in Dale Morgan, *Overland in 1846*, (Georgetown, Calif., 1963), II, 491.

[2] Tamsen Eustis Donner was George Donner's third wife. She was already a widow, a native of Newburyport, Massachusetts. The marriage took place on May 24, 1839. Eliza P. Donner Houghton, in her *Expedition of the Donner Party* (Chicago, 1911) tells a good deal about the personal aspects of the Donner family. Eliza was the third daughter of the union, born March 8, 1843.

edy, she would be the one. The first of her extant letters was written to her sister, Eliza Poor, and it was sent back from Independence, Missouri, a major gathering place of overland parties. This letter is to be found in the Huntington Library, San Marino, California, and it is with their permission that it is published here. Her other letter was published in the same *Sangamo Journal* as the previously quoted ad. It was in the July 23, 1846, edition of the newspaper,[3] having been sent back from the Platte River Valley of present Nebraska. Tamsen Donner was a gracious, educated lady, a competent school teacher.

The other two letters were written by Virginia Reed,[4] a thirteen-year-old teenager at the time of the overland journey. They are not written in a smooth, polished way, but their very naivete is part of their charm. They were written respectively from Independence Rock, in present Wyoming, on July 12, 1846, and from Napa Valley, California, on May 16, 1847. They are both located today in the Southwest Museum Library in Los Angeles. The 1847 letter, the most interesting of all, is in photostat form, the original having disappeared. It is with the permission of the Southwest Museum that they are reproduced here.

---

[3] The July 23 edition of the paper was supplied to us by the Illinoiis State Hist. Soc., Springfield. It is also to be noted that in several books about the Donner party a second "letter" or "extract" of "part of a letter" is included which was supposedly written by "Mrs. George Donner" and appeared in the same newspaper of July 30, 1846. This was published in Houghton on page 26, and in C. F. McGlashan, *History of the Donner Party,* Fourth Ed., (San Francisco, 1881), reprinted by the Stanford Univ. Press in 1947, p. 27. The staff of the Illinois State Hist. Soc. has kindly searched the files of the old newspaper and found the quote is not from a letter written by Mrs. Donner, but by James Reed.

[4] Virginia's age is sometimes referred to as 12-years-old. However, Dale Morgan corrects this to 13 on Virginia's own say-so, *Overland in 1846,* I, 249. Virginia was the only daughter of Lloyd C. Backenstoe and Margret Willson Keyes. Her father died of cholera, and her mother was married to James Frazier Reed on October 13, 1835. (Morgan, I, 248-49).

At first the Donner-Reed letters were not to have appeared in this collection. It was felt that they have been too much published and too lately. A careful study of the photostat of the Virginia Reed letter from the Napa Valley, however, led to the decision to include all four of them. An examination of the photostat led to the conclusion that this letter has apparently never been published exactly as written. There seems to be an inevitable drive when a child's document is inventively spelled and erratically punctuated and capitalized to make a "fair copy" of it, and that is what has happened over and over again in this case. First of all, Virginia's step-father, James Reed, wrote over her words and sentences, emending them between the lines and adding things he thought she had left out. Then the editors of books about the Donner Party did more of the same. One transcriber of the letter marches square brackets across line after line, trying to make more clear what the child is really trying to say. In the same transcription there are also omissions of two or three words at a time that were in Virginia's own copy, and even two omissions of thirteen and fifteen words.[5]

Here Virginia Reed's letter is published as much as possible just as she wrote it, leaving it to the intelligence of the reader to feel the full impact of this very personal message written by a mid-nineteenth-century teenage girl. Sometimes it takes a great deal of ingenuity and a powerful imagination to get at the heart of the child's story of the events of the overland journey and the tragedy in the mountains.[6]

---

[5] George R. Stewart made many changes in spelling, evidently with the hope that the letter would be more easily read, *Ordeal by Hunger* (Boston, 1960), pp. 355-62. The omissions referred to are in Morgan's work, where the letter is published on pages 281-88, vol. I.

[6] Some of the most dramatic of her renditions are "we had to cash [cache] all of our close [clothes]"; "haden bin" for hadn't been; "couldes"

Virginia Reed did write another version of her experience much later in life. It is to be found in the *Century Magazine* in its May-October, 1891 issues. She gave this later reminiscence the title, "Across the Plains in the Donner Party (1846). A Personal Narrative of the Overland Trip to California."

Tamsen Donner was one of those who did not get to the California promised land. She died after tending a dying husband through his last days and hours in the snow-packed Sierra. A day or two after his death the icy cold took her life as well. Virginia Reed, on the other hand, lived a long life in the San Jose, California, area as the wife of Mr. John M. Murphy, to whom she was joined in marriage on January 26, 1850. She died in Los Angeles on March 14, 1921.[7]

TAMSEN E. DONNER: LETTER I

Independence Mo.   May 11th 1846.
My Dear Sister[1]

I commenced writing to you some months ago but the letter was laid aside to be finished the next day & was never touched. A nice sheet of pink letter paper was taken out & has got so much soiled that it cannot

---

for coldest; "cound note had!ey git up" for could not hardly get up; "awl wais" for always; "they raped the children up" for they wrapped the children up. She evidently thought that the "th" attached to a number meant "the," so, logically, she rendered the opening date as July th12 1846" in the first of the two letters published here, and as "May the16 in the second one. Her use of numbers is characterized by a logic all of her own. In the first letter she speaks of the number of Caw Indians as "20050," meaning 250. But, of course, that is the way you say it, isn't it? Near the end of the second letter she writes, "Ma waies 10040," then "Eliza weighs 10070."

[7] Morgan, *op. cit.,* II, 254.

[1] This letter from Mrs. George Donner to her sister, Eliza Poor, is located in the Huntington Library, San Marino, Calif.

be written upon & now in the midst of preparation for starting across the mountains I am seated on the grass in the midst of the tent to say a few words to my dearest & only sister. One would suppose that I loved her but little or I should have not neglected her so long. But I have heard from you by Mr Greenleaf & every month have intended to write. My three daughters are round me one at my side trying to sew Georgeanna fixing herself up in old indiarubber cap & Eliza Poor knocking on my paper & asking me ever so many questions. They often talk to me of Aunty Poor. I can give you no idea of the hurry of the place at this time. It is supposed there will be 7000 waggons start from this place this season We go to California, to the bay of San Francisco. It is a four months trip. We have three waggons furnished with food & clothing &c. drawn by three yoke of oxen each. We take cows along & milk them & have some butter though not as much as we would like. I am willing to go & have no doubt it will be an advantage to our children & to us. I came here last evening & start tomorrow morning on the long journey. Wm's family was well when I left Springfield a month ago. He will write to you soon as he finds another home He says he has received no answer to his two last letters, is about to start to Wisconsin as he considers Illinois unhealthy.

Farewell, my sister, you shall hear from
me as soon as I have an opportunity,
Love to Mr. Poor, the children & all friends.
Farewell

T. E. Donner

TAMSEN E. DONNER: LETTER II

FROM THE CALIFORNIA COMPANY
The following letter is from Mrs. George Donner,
(one of the emigrants from this County, now on the
way to California,) to a friend in this city: It is dated–
NEAR THE JUNCTION OF THE
NORTH AND SOUTH PLATTE,
June 16th, 1846

My Old Friend: – We are now on the Platte, 200
miles from Fort Laramie. Our journey so far, has been
pleasant. The water for a part of the way has been
indifferent – but at no time have our cattle suffered
for it. Wood is now very scarce, but *"Buffalo chips"*
are excellent – they kindle quick and retain heat sur-
prisingly. We had this evening Buffalo steaks broiled
upon them that had the same flavor they would have
had on hickory coals.

We feel no fear of Indians. Our cattle graze quietly
around our encampment unmolested. – Two or three
men will go hunting twenty miles out from camp : –
and last night two of our men laid out in the wilderness
rather than tire their horses after a hard chase. Indeed
if I do not experience something far worse than I yet
have done, I shall say the trouble is all in getting started.

Our wagons have not needed much repair; but I
cannot yet tell in what respect they could be improved.
Certain it is they cannot be too strong. Our preparation
for the journey, in some respects, might have been bet-
tered. Bread has been the principal article of food in
our camp. We laid in 150 lbs. of flour and 75 lbs. of
meat for each individual and I fear bread will be
scarce. Meat is abundant. Rice and beans are good

articles on the road – corn-meal, too, is acceptable. Linsey dresses are the most suitable for children. Indeed if I had one it would be comfortable. There is so cool a breeze at all times in the prairie that the sun does not feel as hot as one could suppose.

We are now 450 miles from Independence. – Our route at first was rough and through a timbered country which appeared to be fertile. After striking the prairie we found a first rate road; and the only difficulty we had has been crossing creeks. In that, however, there has been no danger. I never could have believed we could have travelled so far with so little difficulty. The prairie between the Blue and Platte rivers is abundant beyond description. Never have I seen so varied a country – so suitable for cultivation. Every thing was new and pleasing. The Indians frequently come to see us and the chiefs of a tribe breakfasted at our tent this morning. – All are so friendly that I cannot help feeling sympathy and friendship for them. But on one sheet what can I say?

Since we have been on the Platte we have had the river on one side, and the ever varying mounds on the other – and have travelled through the Bottom lands from one to two miles wide with little or no timber. The soil is sandy, and last year on account of one dry season, the emigrants found grass here scarce. Our cattle are in good order, and where proper care has been taken none has been lost. Our milch cows have been of great service – indeed, they have been of more advantage than our meat. We have plenty of butter and milk.

We are commanded by Capt. Russel – an amiable man. George Donner is himself yet. He crows in the morning, and shouts out, "Chain up, boys! – chain up!" with as much authority as though he was "something in particular." – John Denton is still with us – we find him a useful man in camp. Hiram Miller and Noah James are in good health and doing well. We have of the best of people in our company, and some, too, that are not so good.

Buffalo show themselves frequently. We have found the wild tulip, the primrose, the lupine, the ear-drop, the larkspur, and creeping holyhock, and a beautiful flower resembling the bloom of the beach tree, but in bunches as big as a small sugar-leaf, and of every variety of shade to red and green. I botanize and read some, but cook a "heap" more.

There are 420 wagons, as far as we have heard, on the road between here and Oregon and California.

Give our love to all enquiring friends – God bless them. Yours truly,

Mrs. GEORGE DONNER.[2]

VIRGINIA E. B. REED: LETTER I

Independence rock July th12   1846[3]

My Dear Couzin   I take this opper tuny to Write to you to let you know that I am Well at present and hope that you are well. We have all had good helth – We came to the blue – the Water was so hye we had to stay thare 4 days – in the mean time gramma died. she be came spechless the day before she died. We

---

[2] From *The Sangamo Journal,* Springfield, Ill., July 23, 1846.

[3] The following two letters are from the Southwest Museum, Los Angeles, Calif.

buried her verry decent We made a nete coffin and
buried her under a tree we had a head stone and had
her name cutonit, and the date and yere verry nice,
and at the head of the grave was a tree we cut some
letters on it the young men soded it all ofer and put
Flores on it We miss her verry much evry time we
come in the wagon we look up at the bed for her We
have came throw several tribs of indians the Caw
Indians the saw the shawnees, at the caw viliage paw
counted 20050 Indians We diden see no Indians from
the time we left the cow viliage till we come to fort
Laramy the Caw Indians are gong to War With the
crows we hav to pas throw ther fiting grounds the
sowe Indians are the pretest drest Indians thare is
Paw goes a bufalo hunting most every day and kils
2 or 3 buffalo every day paw shot a elk som of our
compan saw a grisly bear We have the thermometer
102° – average for the last 6 days We selabrated the
4 of July on plat at bever criek several of the Gente-
men in Springfield gave paw a botel of licker and said
it shoulden be opend tell the 4 day of July and paw
was to look to the east and drink it and thay was to
look to the West an drink it at 12 oclock paw treted
the company and we all had some leminade. maw and
pau is well and sends there best love to you all. I send
my best love to you all We hav hard from uncle cad
severe times he went to california and now is gone
to oregon he is well. I am a going to send this letter
by a man coming from oregon by his self he is going
to take his family to oregon We are all doing Well
and in hye sperits so I must close yur letter. You are
for ever my affectionate couzen

Virginia E. B. Reed

VIRGINIA E. B. REED: LETTER II

Napa Vallie
California
May 16th 1847

My Dear Cousan   May the 16 1847

I take this oppertunity to write to you to let you
now that we are all Well at presant and hope this
letter may find you all well to   My dear Cousan I am
a going to Write to you about our trubels geting to
Callifornia; We had good luck til we come to big
Sandy thare we lost our best yoak of oxons   we come
to Brigers Fort & we lost another ox   we sold some
of our provisions & baut a yoak of Cows & oxen &
they pursuaded us to take Hastings cut of over the
salt plain   thay said it saved 3 Hondred miles, we went
that road & we had to go through a long drive of 40
miles With out water or grass   Hastings said it was
40 but i think it was 80 miles   We traveld a day and
night & a nother day and at noon pa went on to see
if he coud find Water, he had not bin gone long till
some of the oxen give out and we had to leve the
Wagons and take the oxen on to water   one of the
men staid with us and others went on with the cattel
to water   pa was a coming back to us with Water
and met the men & thay was about 10 miles from water
pa said thay git to water that night, and the next day
to bring the cattel back for the wagons any [and]
bring some Water   pa got to us about noon   the man
that was with us took the horse and went on to
water   We wated thare   thought Thay would come
we wated till night and We thought we start and
walk to Mr doners wagons that night   we took what

little water we had and some bread and started   pa
caried Thomos and all the rest of us walk   we got
to Donner and thay were all a sleep so we laid down
on the ground we spred one shawl down we laid doun
on it and spred another over us and then put the dogs
on top   it was the couldes night you most ever saw
the wind blew and if it haden bin for the dogs we
would have Frosen   as soon as it was day we went
to Miss Donners   she said we could not walk to the
Water and if we staid we could ride in thare wagons
to the spring so pa went on to the water to see why
thay did not bring the cattel   when he got thare thare
was but one ox and cow thare   none of the rest had
got to water   Mr Donner come   out that night with
his cattel and braught his Wagons and all of us in   we
staid thare a week and Hunted for our cattel and could
not find them so some of the companie took thare oxons
and went out and brout in one wagon and cashed the
other tow and a grate manie things all but what we
could put in one Wagon   we had to divied our propessions out to them to get them to carie them   We
got three yoak with our oxe & cow so we [went] on
that way a while and we got out of provisions and pa
had to go on to callifornia for provisions   we could
not get along that way, in 2 or 3 days after pa left we
had to cash our wagon and take Mr. graves wagon and
cash some more of our things   well we went on that
way a while and then we had to get Mr Eddies Wagon   we went on that way awhile and then we had to
cash all our our close except a change or 2 and put
them in Mr Brins Wagon and Thomos & James rode
the 2 horses and the rest of us had to walk, we went
on that way a Whild and we come to a nother long

drive of 40 miles and then we went with Mr Donner

We had to Walk all the time we was a travling up
the truckee river   we met that and 2 Indians that we
had sent out for propessions to Suter Fort   thay had
met pa, not fur from Suters Fort   he looked very
bad   he had not ate but 3 times in 7 days and thes
days with out any thing his horse was not abel to carrie
him   thay give him a horse and he went on   so we
cashed some more of our things all but what we could
pack on one mule and we started Martha and James
road behind the two Indians   it was a raing then in
the Vallies and snowing on the montains so we went
on that way 3 or 4 days tell we come to the big mountain or the Callifornia Mountain   the snow then was
about 3 feet deep   thare was some wagons thare   thay
said thay had atempted to cross and could not, well
we thought we would try it so we started and thay
started again with thare wagons   the snow was then
way to the muels side   the farther we went up the
deeper the snow got so the wagons could not go so
thay packed thare oxons and started with us carring
a child a piece and driving the oxons in snow up to
thare wast   the mule Martha and the Indian was on
was the best one so thay went and broak the road and
that indian was the Pilot so we went on that way 2
miles and the mules kept faling down in the snow head
formost and the Indian said he could not find the
road   we stoped and let the Indian and man go on
to hunt the road   thay went on and found the road
to the top of the mountain and come back and said
they thought we could git over if it did not snow any
more   well the Woman were all so tirder caring
there Children that thay could not go over that night

so we made a fire and got something to eat & ma spred
down a bufalorobe & we all laid down on it & spred
somthing over us & ma sit up by the fire & it snowed
one foot on top of the bed so we got up in the morning & the snow was so deep we could not go over &
we had to go back to the cabin & build more cabins &
stay thare all Winter without Pa we had not the
first thing to eat Ma maid arrangements for some
cattel giving 2 for 1 in callifornia we seldom thot
of bread for we had not had any since [blot, words not
readable] & the cattel was so poor thay could note
hadley git up when thay laid down we stoped thare
the 4th of November & staid till March and what we
had to eat i cant hardley tell you & we had that man
& Indians to feed well thay started over a foot and
had to come back so thay made snow shoes and started
again & it come on a storme & thay had to come
back it would snow 10 days before it would stop
thay wated tell it stoped & started again I was a
goeing with them & I took sick & could not go – thare
was 15 started & thare was 7 got throw 5 Weman &
2 men it come a storme and thay lost the road & got
out of provisions & the ones that got throwe had to
eat them that Died not long after thay started we got
out of provisions & had to put Martha at one cabin
James at another Thomas at another & Ma & Elizea
& Milt Eliot & I dried up what littel meat we had
and started to see if we could get across & had to leve
the childrin o Mary you may think that hard to leve
theme with strangers & did not now wether we would
see them again or not we could hardle get a way from
them but we told theme we would bring them Bread
& then thay was willing to stay we went & was out

5 days in the mountains   Elie giv out & had to go
back   we went on a day longer   we had to lay by a
day & make snow shows & we went on a while and
coud not find the road & we had to turn back   I could
go on verry well while i thout we wer giting along
but as soone as we had to turn back i coud hadley git
along but we got to the cabins that night   I froze one
of my feet verry bad & that same night thare was the
worst storme we had that winter & if we had not come
back that night we would never got back   we had
nothing to eat but ox hides   o Mary I would cry and
wish I had what you all wasted   Eliza had to go to
Mr Graves cabin & we staid at Mr Breen   thay had
meat all the time & we had to kill littel cash the dog
& eat him   we ate his head and feet & hide & evry
thing about him   o my Dear Cousin you dont now
what trubel is   yet a many a time we had on the last
thing a cooking and did not now wher the next would
come from but there was awl wais some way provided

there was 15 in the cabon we was in and half of us
had to lay a bed all the time   thare was 10 starved
to death   there we was hadley abel to walk   we lived
on litle cash a week and after Mr Breen would cook
his meat we would take the bones and boil them 3 or
4 days at a time   ma went down to the other caben
and got half a hide carried it in snow up to her wast

it snowed and would cover the cabin all over so we
could not git out for 2 or 3 days   we would have to
cut pieces of the loges in sied to make a fire with   I
coud hardly eat the hides and had not eat anything
3 days   Pa stated out to us with providions and then
came a storme and he could not go   he cash his provision and went back on the other side of the bay to

get compana of men and the San Wakien got so hye
he could not crose well thay Made up a Compana
at Suters Fort and sent out we had not ate any thing
for 3 days & we had onely a half a hide and we was
out on top of the cabin and we seen them a coming

O my Dear Cousin you dont now how glad i was,
we run and met them one of them we knew we
had traveled with them on the road thay staid thare
3 days to recruet a little so we could go thare was
20 started all of us started and went a piece and
Martha and Thomas giv out & so the men had to take
them back ma and Eliza James & I come on and
o Mary that was the hades thing yet to come on and
leiv them thar did not now but what thay would starve
to Death Martha said well ma if you never see me
again do the best you can the men said thay could
hadly stand it it maid them all cry but they said it
was better for all of us to go on for if we was to go
back we would eat that much more from them thay
give them a littel meat and flore and took them back
and we come on we went over great hye mountain
as strait as stair steps in snow up to our knees litle
James walk the hole way over all the mountain in snow
up to his waist he said every step he took he was
a gitting nigher Pa and somthing to eat the Bears
took the provision the men had cashed and we had but
very little to eat when we had traveld 5 days travel
we met Pa with 13 men going to the cabins o Mary
you do not nou how glad we was to see him we had
not seen him for months we thought we woul never
see him again he heard we was coming and he made
some seet cakes to give us he said he would see Martha and Thomas the next day he went to tow days

what took us 5 days   some of the compana was eating
from them that Died but Thomas & Martha had not
ate any   Pa and the men started with 12 people   Hiram O Miller CarriedThomas and Pa caried Martha
and thay wer caught in [unreadable word] and thay
had to stop Two days   it stormed so thay could not
go and the Bears took their provision and thay weer
4 days without anything   Pa and Hiram and all the
men started one of Donner boys   Pa a carring Martha
Hiram caring Thomas and the snow was up to thare
wast and it a snowing so thay could hadley see the
way   they raped the chidlren up and never took them
out for 4 days & thay had nothing to eat in all that
time   Thomas asked for somthing to eat once   those
that thay brought from the cabins some of them was
not able to come and som would not come   Thare
was 3 died and the rest eat them   thay was 10 days
without any thing to eat but the Dead   Pa braught
Thom and pady on to where we was   none of the
men was abel to go   there feet was froze very bad
so they was a nother Compana went and braught
them all in   thay are all in from the Mountains now
but five   they was men went out after them and was
caught in a storm and had to come back   thare is
another compana gone thare was half got through
that was stoped thare sent to their relief thare was
but   families got that all of them got   we was one
O Mary I have not wrote you half of the truble
we have had but I hav Wrote you anuf to let you
now that you dont now whattruble is   but thank the
Good god we have all got throw and the onely family
that did not eat human flesh   we have left every thing
but i dont cair for that   we have got through but Dont

let this letter dishaten anybody and never take no cutofs
and hury along as fast as you can

My Dear Cousin

We are all very well pleased with Callifornia par-
tucularly with the climate   let it be ever so hot a day
thare is all wais cool nights   it is a beautiful Country
it is mostley in vallies it aut to be a beautiful Country to pay us for our trubel geting there   it is the
greatest place for catle and horses you ever saw   it
would Just suit Charley for he could ride down 3 or
4 horses a day and he could lern to be Bocarro that
one who lases cattel   the spanards and Indians are
the best riders i ever say   thay have a spanish sadel
and woden sturups and great big spurs the wheel of
them is 5 inches in diameter and thay could not manage
the Callifornia horses witout the spurs, thay wont go
atol if they cant hear the spurs rattle   they have littel bells to them to make them rattle   thay blindfold
the horses and then sadel them and git on them and
then take the blindfole of and let run and if thay cant
sit on thay tie themselves on and let them run as fast
as they can and go out to a band of bullluck and throw
the reatter on a wild bullluck and but it around the
horn of his sadel and he can hold it as long as he wants

a nother Indian throws his reatter on its feet and
throws them and when thay git take the reatter of of
them they are very dangerous   they will run after you
then hook there horses and run after any person thay
see   thay ride from 80 to 100 miles a day & have
some of the spanard have from 6 to 7000 head of horses
and from 15 to 16000 head Cattel   we are all verry
fleshey   Ma waies 10040 pon and still a gaing   I
weigh 80   tel Henriet if she wants to get Married

for to come to Callifornia she can get a spanyard
any time that Eliza is a going to marrie a a spanyard
by the name of Armeho and Eliza weighs 10070 We
have not saw uncle Cadon yet but we have had 2 letters from him he is well and is a coming here as soon
as he can Mary take this letter to uncle Gurshon and
to all tha i know to all of our neighbors and tell Doch-
ter Meniel and every girl i know and let them read
it Mary kiss little Sue and Maryann for me and give
my best love to all i know to uncle James and Lida
and all the rest of the famila and to uncle Gurshon
aunt Percilla and all the Children and to all of our
neighbors and to all she knows so no more at present
pa is yerbayan [Yerba Buena]

My Dear casons
Virginia Elizabeth B Reed

Two Letters ⸲ Phoebe Stanton

INTRODUCTION

In the manuscript collection of the Oregon Historical Society in Portland are two letters written by Phoebe Stanton. One, the actual original, was written in 1847 while traveling in a wagon train in Missouri enroute to far-away Oregon. The second letter was written in 1856 from that far-away land telling of life in their new surroundings near Salem in the Willamette Valley. The first part of the second letter is really written by her husband, Alfred Stanton. Although it is our purpose to publish women's diaries and letters, the husband's is in this case so much a part of the whole that it is included as well.

Part way through her 1847 letter Phobe Stanton wrote as follows: "May 10th another pleasant morning to morrow makes me 32." This tells us her birth date: May 11, 1815. Her maiden name had been Phoebe Fail, and her birthplace, according to the 1850 Federal Census, was somewhere in Virginia. She was married to Alfred Stanton, a native of Ohio, on January 9, 1831, in La Porte, Indiana, several months before her sixteenth birthday. The bridegroom was a 23-year-old farmer, his birth date being July 23, 1808.

They lived in Indiana for the next sixteen years, and in April, 1847, they left for the trip over the Oregon Trail with five children: Marietta and Rocena, 14-year-old girls, evidently twins; Francis (or Frank), 11 years; Sarah, 8 years, and Lydia, 4.[1]

---

[1] The names of the children were taken from the records of the 1850

There is one fact that does not appear in Phoebe Stanton's letters, but it can be deduced by historical detection: She was pregnant during the long westward journey, for the 1850 Federal Census lists a little boy, Philip, three years old, born in Oregon.

This was a farm family, typical of those participating in the overland trail migration to the Willamette Valley of Oregon, where they could look forward to settling on a sprawling acreage of rich land. Alfred Stanton was an experienced farmer and nurseryman. The same Federal land records inform us that one year after reaching Oregon they filed on 640 acres just east of the new little town of Salem on November 3, 1848. They got that much because, as the record shows, they were husband and wife, each of them being entitled by law at that time to settle on 320 acres.[2]

Another thing we learn from the land records: Alfred Stanton ran a nursery business, for in signing a verification for a neighbor, James Downs, an Englishman, Alfred testified, "he purchased fruit trees from my nursery in the Fall of 1851." [3] He has much to say about growing fruit trees in his letter below.

Over and over again there were printed during the following decades items in the Salem newspaper, the *Oregon Statesman,* telling of the participation of the Stantons in first the Marion County Agricultural Society, and then, beginning with the first Oregon State Fair in the autumn of 1861, in that growing institution.

Phoebe Stanton was a perennial prize winner with her

Federal Census of Marion County, Oregon. The ages on the journey were extrapolated from the same record. A most helpful book on this subject is Elsie Youngberg, *Oregon Territory, 1850 Census* (End of the Trail Researchers, Lebanon, Oregon, 1970).

[2] *Genealogical Material in Oregon Donation Land Claims,* I (Portland, Ore., 1957), Claim Number 28.

[3] *Ibid.,* II (Portland, 1959), Claim Number 2637.

preserved fruits and with her flowers. She often brought
gifts of the same to the editor of the newspaper, which he
duly noted:

> FRUIT AND FLOWERS. – We are indebted to Mrs. A. Stanton,
> of this county, for a basket of choice peaches, pears and plums,
> of huge sizes and rich flavors capped with a most elegant bouquet.
> Many thanks.
>
> *Oregon Statesman,* September 29, 1859.

There appeared in the same newspaper on October 6,
1862, a tribute to Phoebe Stanton's talents, with a statement about the fair, that "A crab-apple jelly, in fancy
mould, by Mrs. Stanton, was particularly admired." On
June 15, 1863, the fair's board of managers met in Salem
and designated Phoebe Stanton to be one of those in charge
of "Class 10 — Miscellaneous Home Work" at next fall's
fair.[4] That year she won premiums with her dried apples,
dried plums, preserved peaches, preserved pears, cucumber
pickles, vinegar, and finally with her currant wine. So it
went on year after year.

The Stanton family was active in the Christian Church.
They took an interest in the developing educational program of that church. The *Oregon Statesman* reported on
July 2, 1865, that a "Christian College" had been approved
at the annual meeting of the Christian Church of Oregon
held at Bethel, Polk County. The college was to be established at the town of Monmouth. Albert Stanton of Marion
County was appointed as a trustee of the new college. That
institution has continued to the present with a strong em-
phasis on training teachers. It was later turned over to the
state and became successively Oregon Normal School, Oregon College of Education, and now Western Oregon State
College. If the two letters here published show something
to be desired in the use of the English language, these

---

[4] Reported in the *Oregon Statesman,* June 15, 1863. The premiums are
listed in the same newspaper for Oct. 26, 1863.

parents wanted to see to it that their children did not suffer from the same disadvantage.[5]

The Stantons also took an active part in the commercial development of their new homeland. One thing they did was to support the founding of the Willamette Woolen Manufacturing Company in Salem from the date it was organized in December, 1865.[6] Another project they shared with others was the Capital Lumbering Company, whose voluminous records are located in the manuscript collection of the University of Oregon Library, Eugene. There are a number of Stanton items among the company's papers.

Their retirement from active farming is noted in the 1880 Federal Census records for Marion County, when on June 8 of that year a census taker named J. W. Cox recorded that Alfred Stanton, age 71, was now a "Retired Farmer," and that "Phoebi" [sic], his wife, was living out her role to "Keep house." Persons seemed to have a knack for finding different ways to mis-spell "Phoebe."

The same *Oregon Statesman* newspaper that had recorded a scattering of events through the lives of Phoebe and Alfred Stanton also recorded their deaths with proper obituaries. The one for Phoebe came first, as the newspaper reported on March 19, 1886, that she had died "At her home in this city at about 6 o'clock last (Thursday) evening, March 11th, 1886, Mrs. A. Stanton, aged about 73 years." She was one of the "early pioneer ladies of Oregon." Six years later, on June 17, 1892, the *Statesman* reported Albert Stanton's death, age 84 years, on June 11.

We are grateful to the Oregon Historical Society for permission to publish the following pair of letters. Phoebe Stanton was the principal author in this case, and Albert played a somewhat smaller part in the letter writing.

---

[5] Ellis A. Stebbins, *The OCE Story* (Monmouth, Ore., 1973), 9 and *passim*.

[6] Oregon Archives, Manuscript 7695, "A Bill – To incorporate the Willamette Woolen Manufacturing Company . . . Joint Stock Company."

I. A LETTER FROM MISSOURI: 1847

May the 9th   1847

Dear Brothers and Sisters   I now take this oportunity of in forming you that we are all well at present and hope these few lines will find you enjoying the same blessing   we are now one hundred and ten miles from St. Joseph   it will be 4 weeks to morrow since we left home   we have delayed some on account of our company be hind   the roads have been extremely good the wather fine   we could of traveled it easily to St. Joseph in four weeks and a half if we had not layed by so much as much as 4 days   we have had a pleasant journey   we have never been weary and tired yet we are now twenty one waggons strong   hundreds behind and before   we have had a hard time to get food for our catle its being so scarce on acount of such emigration   we have paid from 5 to 10 cts a head for hay when we could get it   some time went with out anything but now since the fifth of may we have had plenty of grass   our cattle looks well as when we started   there is a great deal said about the Mormans they say they have gone on and joined three tribes of Indians and are going to cut us all off   they are raising a company of volunteers and 3 hundred have volunteered to go and guard us through   they are going to all start from St. Jo   we have not heard of any going by Councilbluff   we are asked a gret many time if we are mormans   when we tell them no they say I know you are but you wont own it   your wagons looks like it and will say I hope you are not for their road is marked with stolen property and all maner of wickedness   we could not get any kind of acommo-

dations if we were known to be mormans some
would tell us the mormans will rob you before you get
half way through but we are not afraid of them we
tell them there is a great deal done on their credit
has ben a very backward spring here we was in Illinois it was as forward as it is here now all except
wheet in Ioway and Masourie looks better than in
Illinois some are planting corn here now and corn
is up in some places last Sunday and Monday night
we have hard frosts there is a great deal of wild
fruit in this country. the people looks course and plain
here but apear to be clever last Saturday we layed
bye and the men went 6 miles to Town on the Desmoin
river kesoqua and bought provision 5 cts a pound for
pork one dollar and seventy five cts for flour 7 cts rice
10 cts sugar then we crossed the Desmoin at Ioway-
ville 17 miles above the water was clear in their
stream and very shallow so that we could of taken the
bed of the river for our road I believe here we was
detained half a day on acount of some blacksmithing
   the boys and girls went on the river to have a ride
and run on a sand bar and they thought they would
soon get over that place and the girls pushed and the
boys got out and pulled and finally they boys had to
carry the girls to shore you may guess the rest laughed
so much for that place and a poor litle place it was
well it is gett so dark in my waggon I must wait untill
morning to finish May 10th another pleasant morning to morrow makes me 32 Lydia has the chils off
and on ever since we left home and 2 wks before some
others complaining this morning myself a litle head
ache the water has been very bad for more than a
hundred miles scarcely anything but slowholes enough

to make the catle sick   I want very much to see you all   I saw all of my relations but Alpheus and Eleanor and Cyntha and children   perhaps you often pity our condition but it had not been pitiable yet sofar it has been pleasant   wev not had any Company but our Laport friends but 2 nights to do our laport boys justice   I must say they are a fine decent set of fellows very unlike our Suckers   when they stop at night they have their jug and cards and fidles and they are a ruff set   I think it will be disagreeable traveling in a large company which we have avoided untill now   nothing more of interest now as I have to close my letter before we start and the catle coming now my oportunyty for writing is poor as I have to write on a small box in the waggon with every kind of noise around me but I would write I thought to you as I did not see you before I started   forgive my scribling for I have written the most of it with the oxen hiched to the wagon I am now writing so I hope you will get ready bye next spring and come   Fare well   remember I am your affectionate Sister

   Phoebe Stanton
      [To] Alpheus Traggoner Eleanor
      Benajah and Cyntha Stanton
The girls wanted me to tell you all very much and sent their love to you all   Alfred sends his love to all as he is on a high hill and cannot leave his oxe long enough to write and we will soon start   I want some of you to write to Oregon city perhaps we may get it   I want to hear from home verry bad   May the 12th at night
   I did not come to a post office as soon as I expected
   I told you of what fine roads we had but now I will tell of what bad roads we have had   we have been

crossing the 3 branches of the Grand River all the way
through thick timber and barrens to gather and Seventh at night it comenced raining when we were
camped on bank of the first branch and raine all night
next morning the ground was covered with watter
and the folks that layed in the tents were all most a
drowned some rung their beds some layed them on
brush to drean the watter half shoe deep then we
traveled 25 miles of the worst road I ever traveled
in my life sometimes the whels rolled on the ground
sometimes the wagon stood on 2 wheels some times on
one end and we overtook 5 more wagons and after
26 waggons passed I cannot compare it to any thing
yove ever saw finally we are safe over the last branch
and what's a head I cant tell

　　Now dark again

II. A LETTER FROM OREGON: 1856

　　　　　　　　North Bend Farm, Marion Co.
　　　　　　　　　April 13, 1856.
Dear Brother & Sister.

　　I thought i wood breake they long silance that has
prevailed between us, I received your kind letter some
time ago, which informed us that you ware all in good
health, We are all in good health at this time & all of
our folks are far as i know. The weather is verry fine at
this time, and crops bids fair to be verry good this
season. We had verry cold weather for about two weaks
which froce harder than I ever saw in Origon before,
it froze all the wheat out so that the people had to
sow agane this spring. We have a fair prospect for a
large crop of fruit this season. Wheat is worth one

dollar pr bushel oats 60 cts potatoes 1 dollar pr bus. Good work horses are verry high good american cows are worth from 50 to 60 dollars a piece good sheep is worth from 7 to 8 dollars a head hogs are verry cheap. We have had a great deal of Indian difficulty both North and South,[1] thare has bin a great many men and women and children kiled in Oregon. Great many families have been murdered and [t]hair Houses burned and cattle driven off and distroyed. They have several woman and children prisoners at this time, Our young men and a good many oald men have gone to Fight Indians. Our Indian war commenced about the first of September last, and we have had a great deal of difficulty with them ever since, and thare is no telling when it will be over, this war caused labour to be high and money scarce. The farmers of Oregon have turned thair attention a great deal to raising fruit, thare being a good market at this time and wee think that it will continue for a long time to come, for California does not rais as good fruit as wee doo, also the Sandwich [Hawaiian] Islands will be a good market for fruit Sanfracisco is a city of nearly one hundred thousand inhabitance at this time, and Apples are worth one dollar a pound and it takes about 44 lbs for one bushel this is no small sum for one bushel of apples Just think of that and just wish your Selves in Oregon with a good orchard. I have now over two thousand fruit trees set in an Orchard and expect to set untill I get forty acers compleetly set out. I am

---

[1] This was the time of the so-called "Yakima War," which took place north of the Columbia. A balanced treatment of this conflict may be found in Dorothy Johansen and Charles M. Gates, *Empire of the Columbia,* 2nd Ed. (N.Y., 1967), 246-58.

a setting 80 trees to the acre which will make upwards of three thousand trees. I think if the late frost dont hurt the fruit this year I shall have about three hundred bushels of Apples   I judge from what I had last year. I had two hundred bushels of Apples for which I sold for eleven dollars pr bu. this is a fair price for fruit. I have about 20 thousand fruit trees which will fetch a fair price, nothing more about fruit. I have one thing more to rather bost of that is, we have a fine son to bost of at this time [2] he is two months oald yesterday. Marietta [3] has a son three months oald and Calls his name Frank Newton. We have not named him yet. I have not much more to wright. I want you to wright and let me hear all the news. I doant expect that we shall come back this year, but I want to be ready nex year. I think the little boy will be too small this year to travil. I have nothing more at this time   I remain your affecionate Brother

Alfred Stanton.

To B. S. Stanton.

Dear Brother & Sister   seeing Alfred has not filled the sheet I will try & do it, I have nothing of great

---

[2] The *Oregon Statesman* of Salem reported in its May 20, 1856, edition, "DIED Near Salem, May 13, WILLARD, infant son of Alfred and Phebe [sic] Stanton, aged three months and one day."

[3] The Oregon City *Spectator* newspaper carried the following story in its April 18, 1850 edition:

MARRIED

By Rev. S. M. Fackler on the 27th of March, Mr. ISAAC GILBERT and Miss MARIETTA STANTON, both of Marion County.

The happy pair were determined that the Printers should in some way share in their rejoicing, and accordingly accompanied the above notice with lots of cake. May their lives be long and their mutual happiness increase with increasing years.

importance to write unless I tell you how much work
I have to do. Alfred has told you all of the good &
left out the bad & so ill tell that, from this you would
naturally supose we were a getting rich   our expences
are very great Mens labour $100 for 3 months work –
$3 per week for a girl when you can get one, I am
doing my work my self cooking for four men & got
a cross child   the children are all going to school
except Olive J   she is all the help I have, you had
better think Alfred has to come to the pounding barrel.
Francis M is going to school west of the Willamett
to Bethel Institute [4] one of the best schools in Oregon;
Well bettween the indians & grass hoppers we have a
continual war   we are looking for both & indeed this
is no joke   the Indians have entirely destroyed the little
village at the cascade falls (but the Whites have re-
taken it) & killed a good many of its inhabitants before
they could get in to the fort [5] they few in number had
to defend the fort several days before they could get
assistance   that is only from 80 to 85 miles from here
   we were acquainted with a good many that are now
murdered by the savage foe   amongst the first to fall
was young Bellshaw from Rolling prairie IA [6]   he

---

[4] Francis M. Stanton was reported to be 14 years old in the 1850 Federal
Census. At the time of the writing of this letter he was 20. Bethel Institute
was a school established by the Disciples of Christ or Christian Church in
the Willamette Valley west of the river in present Polk County. There is
still an empty building out in the green farmland. Some organization of the
Institute still remains, however, and the defunct school has a board that
meets for some purpose occasionally. It is about 13 miles north of Monmouth,
just to the east of Highway #99.

[5] This was the notorious "Cascades Massacre," which took place upstream
from Fort Vancouver on the north shore of the Columbia. Tragically both
sides, white and Indian, mutually massacred each other. See Howard Mc-
Kinley Corning, *Dictionary of Oregon History* (Portland, 1956), 47.

[6] So far this young man is unidentified.

left here four week before with a load of aples going
South   they killed the whole company up set wagons
took the horses & strewed the aples in every direction
    O what horible crimes they have committed   it
would chill your blood to hear – – – they have mad
several efforts to come into this valley   they warned
the whites that had squaws & one in particular near
Vancouver to flee if he wanted to save his self & family
for they would not regard any of his colour   his wife
was the Chiefs sister   the families all fled to Portland
& Oregon City along the Columbia but some of them
have gone back   they have to keep rangers out all the
time – how long matters will continue this way we
cannot tell   The Indian Agent has brought seven or
eight hundred Indians in to this Valey & boucht a
tract of land & placed them on it & there is already
doubts as to there friendly disposition there is no trusting them [7]   those you think to be the most friendly
are the first to murder the whites, the indians near
by always com off victorious   the whites careless &
very reckless & the indians always take the advantage
they dash down from the mountains & commit their
depredations & back to the mountains before the whites
are aware of them but it is of no use for me to try
to describe affair to you for I can not do it & so I will
come to a close after I inform you that William [8] lives

---

[7] This was the Grand Ronde Indian Reservation, some 60,000 acres on
the eastern slope of the Coast Range. It was established in 1856. Some 2,000
Indians from all parts of the region were placed there by the Federal Government. There is still a Grand Ronde Reservation of a much smaller
acreage and population.

[8] William and Sarah were William Lerwell and his wife, Sarah. She
was Alfred Stanton's sister. He is listed in the 1860 Federal Census as a
miller, born in England, and between the writing of the 1856 letter and the
1860 census, Sarah had died.

five miles north of here & is doing very well   he is
tending mill him self for $80 a month & hires a man
on his farm   Sarah is not very well at present   Anna
& William [9] lives at Ugene City & are well the last
account   can any of you tell any thing about Mr. Hunt
we heard he was dead   he owes a poor man here
some one hundred & fifty dollars & does not know any
thing where to write   please inform us about him the
first one that writes.

Phoebe Stanton

please remember us to all of our friends   we receive
3 letters dated within 9 days of each other one from
Alpheus one from Philip & one from you   We learn
you have had a very cold winter & so have we   We
are going to write to alpheus soon   tell Moses we
would like to see some more of his composition.

---

[9] Anna and William are so far unidentified.

Letters from a Quaker Woman

❦ Rachel Fisher

INTRODUCTION

The key word is "poignant" when describing the letters that follow.

As a 15-year-old girl, Rachel Joy (b. April 20, 1822), had emigrated with her parents, Reuben and Rachel Joy, from Henry County, Indiana, to the budding Quaker community of Salem, Iowa. That was in the year 1837.

On January 6, 1841, she and John H. Fisher were married. Over the next four years she would give birth to four children: Angelina, b. December 17, 1841; Thomas Clarkson, b. November 24, 1843, both of whom died on April 14, 1844, probably during an epidemic. Then there were twin girls, Anna Jane and a second Angelina, born on February 5, 1845. Anna Jane died on December 7, 1846, just over one year old.[1]

John and Rachel Fisher started over the plains to Oregon in the spring of 1847 in a wagon train led by Henderson Luelling, a close family friend. Angelina was in excellent health. The first of Rachel's two letters here published was written to tell the folks back home of the death of her husband, John, on June 6, 1847. It was sent from "Sixty miles from Fort Larima" early in July.

Rachel traveled on, aided by other members of the wagon train. The second letter, written in "Tualaty County, Ore-

---

[1] This information was gleaned from the Iowa historical collections in different localities by Frances Fuller Meltebeke. See also Mary Elizabeth Way, *The Way Family* (Martinez, Calif., 1969). Rachel's middle name was Way.

gon," on March 18, 1848, told of the death, probably
somewhere in present Idaho, of the second little Angelina.
Rachel had discovered the child's illness, a kind of paralysis,
on August 11, and Angelina had died the next day.

Rachel Fisher decided to stay on in the Tualatin Valley
(present Washington County, Oregon). There she met
William A. Mills, a young farmer who had just attained
the age of 21 years on September 1, 1847. They were
married on March 2, 1848. William was described by a
contemporary much later in life as follows:

> To quote his own words, he was "born in Tennessee, but was
> raised on the road, with little opportunity for education, having
> attended school but five months." Hence we have before us the
> unfolding of a self-educated and self-made life, which is always
> interesting to a student of human nature.[2]

That marriage, too, early on suffered from tragedy as
there was reported in the *Oregon Statesman* newspaper of
Salem, Oregon, in its issue of September 13, 1851, that there
had died "on the 14th inst., of croup, Rachel, daughter of
Wm. A. and Rachel Mills, aged two years and six months."
There was a second child, a baby boy, John Milton, who
had been born on February 18, 1851.

There would follow Mary Ellen, b. December 9, 1853;
Laura Alice, b. November 8, 1854; Elva Jane, b. January
20, 1856, and Albert, b. April 13, 1861. All of these lived
on to fairly ripe ages.

Rachel was all her life a devout Quaker, quite lonely
because, though there were individual Quaker neighbors in
Oregon, there were no meetings as yet. In her letters she
uses the Quaker method of dating. They had originated the
numerical way of recording dates because they simply would
not use the names of days and months derived from pagan

---

[2] H. K. Hines, *An Illustrated History of the State of Oregon* (Chicago,
1893), 280.

[3] Meltebeke, *op. cit.*

gods such as Woden, Thor, Janus, and Mars. Occasionally
there strays into her letters a "thee" or "thy."

Rachel Mills died on the 11th of 12th month, 1869, at
her home in the Tualatin Valley. The third item published
below, another letter, is an obituary written on March 19,
1870, by Edward Luelling, a dear friend, and son of Henderson and Elizabeth Luelling. It was sent to the editor
of the *Willamette Farmer,* of Salem, Oregon, an early
agricultural newspaper.[4] Edward Luelling told of the death
of Rachel and went on in poignant words to describe the
tragedies that dogged her early life and of the "plainness
in dress and address" of her later years.

The two "Rachel letters," as we have come to call them,
are printed with the permission of George Joy of Hays,
Kansas. They were the property of Mrs. Rossie Stackhouse,
since whose death George Joy has been the administrator
of her estate. We are grateful for permission to publish
these significant documents of nineteenth century American
life.

Other information has been supplied by Miss Rhoda
Mills, Portland, Oregon, and we have had the use of information on births, marriages, and deaths worked out in great
detail by the genealogical researches of Mrs. Frances Fuller
Meltebeke, of Springfield, Oregon.

RACHEL FISHER MILLS: LETTER I

Sixty miles from Fort Larima 7th *mo* 2th 1847
Dear parents I will again endeavor to prepare A
letter for you not withstanding the anguish and bitter
mourning it exites when I recall the past think of the
present and imagine the future. John still continued

---

[4] There is a rare file of the *Willamette Farmer* in the Salem, Oregon,
Public Library.

sick some times better and then worse untill the 7th of
6th *mo* he appear worse and the 5th the com[pany]
stoped before night for he still grew worse. 6th I had
to bid him farwell and see him breathe the last breath
of Earthly Life without A strugle or groan. appearing
to fall into a sweet sleep of eternity. he did not appear
to have a recollection of things as they pass for something over a week before his death but had at the same
time had his right reason of what pass before. he appear
to have some knowledge of his death but could not talk
much he had become so much affected in his nerves.
the place were we left him was nine miles from whare
we had come to platt river close to the road side by a
small grove. I thought of returning but I had no one
to take me back and I could not see how I could do
better than to go on. I have fared as well as I could
have expected. I have laid with Rachel Hockette in
their waggon and cooked by their fire since I was left

Thomas Hockette has drove for me mostly.[1] since
we passed the Fort I got Th. Williba [Wilbur?] to
drive for me through if I do not with an opportunity
turning back. We are in company with 19 waggons.
Luellings [2] are behind. we are stopt to day for the cattle

---

[1] The Hocketts were also Quakers from Salem, Iowa. Rachel Hockett's
husband, Thomas, would also become a casualty of the frontier. We do not
know the details of his death, but by the 1850 U. S. Federal Census in
Oregon, she would be remarried to John Griffith, a 25-year-old farmer, a
Kentuckian.

[2] Different members of the family spelled their name variously Luelling
and Lewelling. Henderson Luelling was the leader of the wagon train of
which Rachel Fisher was a member. He became a nurseryman in Oregon.
He had been a community leader in Salem, Iowa, and very active in the
Underground Railroad by which slaves were aided in their escape from
the South to Canada. Elizabeh, his wife, was Rachel's best friend. The
Luellings brought out a wagonload of fruit trees, 800-1000 of them, on the
1847 migration. He also had a number of scions for grafting onto trees,

to rest. their is good feed and water here but it is the
first grass since we come to the   [?]   Yes my cattle
all stand the journey well   have not lost any. have had
better roads than expected some verry hilly and rough

not much warm wether and no rain of consequence
since the 6th of 6 *mo*   considerable before then mostly
at night. we have not laid by but one day. on the account
of high water which was the ten of 6th *mo*   it is a
somewhat memmerable day to com[pany]. soon as the
men got their breakfast some went a hu[n]ting and
some at one thing some another and the first we knew
there was about 40 Indians runing past the campt trying to take the horses   all the men that was in campt
took after them

they [*sic*] men soon all come back except four that
had gone a hunting and three that took horses and went
to try to rescue the others   Indians went over the bluff
found two of the men T Hockette and J. M. Robison [3] took guns and all their clothing except boots and
hats. found the other two men   did not take any thing
but their shot pouches all come up in time for dinner.
We have not seen any pawnee Indians since. We got
to Fort Larima yesterday   was a week ago, it being
first day the Indians came out and meet   they expect
gifts   the Oregon fellows has now passed by us   will
not pas us   we send our letters after them − 7th *mo*
5th 1847   your affectionate daughter
                                              Rachel Fisher
    my little daughter & myself is in good health at this
time

literally a moving nursery. Morton E. Peck, "Luelling, Henderson," *Dictionary of American Biography* (New York, 1933), IX, 498-99.
    [3] J. M. or I. M. Robison is so far unidentified.

7th *mo* 5th 1847

I have just closed my letter in a hurry.

But two more Oregon men has come up   will wait a few minutes I want you to come if you can and as son [soon] as you can for no doubt but I shal feel my self verry lonesome   I began to say something about the Sous [Sioux]   They complain that the Buffaloes has all left from near the road   they have to go 30 miles for their subsistence there fore they Expect a Smal contribution from each co of the emegrants but they are verry thakfull of the smalest gift but yet they are Friendly & Beggarly and thieveish   they have stelen several horses in our knowlede   Their women are generally neatly dressed in their way   there are about 50 white looking men but call them selves French men about the fort

from your daughter   Rachel Fisher

and now a few lines to John Lewelling[4]   I want him to settle all our business that was in trusted with him a cording to law   I want him to let Stephen Frazier[5] have the amount of a note of 35 dollars that is due us from John Rader[6] for the purpose of fixing him to move if he wishes   if the[e] can make thy self safe

Rachel W. Fisher

---

[4] John Lewelling was Henderson's brother who had stayed home in Salem, Iowa. He and a third brother, Seth, would later travel to Oregon to join the nursery business. Seth was to become responsible for the development of the Bing and the Black Republican cherries. The Bing was named for a faithful Chinese workman beloved by the entire family. Howard M. Corning, Ed., *Dictionary of Oregon History* (Portland, 1956), 146, 157.

[5] Stephen Frazier, husband of Anna Joy, Rachel's sister. The Joy family was very acive in the Underground Railroad, as were many Salem, Iowa Quakers. Charles Arthur Hawley, "For Peace and Freedom," *The Palimpsest,* XVI (Nov. 1935), 337-346; O. A. Garretson, "Travelling on the Underground Railroad in Iowa," *Iowa Journal of History and Politics,* XXII (July 1924), 418-53.

[6] So far unidentified.

RACHEL FISHER MILLS: LETTER II

Oregon Teritory   Tuality County   3th *mo*. 13th 1848
Much respected Parents & often thought of Brothers
& Sisters   I again sit down to write to you to let you
know something of me   I arived at Portland on the
willamet river 13 miles below Oregon City about the
15 of 11 mo. making 7 mo. from the time I started
untill I arived at A place to stop, near two months of
which I spent getting down the Columbia river. you
may imagine some thing of my feeling since I left you,
but you can only imagine. you may think I had seen
trouble before but my trouble in Iowa was nothing to
what I have experienced since I left there being deprived of one of the two objects which I held more
dear then any other earthly object, on the Plat river
I then thought that little Angeline was more dear to
me then any thing ever had been she being the last one
of my family. but alas the day was soon to come when
I should see her laid in her silent grave. I wrote to
you since her death but thinking it unceratin as to you
getting it, I will give you some account of her sickness
& death   I discovered her sickness the 11th of the 8th
mo.   she appeared well and very playful in the morning, when we stoped to eat dinner she was lame but
still was very playful & eat her dinner apparently
about as usual. soon after eating she became feverish
which increased very rapidly   her lameness (which
we soon found to be in her thigh just above the knee)
became very painful, getting worse through the night
the following morning she commenced having fits and
died about noon. the disease seemed strange but It was
not more so then It was distressing. A mortification

appeared to take place before her death. You may
judge of my lonely situation and render more lonely
by my driver being drown on the third day of the
week following. (he was drowned in Snake river 3
or 4 days travel before we came to the first crossing
by attempting to swim over to the other side to A
spring which he wished to see, it appearing to be quite
A curiosity he only got about half way across) his
name was I M Robison. I was taken sick soon after
crossing Snake river & was about six weeks not able
to do my work I have been midling well since I
recovered though not well as I was be fore

I stoped at Portland near a month after I got there
but my cattle were not doing well where they were
& hearing that the range was better on the plains I
concluded to move out there and winter at Isaac
Mills.[7] (A brotherinlaw to William Lech of Economy)

Enos T. Mendenhall [8] was teaching school at Millses
& I commensed attending school the 20th of 12th mo.
& continued on to the 18 of 2 mo. I went nearly half
way though Smiths Arithmetic. But Enos & myself
both taking up another subject to consider the school
was stop & the second day of the third month we both
joined hand in wedlock – I with William A. Mills
Isaac youngest son, aged 22 years, & Enos to A sister
age 16 years [9] William & I are living at his Father

---

[7] Isaac and Rachel Mills had brought their family to Oregon in 1843.
They settled in what was then called the Tualatin District, named for the
Tualatin River, which flows into the Willamette. This is present Washington
County, Oregon. Miss Rhoda Mills of Portland, Oregon, kindly shared with
the editor a family history of the Mills clan, a four-page transcript, and
other family papers.

[8] Enos Thomas Mendenhall, of the Quaker family of Salem, Iowa. Mills
family transcript, *op. cit.,* p. 4; also Louis Thomas Jones, *The Quakers of
Iowa* (Iowa City, 1914), 43.

in A house to ourseves. we have some prospect of going
up the Willamet this fall but we do not know whether
we will or not   it is so unhandy to market   I must now
leave you to conjecture the cause of my changing my
way of liveing And tell you something else. Health
appears to be good on the plains   people look well
and there appears to be but little use for grave yard
At Portland (which is 24 miles from here) they have
the ague some, but the second person was buried there
while I was stoped there that had ever died neer the
place & that person was an emigrant   there has been
A great many deaths on the road this season & still
more among the emigrant after they stoped on the
Columbia river & Willamet   I have knew as many
as 3 or 4 deaths in different families   those that got
to the [Tualatin] plains fared better generally   I was
at Oregon City soon after I came down the river   I
staid with Abrilla Trimble [10] while there   she was
midling well & in midling good spirits. she told me
that she had never felt satisfied in her mind since the
news came to her that Edward was on the road coming on before that   that she had no doubts be what
he was killed out of his misery

since that she has learned things about the circumstances that she had not learned before   I think from
the best that I learn that he was wounded and dragged
himself away and suffered to death   Oregon City
appears to be quite A flourishing little town   there

9 The sister who became the bride of Enos Mendenhall was Rachel Emily
Mills, born April 27, 1832, usually called Emily. Mills family transcript,
op. cit., p. 4.

10 Our search takes us to an "Arilla Tremble," listed in the 1850 Federal
Census as the wife of Thomas Powell of Marion County, Oregon, with four
children, all "Tremble" by name.

is something of A spirit of reform existing there, there
is A temperance meeting A licium two common day
schools, & two diferent religious meeting up there.
the situation of the place seems to me to be rougher
than any place that I ever seen in Iowa. the bluff coming up to within a stonethrow of the river, leaves A
small space for A city, but is advantages of mill priva-
leges can not be exceled in any place the falls of willamet being just at the upper edge of town. Portland
is the head of ship navigation   there has been between
15 and 20 ships there within the last twelve months   it
is A better situation for A town than Oregon City
notwithstanding it is very heavy timbered. there seem
to be but little thought of in Portland but to get rich
nor does there seem to be much else thought of in Oregon as far as my knowledge extends for I have not
been in reach of A meeting for any kind since I came
here except it was something like A dance & that did
not interest me enough for to cause me to attend.
There is a great call for machanics of different kind,
(vis) Cabinet, Chair, Sadling, coopering, shoemaking,
fanmaking, thrashing, tanner brickmaking & laying,
hatting wheelmakeing housejoiner & Millright   these
are all in good demand & perhaps others that I do
not think of. common mens work is [blank] per day,
making rails   women work is from one to three dollars per week. wheat is $7 per bu, pork from 6 to 10
cnts per lb, bacon from 16 to 20 salt 50 cents per bushel
masured at that, Sugar from 5 to 12 cents per lb, coffee from 3 to 5 lbs to the dollar, factory [11] from 10 to
20 cents per yd, beef from 2½ to 3 cents per lb. cattle

---

[11] Factory-made cloth, usually cotton.

such as work oxen are cheap, & American cows fetch
A good price. waggons are cheap. good American
horses are in good demand. mules are in good demand.
there is A plenty of hogs here but they are A good
price   they do not feed here like they do in Iowa
Isaac Mills killed hogs that never were fed A day
that weighed from 2 to 300 hundred   Cattle are in
good order   my cattle are doing well. the little cow
has give milk ever since we left Iowa And now gives
milk & butter enough for us. the climate is fully as
good is I anticipated. I have not been colder since I
stop traveling then I have been in Iowa in June. it
has been sun shiny nice weather considerable of the
winter although there has been some rain & snow. the
deepest snow that I have seen here has not exceeded
three inches deep laid over one day. some winters is
said to be much colder than this has been. Vegetables
grow well here. (Mother I have lived this winter
where I could have mustard and other greens all the
time & I have live with A woman for the last three
months that I have never heard scold one word on any
occasion. that is Wm. mother   she has seemd more like
A mother than any one I have ever seen since I left
thee   Fruits of some kind grow in abundance such as
strawberries, gooseberries, rasberries, blackberries,
hucleberries, cranberries, dewberries, sallal berries,[12]

---

[12] Salal is an Indian name for *Gaultheria shallon,* a coarse-growing
ground cover, knee-high and higher, that covers the ground all through
northwest forests. It was a staple in the Indians' diet. The blue-black berries
tend to be rather bland but are large and abundant. Lewis J. Clark, *Wild
Flowers of the Pacific Northwest* (Sidney, B.C., Canada, 1976), 376, 395.
The Indians chewed the leaves and spread the product on burns, which was
not bad medical practice as the leaves contain tannic and gallic acid. Erna
Gunther, *Ethnobotany of Western Washington* (Seattle, 1973), 43-44.

sarvis berries,[13] &c   there is not much fruit that grows
on trees unless it is planted. there is no plumbs nor
graips that I have heard of. there is crab apples. they
are very small. The growth of timber is pine, fur,
cedar, hemlock, white oak, alder, ash, cottonwood, dog
wood, cherry, maple & hazle, the main growth of
which is Evergreen. they make brooms, barrel hoops
& withs of hazle   they also use cherry for brooms, &c

Wm says that he has seen wheat sowed in ever month
in the year except July & August & produce good wheat
he has been here 4 years & likes the country very
well. I cannot say much whether I like it or not for
I have not seen much of it   as far as I have seen the
face of the country does not look as butiful as Iowa,
but perhaps the health & mild climate make amend
for the want of beauty of the country & perhaps when
I see more of it I will be better pleased. there is salmon
& trout fish here plenty & there is deer, bear, tigar elk
panther & wolves plenty   there is chickens turkeys &
ducks that is tame & wild fouls about as they were
there except wild turkeys   there is none of them here
[Only part of the next page is still extant.]
& if any of you are on the road & chance to see this
write me word which way you are coming & whether
you are likely to need assistance or not & I think that
I will meet you if sickness does not hinder. I must now
bring my letter to A close trusting that the Great ruler
of the universe may guid us so that we will meet here
or herafter so I bid you all Far well   Parents & relations all.   Wm. A. Mills
                                               Rachel Mills

---

13 Rachel's "sarvis berries" would be service berries, a common Pacific
slope shrub, *Amelanchier alnifolia,* a member of the rose family. Clark,
op. cit., 233, 239.

EPILOGUE

The following letter was written, not by Rachel Mills, but by Alfred, the oldest son of Elizabeth and Henderson Luelling, her dearest friends from back home in Salem, Iowa. Evidently the editor of the Oregon farm newspaper, the *Willamette Farmer,* of Salem, Oregon, had heard of the death of Rachel Mills and sought information about it from the Luellings as to details. This letter is in answer to the editor's enquiry and was published in the *Farmer* on Saturday, March 26, 1870 (page 37). It has a one-word headline: "Obituary."

DAIRY CREEK,[14] March 19, 1870.
DEAR FRIEND: – Yours of Feb. 18th is received, after considerable time, occasioned by my removal to this place and the consequent necessity of forwarding it to Forest Grove. Mrs. Mills was born in Wayne county, Indiana, April 20th, 1822; died Dec. 11th, 1869, her age was, therefore, 46 years 7 months, 21 days. Her parents removed in 1837 to Henry county, Iowa. She was married in 1842 [1841] to Mr. John Fisher, with whom she started to cross the Plains to Oregon in 1847. Mr. Fisher died, June 6th, on Platte River. In August, and on Snake River, she buried a bright little girl, something over 2 years of age. She arrived in Tualitin Plains late in the fall; during the following winter made the acquaintance of a Mr. W. A. Mills, who had been here since 1843. They were married the next spring, since which they resided most of the time in this county, until her death. Her

---

14 Dairy Creek is a stream flowing into the Tualatin River in Washington County, Oregon. The most prominent Oregon community that stands on its banks is Hillsboro. The Hudson's Bay Company is supposed to have operated a dairy in that area. Lewis A. McArthur, *Oregon Geographic Names,* 4th Ed. (Portland, 1974), 203.

parents were members of the Society of Friends (or-
thodox Quakers) and brought her up in the faith,
which was evinced by her consistent practice of the
cardinal injunctions of the discipline, and, notwithstanding her isolation from those of like Faith, she
continued the characteristic "plainness in dress and
address," to the close of her life. She leaves Mr. Mills
with five children, the eldest and youngest sons aged
19 and 9 years respectively, the three daughters of
intermediate ages, and many devoted friends, to mourn
her loss.

Yours truly,
ALFRED LUELLING.[15]

----

[15] Alfred Luelling was the oldest son of Henderson and Elizabeth
Luelling.

The Diary of ⸋ Elizabeth Dixon Smith

INTRODUCTION

Elizabeth Dixon Smith's diary is one of the classics of western history. It was published first in the *Transactions* of the Oregon Pioneer Association for their 35th annual reunion in Portland in June, 1907, published in 1908. This is the copy that historians have worked with and quoted from. It is not an accurate copy. These transcribers corrected Elizabeth Smith's spelling, punctuated her sentences and capitalized words where she had not done so. We have gone back to the original [1] in the Oregon Historical Society's manuscript collection and transcribed it as accurately as possible. It is published with their permission.

Now, as to the manuscript itself: It is written as a letter with the diary entries following each other line after line, with no diary format at all. Elizabeth Smith had kept a diary all right, but this document is a letter to two friends in Indiana in which she copied her original diary, and, evidently because of a shortage of paper, she used every square inch of space as efficiently as possible. Her writing is clear and easy to read for the most part, but it is very small. She wrote the last entry in her actual diary on February 24, 1848, and she dated the letter copy May 25, 1848. She also inserted some comments about events that had taken place in the meantime, such as the Whitman Massacre. These are fairly easy to discern, as her language gives them away.

So far it has been impossible to learn the exact date of

---

[1] Postal Mss 641.

her birth. Her daughter, Mrs. Martha Smith Marsh, the baby carried over the trail, told Fred Lockley, a writer for the Portland *Oregon Journal* in 1925 [2] that her mother had been 40 years old in June, 1849, so one would suppose that she was born in 1809 and was 38 when she crossed the plains in 1847. The report of her death in the March 18, 1855 issue of the Salem *Oregon Statesman* did not give her birth date but indicated that she was 47 years old when she died, which would mean that she was born in 1808.

Her husband at the time of the overland journey was Cornelius Smith. He took seriously ill upon arrival in Oregon, and she wrote in her diary on February 1, 1848, while staying in a wooden lean-to shack in Portland, "rain all day this day my Dear husband my last remaining friend died."

The Smiths took the long road to Oregon in 1847 with eight children, yet she found time to write something in her journal nearly every day. Some of the entries were quite short, but others were long and literary. She never listed the children and hardly ever mentioned them. We have been able to put together a list by name and age with the aid of the *Oregon Journal* interview with her daughter and by reference to the early Oregon census records: [3]

> Susan Welch, who traveled the trail with her husband, Russell
>   Welch, and their tiny son, Thaddeus, 3 years old. Susan was
>   20 at the time of the journey, and Russell was 30 years old.
> Erastus Smith, 17 years old.   Jasper, 5 years old.
> William Smith, 16 years old.   Seneca, 3 years old.
> Perley Poore Smith, 14 years old.   Eliza Marie, 1 year old.
> Eleanor or Ella, 8 years old.

Some comment is due on the Welch family. Russell Welch,

---

[2] Fred Lockley "Impressions and Observations of the Journal Man," March 3-5, 1925; also April 9, 1935.

[3] Elsie Youngberg, Ed., *Oregon Territory, 1850 Census* (Lebanon, Ore., 1970).

who was the husband of Sarah, the eldest daughter, had also been the business partner of Cornelius Smith, his father-in-law. They had owned a large lumber mill near LaPorte, Indiana, and it was the burning down of the mill that set the two partners and their families to moving on westward in 1847. Russell Welch was born of mixed Indian-white parentage. He is described by those who knew him as a gigantic man and a logger of no mean ability. The Welch family settled in Oregon on a donation land claim on Panther Creek, between present McMinnville and Carlton. Russell gained fame as an outstanding axeman, and it was said that he could demonstrate it by "chopping a tree six feet in diameter without changing his position; first swinging his axe to the right and then to the left." These are the words of his son Thaddeus.

Now, Thaddeus accompanied his parents on the overland trip of 1847 as a 3-year-old (born July 14, 1844). He grew up to become a well-known California painter of landscapes, having had training as an artist in Europe. His paintings are to be found in several west-coast museums. The Oakland, California, Art Museum has some of them. Much of his later life was spent in Marin County, California; then he and his wife, Barbara, moved to Santa Barbara, where he lived out his life. He died on December 19, 1919.[4]

Nearly a year and a half after the death of Cornelius Smith, Elizabeth married a widower named Joseph Cary Geer (February 5, 1795 - August 28, 1881). Geer's first

[4] Story on Thaddeus Welch in Portland *Daily Oregonian,* April 24, 1875, p. 3, col. 1; Eufina C. Tompkins, "Story of Two California Artists," *Sunset Magazine,* XIII, no. 2 (June 1904), pp. 131-36; a series of articles by Helen Vernon Reid, "Thad Welch – Pioneer and Painter," appeared in *Overland Monthly and Out West Magazine* during the year 1924, Volume LXXXII, March-July. The *Overland Monthly* series was republished in a book by the Oakland, Calif., Art Museum, in 1966, the author's name being given as Helen V. Broekhoff, Helen Reid's later name. There is a very brief entry on Thaddeus Welch in James D. Hart, *A Companion to California* (New York, 1978), p. 474.

wife, Mary, had died soon after reaching Oregon on December 6, 1847. The Geers moved to Joseph's donation land claim just across the Willamette River in Yamhill County from Butteville, Marion County.[5]

Joseph Geer was ten years older than Elizabeth and was already father of ten children. Elizabeth gave birth to three more in the years following:

Orlando Thurston Geer, born January 22, 1851; died December 29, 1851.

Lucien Geer, born February 16, 1854.

Joel Palmer Geer, born March 7, 1855..

It was just after the birth of Joel Palmer that the pioneer *Oregon Statesman* newspaper of Salem carried the news of Elizabeth Geer's death:

DIED Near Buteville, in Yamhill county, Oregon, March 18, 1855, Mrs. ELIZABETH GEER, wife of J. C. GEER, Sen. aged 47 years of inflamation of the brain.

There need to be some comments on the most famous and oft-quoted entry in Elizabeth Dixon Smith's diary, that of Wednesday, September 15, 1847, which reads as follows:

layed by this morning one company moved on except one family the woman got mad and would not budge nor let the children he had his cattle hitched on for 3 hours and coaxing her to go but she would not stur I told my husband the circumstance and him and Adam Polk and Mr. Kimble went and took each one a young one and cramed them in the wagon and her husband drove off and left her siting she got up took the back track travled out of sight cut across overtook her hus-

---

[5] Lockley, op. cit.; Walter Geer (comp.) *Genealogy of the Geer Family in America* (New York, 1914), pp. 213-16; Joseph C. Geer, Sr., (Obituary), Portland, *Daily Oregonian,* August 31, 1881. On Butteville see Howard McKinley Corning, *Willamette Landings: Ghost Towns of the River* (Portland, Ore., 1947), pp. 74-80; and Randall V. Mills, *Stern-Wheelers up Columbia* (Palo Alto, Calif., 1947), *passim.*

band   meantime he sent his boy back to camp after a horse that he had left and when she came up her husband says did you meet John   yes was the reply and I picked up a stone and nocked out his brains   her husband went back to asertain the truth and while he was gone she set one of his waggons on fire which was loaded with store goods   the cover burnt off and some valueable artickles   he saw the flame and came runing out and put it out and then mustered spunk enough to give her a good floging   her name is Marcum she is cousin to Adam Polks wife

Two things need comment in this quote:

The first has to do with the boy, John. He did not get his brains "nocked out." His name turns up in the 1850 federal census of Oregon, and he lived many years after that.

Then there needs to be a word about the family, "Marcum," as Elizabeth Smith spelled the name. She was referring to Samuel and Elizabeth Markham, who are listed in the 1850 census as living in Clackamas County and having six children: Daniel, 26 years old; John, 18; Warden, 15; Henry, 9; Mary, 6; and Columbia, 3. The last named is listed as having been born in Oregon Territory, which means that Mrs. Markham must have been pregnant during the overland crossing.

A seventh child was born in Oregon City on April 23, 1852. They named him Charles Edward Anson Markham. Many years later he took the name, "Edwin" Markham, and would become world renowned as the poet who wrote "The Man with the Hoe," and many other poems. Not long after "Charley" was born, Samuel Markham left the family for good, to go to California (having been there before), and a divorce ensued. In 1859 Elizabeth Markham would take her children to California, and in that year she married once more. The new husband was one John Whitcraft. They, too were divorced in 1872, he having left her ten years before. Many questions have been posed about the relationship of Edwin Markham to his mother, the latest and most thorough study being Louis Filler's *The Unknown Edwin Markham: His Mystery and Its Significance*.[6] It was from this book that much of the information given above is taken.

Certainly Elizabeth Dixon Smith's comments about the activities of Elizabeth Markham on September 15, 1847, add some insight, or pose even more questions about this unusual woman.

We have added an epilogue after Elizabeth Smith's diary in which are reproduced three of Elizabeth Markham's poems from the *Oregon Spectator*.

THE DIARY

[Lafayette, Yamhill County, Oregon, May 25, 1848][1] Mrs. Paulina Foster   Mrs. Cintha Ames   Dear Friends

by your request I have endevered to keep a record of our journey from the States to Oregon though it is poorly done owing to me having a young babe and besides a large family to doo for and worst of all my e[d]ucation is very limited

April 21, 1847 [Wednesday]   Commenced our journey from Laporte Indiana to Oregon and made 14 [19?] miles

April 22   made 12 miles rain all day
April 23   made 19 miles travled untill dark   eat a

---

[6] Antioch Press, Yellow Springs, Ohio, 1966.

[1] This date is nowhere to be found in connection with the manuscript diary of Elizabeth Smith. However, it does appear in the printed rendition of the diary in the Oregon Pioneer Association *Transactions,* 35th Session, covering the meeting of June 19, 1907 (Portland, Ore., 1908), p. 153. One can only assume that the address and date were on an envelope that has been lost.

cold bite and went to bed chilly and cold which is very disagreeable with a parcel of little children

April 24   made 12 miles to

April 25 [Sunday]   last night our cattle ran off concequently only made 11 miles

April 26   made 16 miles had a view of Mount Juliett it is some of the great works of nature   we see a great deal of admirable works of nature and art as we pass through Ill.

April 27   made 18 miles through a beautiful country Ill.

April 28   made 18 miles   encamped on the bank of the Ill River   beautiful place

April 29   made 16 miles through a delightful country encamped on the Ill   cold and rainy.

April 30   made 19 miles   passed through Peru travled through a beautiful and fertile country   cold and rainy

May 1 [Saturday]   made 14 miles   passed through Princeton Buro [Bureau] County Ill   rich soil   hundreds of acres not oned or cultivated by any one

May 2   made 20 miles exceding cold for the season

May 3   made 20 miles   cold and dry   all in good spirits

May 4   made 20 miles   pleasant weather

May 5   made 16 miles   passed through Henderson Ville and Gales Burg Nox County, Ill   Good roads fine weather.

May 6   made 18 miles   passed through Monmouth Ill   good weather

May 7   made 12 miles   rainy weather

May 8   crossed the Mississippi   delayed in Burlington   made 7 miles   in Burlington I saw Perley Mitchells first wife

May 9   [Sunday]   passed Augusta a small village ferried Skunk river Ill [Iowa]

May 10   fine weather   layed by to wash

May 11   layed for rain

May 12   made 20 miles   passed West Point IOA

May 13   made 18 miles   encamped on Desmoins river

May 14   forded the Desmoins   made 18 miles

May 15   fel in with 7 oregon waggons made 20 miles

May 16   [Sunday] Made 15 miles   rained all day.

May 17   layed by for rain

May 18   made 20 miles   good weather

May 19   last night one of our cows went back one dayes journey to see her calf that we had given away that morning.

May 20   made 18 miles   rainy weather   bad roads.

May 21   made 7 miles   water bound by a branch of Grand river   hilly and bad roads.

May 22   made 7 miles   water bound by creek called the mudy.

May 23   [Sunday]   made 7 miles   crossed Weldon river   Missori State.

May 24   made 12 miles   rain all day   encamped in a marsh   Shoe mouth deep in water   the men peeled bark made a floor   built a fire on it to dry themselves and get supper by.

May 25   made 2 miles   water bound.

May 26   made 22 miles.
May 27   made 14 miles   crossed big Creek   it has
on it one saw mill one grist mill.

May 28   made 20 miles   crossed Samson creek   [it
has] one flouring and one saw mill on Grand river
crossed Grand river   encamped with out wood or
water in a large prairie   eat a cold bite and went to
bed.

May 29   travled until dark crossed the little Platt
it was raining and we went to bed without super

May 30 [Sunday]   rained this morning untill late
made 8 miles crossed a river called the Hundred and
two on a dangerous bridge and encamped

May 31   layed by to wash
June 1   [Tuesday] lying by.
June 2   made 7 miles.
June 3   passed through St Joseph on the bank of the
Missouri   laid in our flour cheese and crackers and
medicine for no one should travle this road without
medicine for they are al most sure to have the summer complaint   each family should have a box of
phisic pills and a quart of caster oil a quart of the best
rum and a large vial of peppermint essence. we travled
4 miles the river and encamped   here we found nine
waggons bound for oregon.

June 4   crossed the Missouri   doubled teems with
difficulty ascended a hill or mountain   travled 3 miles
& encamped   we are now in Indian territories.

June 5   made 9 miles   at present 22 waggons.
June 6 [Sunday] made 18 miles   passed 70 oregon
waggons as they were encamped.

June 7   good roads   made 20 miles
June 8   made 20 miles   crossed one creek very high
and steep banks where I know the names of streams
I give them.

June 9   made 14 miles   crossed one creek
June 10   made 13 miles.
June 11 made 18 miles   crossed the Blue earth river
one waggon turned over just at the edge of the water
happyly nothing got wet.

June 12   layed by to wash   had 2 horses stolen last
night out of company by Indians.

June 13 [Sunday]   made 18 miles.

[June] 14   made 18 miles   we are continuly finding
elk horns buffalows skulls and carcases.

[June] 15   made 18 miles.
June 16   17 miles   saw one grave day before yesterday and one to day by the lonely way side made this
spring.

[June] 17   made 12 miles   fel in with 18 waggons
broke an exeltree layed by and made a new one   stood
guard all night in the rain.

June 18   finished the broken exel   made 5 miles
encamped in a circle as it is our custom   put out
guards and retired to rest.

[June] 19   made 20 miles   evry night we encamped
we locate quite a village but take it up next day   we
have plenty music with the flute and violin and some
dancing.

June 20 [Sunday]   made 20 miles   encamped on the
Platt   the ground here is covered with a white sur-

face   something between salt and salts   the cattle are fond of it.

[June 21]   made 18 miles   last night had 2 more horses stolen one belonging to the same man that lost one of those first ones   it was a fine horse and his last one   our road a long the Platt is beautiful & level the river is wide a mile or more and very rily & shallow.

June 22   made 15 miles   see antelope evry day.

[June] 23   made 18 miles   at present there is one hundred and forty persons in our company.   we see thousands of buffalow and have to use their dung for fuel   a man will gather a bushel in a minute   3 bushels makes a good fire.

[June] 24   made 10 miles   stoped to kill a buffalow but did not succeed   saw hundreds of prairie dogs barking a bout   they are a bout as large as a grey gofer – saw another grave.

June 25   made 18 miles   our road is like a floor for miles and miles to gether   we found the sensetive plant growing here.

[June] 26   made 10 miles   killed 3 buffalows   their flesh is generly coarser and dryer than beef but a fat buffalow heifer is as good meat as I would wish to taste of.

June 27 [Sunday]   made 15 miles   killed 5 buffalow   at the least calculation we saw 3000 buffalow today   a buffalow gallops and rolles like a horse.

[June] 28   made 18 miles   saw thousands of buffalow   caught 2 of their calves   one ran away   the other they drove a long with the loose cattle several miles   it finely left them.   9 more waggons over took us

June 29   this morning 8 of our largest and best work oxon was missing besides 2 yoke of Welches[2] 3 yoke of Adam Polk's[3] and a bout 30 head blonging to the company   all work oxon right out of waggons   here we was thousands of miles from any inhabitants and thus deprived of teams   was an appalling situation we had only one yoke left   we hunted evry direction without success.

June 30   hunted all day   our cattle hunters my husband among them were so far from camp some 30 miles that they stayed a way all night.

July 1   [Thursday]   today when our hunters came in they brought one dead man   he had shot himself last night accidentily   he left a wife and six small children   the distress of his wife I cannot describe he was an excelent man and very much missed   his name was Smith Dunlap[4] from Chicago Ill.   they found no cattle.

---

[2] Russell and Sarah Welch. Sarah was the oldest child of the Smiths, at the time of the journey, 20 years old, and Russell was her husband, eleven years her senior. These figures were extrapolated from the records of the 1860 census. They are not listed in the 1850 census, as they had gone to California for a time. The Welches had with them their only child at the time of the overland trip, Thaddeus, age 3. Thaddeus Welch grew up to become a well-known artist, a painter who studied in Europe. See the introduction to this diary for more informaion on the Welch family, especially Thaddeus.

[3] Adam Polk died on November 8, 1847. See Mrs. Smith's diary entry for that date, below. What happened to Mrs. Polk is so-far unknown. She was staying in the same house as Mrs. Smith in Portland as Mrs. Smith's diary entry shows in the entry for November 30, 1847. According to Elizabeth Smith, Mrs. Polk was a cousin of Mrs. Elizabeth Markham, future mother of the poet, Edwin Markham, diary entry of September 15, 1847. See also our introduction to Mrs. Smith's diary for a discussion of the Markham family, above.

[4] So-far we have been unable to find the widow of Smith Dunlap from Chicago, Ill. This is a case in which she probably married soon, and, in taking on another name, disappeared from official view. The change of names is one of the problems associated with research on women.

July 2   a trying time   so many of us having to get
teams had hire borrow buy just as we could   had to
take raw cattle cows or any thing we could get   some
had to apply to others companys for help   at last we
moved off   made 15 miles.

July 3   made 13 miles
July 4 [Sunday]   last night had some rain which is
very uncommon in this region   we forded the platt
yesterday   today passed over from south to north
branch of the Platt   it is the ruffest country here that
the mind can conceive of indicative I think of shapes
of the earth   no level land all ridges mounds and deep
hollows covered with no herbage whatever but you
will see now and then in some deep hollow a scruby
ceder growing   made 16 miles   encamped on north
Platt botom   midling feed   found old trunks of ce-
ders to burn.

[July] 5   Made 17 miles   hot water   sandy roads
the road continues along the river

July 6   made 18 miles   many of our cattle is lame
it is plain to my mind what makes their feet wear
out   it is the lyey nature of the ground.

[July] 7   made 18 miles   this country is full of curi-
oseties hundreds of acres seems to have been bursted
and thrown up by volcanic eruptions   the earth along
here is strong with ly   after a shower if the little ponds
were not rily one could wash linen without soap

July 8   made 12 miles   saw chimney Rock it is
a curiosity in deed a rock or rather a hard clay standing alone towering in the are perhaps 300 feet   all
of the lofty rocks alone here is composed of the same

meterial   some of them resemble old demolished vil-
ages half sunk in the ground with stoves pipes sticking
out at the top. to day we the dredfulest hail storm that
I ever witnessed which me and a young woman had
like to have been caught in as we went out to visit the
famous chimney rock   fortuneately we reached one of
the foremost waggons just as the hail began to pelt us.
it tore some of their waggon covers off broke some
bows and made horses and oxon run a way & made
bad work   they say a bout it is subject to tornadoes.

July 9 to day we saw by the way side a bout 2 acres
of fine white stone all cut up compareitively in to
pieces a bout 10 feet square and 2 feet thick   I ran
bear footed to get on to them but got my feet full of
stickers and was glad to get back to my waggon   all
the herbs in this region is prickry and briery the sage
dredful on ones clothes it grows from 1 to 6 feet high
has a stalk like our tame sage or sedge the leaves are
smaller and very narrow   it has a sage taste though it
is very biter. besides we travle through a shrub called
greece wood jenerly not so large as the sage   it is very
thorny   we have to use it sometimes to burn. then there
is the prickly pair   it is any and every where   lookout
for bare feet   made 20 miles   encamped at Scots
bluffs   here is starvation   no feed and little water
here after traveling 20 miles we chained up our oxon
to our waggon wheels and started next morning by
sun rise.

[July] 10   made 12 miles through a barren destitue
region   encamped on a creek   found feed and willows
July 11   made 18 miles on dry and barren land.
July 12   made 10 miles   encamped at a french and

Indian residence as soon as we had careled the indians flocked in spread their blankets and beged for present we gave them meal meat flour and beans for which we afterwards suffered

July 13 this morning 5 of our work cattle was missing the men hunted and hired indians to hunt but found no cattle empted one waggon and left it and moved on passed Fort Larama made 5 miles encamped the indians came as before and set down in a circle and spread a blanket in their midst and beged presents we gave them provision and they dispersed.

July 14 layed by found the lost cattle payed the indians for hunting 15 dollars although our men found them

July 15 made 20 miles through a barren desert found wo[o]d and water but no feed to night. I intend to state all the rain we have.

[July] 16 made 6 miles found feed layed by to paster our cattle.

July 17 made 15 miles disentary pervails in our company we are travling through destitute land no vejitation except at our camping places but the sage and a little stunted pitch pine.

July 18 [Sunday] made 15 miles through what is called the black hills they are intirely barren except now and then a stunted ceder there are a great many old pine logs lying a bout on them some of these hills are clear stone others coarse sand.

July 19 passed through a bason of 30 or 40 acres of level land with in this bason is a surface of stone about 15 feet in diameter white as marble but porious like burnt bone and brittle the earth resembles spanish brown made 6 miles layed by to bait our cattle nature has provided a occasionaly for poor hungry cattle.

July 20 made 15 miles black hills
July 21 made 20 miles encamped on the Plat.
[July] 22 made 15 miles
[July] 23 made 16 miles.
[July] 24 made 15 miles encamped near the red Butes it is nothing more than a red side hill the earth is red.

July 25 [Sunday] made 12 miles encamped at the willow springs a handsome little place of grass and willows today we crossed a little mudy branch along the sides of it we could have gethered pailes full of clean salt peter. many of our cattle are sick and dying

July 26 passed the noted saleratus bed [5] made 20 miles encamped on Sweet water. this saleratus is far from being equeal to artificial saleratus although looks as good we got a great deal of it some kept and used it others threw it away it will not foam buter milk one bit I knew a person to fetch some through and sell it to a merchant for 50 cents per pound not telling him what it was.

July 27 we at rising this morning baked a lot of light bread moved on passed Indipendance Rock made 7 miles.

July 28 made 20 miles
[July] 29 made 18 miles I could have writen a

---

[5] Saleratus is an old term for baking soda or sodium bicarbonate.

great deal more if I had had the opertunity some times I would not get the chance to write for 2 or 3 dayes and then would have to rise in the night when my babe and all hands was a sleep light a candle and write.

July 30   made 10 miles   sage still to cook with.
July 31   passed over one mountain   encamped at the foot of the South pass   here we found some goos berries and they were as smothe as currents and tasted much like fox grapes   all the goose berries this side the Missouri is smothe   Still we have sage to cook with   I do not know which best it or buffalo dung jest step out and pull a lot of sage out of your garden and build a fire in the wind and bake boil and fry by it and then you will guess how we have to doo.

August 1 [Sunday]   passed over the Rocky mountain the back bone of America   it is all rocks on top and they are split in to pieces and turned up edge ways Oh that I had time and talent to describe this curious country   we wound over the mountain a very crooked road   made 18 miles   had rain and hail to day which made it disagreeably cold.

August 2   made 15 miles
August 3   saw the ground covered in many places with epsom salts but so shallow and thin on the ground that we could not collect it and indeed having no expectation of ever kneeding it any more we left it there made 25 miles   encamped on little Sandy river we 2 days journey in the Territory of Oregon and have found no timber except on streams since we left the Missori.

August 4   made 8 miles   encamped on big Sandy layed by to let our cattle feed and rest.

August 5 made 19 one of our cows got drowned
August 6 crossed Green river a large and beautiful
stream bordered with considerable timber quaking
asp made 12 miles encamped on green river

August 7 made 15 miles encamped on Blacks fork
a small river bordered with willows this large waste
of country in my opinion has once been a see my husband found on top of a mountain sea shells petrified
in the stone the creaces in the rocks show the different stages of the water.

August 8 [Sunday] made 20 miles encamped on
Blacks fork

August 9 made 16 miles encamped at fort Bridger
this is a pretty place to see in such a barren country perhaps there is a thousand acres of level land
covered with grass interspersed with beautiful stony
brooks and plenty of timber such as it is quaking asp.
one of the superintendents of this place travled with
us from fort Larimy to this place he is a good and
inteligent man his name is Vascus [6] he has a white
wife. long will he remember the Capt of our company
Cornelius Smith they were good friends.

August 10 layed by to purches teems that we might
have teems of our own.

August 11 fort Bridger
August 12 still at Bridger here we have a good

---

[6] This would have been Louis Vasquez, partner with Jim Bridger at
the fort. There is an excellent biography of Vasquez by LeRoy R. Hafen
in *Mountain Men and the Fur Trade,* (Glendale, Calif., 1965), II, pp. 321-28.
Louis had been on a trip east just before this meeting and married at St.
Louis, 48-year-old Mrs. Narcissa Land Ashcraft, a widow with two small
children.

time for washing which we women deem a great privildge.

August 13   Left fort bridger   made 19 miles encamped on mudy creek.

August 14   made 12 miles   encamped on mudy creek.
August 15 [Sunday]   passed over one high mountain   made 20 miles   encamped without feed water or super.

August 16   started without breakfast   made 9 miles encamped on bear river   plenty feed and willows.

[August] 17   made 18 miles   camped on bear river found some currents better than tame currents   they were yellow.

August 18   made 12 miles   camped on a creek.
August 19   travled over a high rocky mountain made 12 miles.

August 20   passed over another mountain   camped on bear river.

August 21   made 10 miles.
August 22 [Sunday]   saw some of natures curious works   here are mounds of perhaps 40 feet in diameter and 10 feet high composed of a shelly stone   in the middle of the mound stands a I know not what to call it   it looks like a stump a bout 3 feet high   it has a hole in the top full of water roiling and runing over all the time   it [is] this water that makes the mounds   the water is blood warm and has a little of the soda taste   a mile or so from here are the famous Soda springs   they are not so good as has been represented   only one or two of our company like it tasts like weak vinegar with a little saleratus in it

they are jenerly ten or twelve feet across and resemble hog wallows more than springs though I saw one that was clear. A bout 2 hundred yards below the soda springs is a boiling spring it boils and foams and runs over 30 barrels in a day   it boils up out of a stone the hole is a bout as large as a large dinner pot evry few minutes the water will bounce up 3 or 4 feet high the water slightly warm.

August 23   left soda springs   a bout 3 miles further is a rock perhaps 30 feet long 8 feet high 8 feet wide at the base   it was shattered so that we could look in to it and it was hollow   a mile or so further on the earth is cracked for a great many feet in length the boys rolled down stones and they would rumble a long time. made 16 miles   encamped with nothing but green sedge to cook with   good feed   this sage is larger than the tame sedge but very much like it in appearance   has a little of the taste   it grows some times 6 feet high.

August 24   made 16 miles   camped on a creek called port niff [Portneuf].

August 25   made 12 miles   have cold nights and warm days.

August 26   dusty roads   made 14 miles   camped on Snake river   it is soft water   plenty quaking asp   no feed.

August 27   made 20 miles   camped on snake river plenty feed

August 28   passed fort Hall   Capt Grant[7] is not

7 This was Richard Grant, a Scot born in Montreal, and a major figure in the Rocky Mountain fur trade for the Hudson's Bay Company. His biography has been very ably written by Merle Wells of the Idaho Historical Society in *Mounain Men and the Fur Trade, op. cit.,* IX, pp. 165-86.

that charitable jentleman that we expected to see but a boasting burlesquiing unfeeling man. made 15 miles.

August 29 [Sunday]   made 16 miles   camped on snake river   plenty grass and willows   very dusty roads   you in the states know nothing about dust   it will fly so that you can hardly see the horns of your tongue yoke   it often seems that the cattle must die for the want of breath and then in our waggons such a specticle beds cloths vituals and children all compleetly covered.

August 30   passed some large cold springs 20 or 30 feet in diameter boiling up all over the botom   passed Snake river falls   bad roads hilly and rocky camped without feed.

August 31   made 16 miles   bad roads and very dusty camped on Rat River   green grass and willows

September 1 [Wednesday]   rough roads   very rocky all apearance of this land being burnt up   once some places will be surface of black stone and look like thick black for some rods square and look as if it had boiled and bubbled for months.   made 18 miles camped at Swamp Springs   plenty of grass and sedge.

Sept 2   layed by to rest our cattle   had rain last night enough rain to lay the dust.

Sept 3   made 18 miles   camped on Goose creek.
Sept 4   made 14 miles   camped with out feed   had ceder to burn.

Sept 5 [Sunday]   made 16 miles   camped on Rock willows to burn.

Sept 6   made 12 miles over rocks and dust   camped
on Rock.

Sept 7   nooned at Snake river   watered our cattle
moved on 2 miles and camped, 2 men were left be hind
which was always the case with them they had such
heavy loads   they came up afterwards and while
watering some of their cattle swam over the river
one of the men swam after them and before he got
a cross he sunk to rise no more   he left a wife and 3
children [8]   the other came runin to camp to let us
know some men went back and stayed with them   by
this time another company had overtaken them   next
morning my husband took a horse and went back to
swim the horse over after their cattle   The man that
owned the cattle took the horse and swam after the
cattle and while comeing back by some means got off
of the horse and sunk and was seen no more he left a
wife and 6 helpless children [9]   my husband stood

---

[8] This was a man named Sturges (given names so far not known). The
following brief newspaper story appeared in the March 23, 1848, issue
of the *Oregon Spectator* of Oregon City:
    MARRIED – In his city on the 18th inst, by Rev. David
    Leslie, MR. MOSES K. KELLOGG to MRS. ELIZABETH STURGES,
    aged 28 years each.
They are listed in the 1850 census of Washington County, Oregon, as
M. K. Kellogg, farmer, and Elizabeth, both from New York State. There
were three children, according to Elizabeth Smith, and, sure enough, the
census lists Sarah J. Sturges, 13, Eudora, 7, and George, 5 years old.
Another child had been added since the wedding, Ellen Kellogg, one-year-
old. According to the "Provisional Government Land Claim Records" in
the Oregon Archives, they are recorded for February 14, 1848, to have
laid claim to 640 acres on the Cowlitz River at its juncture with Coal
Creek, in present Washington State, north of Vancouver, Washington. There
was another story in the *Oregon Spectator* for March 23, 1848, saying that
Moses Kellogg had discovered coal. That section of Washington is today
an active producer of coal.
[9] This man was a Mr. Green (given names so far not known). His wife,
whose given name is variously spelled Philenda, Felinda, Philinda, later

watching him   it is supposed that there was a suck in the bottom of the river.

Sept 8   we moved on for we had neither feed nor water   made 10 miles   camped on Snake river   at 10 oclock my husband came up and told the shocking news.

Sept 9   made 4 miles   camped on Clarks river   Clarks River is a small creek

Sept 10   layed by to wait for those two widowed women.

Sept 11   while moving a long to day we saw on the opposite side of snake river   the bank was a bout 80 feet high and a bout half way to the top was a large river emptying in to Snake river. it was a half a mile wide   it came out on the same highth all a long and was one continued sheet clear down. made 12 miles camped on little feed and no water.

Sept 12 [Sunday]   made 11 miles   one of our oxon died   the indians a long snake river go naked except an old rag tied a bout their hips they have few horses no blankets   the emegrants trades them old clothes for fish witch was dead no doubt when they caught them.

Sept 13   layed by to rest our cattle.

Sept 14   blocked up our wagon beds   forded snake river which was wide deep and swift   made 9 miles

---

married a brawny blacksmith named James Terwilliger in April, 1848. They were among the earliest settlers of Portland, and "Terwilliger Boulevard" in that city is named for the family. Percy Maddux, *City on the Willamette* (Portland, 1952), p. 17; H. W. Scott, *History of Portland, Oregon* (Syracuse, N.Y., 1890), p. 89; H. K. Hines, *Illustrated History of Oregon* (Chicago, 1893), pp. 413-15.

camped on good grass at a spring   here we over took
2 companies.

[Sept] 15 layed by this morning   one company
moved on except one family   the woman got mad
and would not budge nor let the children   he had
his cattle hitched on for 3 hours and coaxing her to
go but she would not stur   I told my husband the circumstance and him and Adam Polk and Mr Kimble [10]
went and took each one a young one and cramed them
in the wagon and her husband drove off and left her
siting she got up took the back track travled out of sight
cut a cross overtook her husband   meantime he sent
his boy back to camp after a horse that he had left and
when she came up her husband says did you meet John

yes was the reply and I picked up a stone and nocked
out his brains   her husband went back to asertain the
truth and while he was gone she set one of his waggons
on fire which was loaded with store goods   the cover
burnt off and some valueable artickles   he saw the
flame and came runing and put it out and then mustered
spunk enough to give her a good floging   her name is
Marcum [11]   she is cousin to Adam Polks wife

Sept 16 saw a boiling hot spring clear and good

---

[10] Mr. and Mrs. Nathan L. Kimball and their children: Susan M (16),
Nathan, Jr. (12), Byron E. (8), Sarah S. (6), and Nina A. (1), all stayed
over with Dr. and Mrs. Marcus Whitman at their mission. See this diary
entry for October 12, 1847. Nathan Kimball, Sr., was one of those killed
in the "massacre" on Tuesday, November 30th. The family later went to
the Oregon Country, where Mrs. Kimball married John Jewett. They are
all listed as members of his family in the 1850 census for Clatsop County,
Oregon. Clifford Merrill Drury, *Marcus and Narcissa Whitman and the
Opening of Old Oregon*, (Glendale, Calif., 1973), II, pp. 200ff.

[11] This was none other than Elizabeth Markham, wife of Samuel Markham, who later divorced her. She became the mother of the future poet,
Edwin Markham, later in Oregon City. See introduction to this diary, above,
for a discussion of the Markhams.

tasted water   made 13 miles   camped at barrel camp good grass by driving up the stream a mile or so where 2 cattle got shot with arrows but not mortal

Sept 17   made 15 miles over mountainous roades camped on good grass   scant water.

Sept 18   made 8 miles   camped on Big wood river it is nothing more than a brook.

Sept 19 [Sunday]   made 18 miles over mountains and dust   camped on Bois river a small hansome river good feed.

Sept 20   made 12 miles   camped on Bois river good grass.

Sept 21   made 18 miles   camped on Bois river good feed.

Sept 22   made 15 miles   camped on Bois river good feed and wood   all the wood here is Bamagilead it grows in low places and a long the river banks.

Sept 23   made 20 miles   forded Snake river jest before dark   it was waist deep and very cold   it is a large and swift running river   found good feed and willows   rained last night enough to lay the dust.

Sept. 24   layed by to dry our things which got wet crossing the river   Mr Kimbles oldest son died of tipus fever.

Sept 25   buried the corpse   proceeded on our journey   made 14 miles   camped on Burnt river   some feed and willows

Sept 26 [Sunday]   made 12 miles   camped at a small spring   some feed and sage

Sept 27   made 12 miles   camped on Snake river.

Sept 28   made 12 miles   crossed burnt river 6 times
we are all the time on a hill or in a hollow   camped
on burnt river with mountains on every side.

Sept 29   made 11 miles winding between and over
mountains   camped on burnt river
Sept 30   made 14 miles   camped on Burnt river
dry grass and willows.

Oct 1 [Friday]   woman of our company died as we
were travling a long she had been sick some time.
made 9 miles   camped on burnt river.

Oct 2   buried the corpse   made 16 miles   camped
on south branch of powder river.

Oct 3 [Sunday]   layed by to rest our failing cattle.
Oct. 4   made 15 miles   camped on north branch of
Powder river   midling feed.

Oct. 5   made 12 miles   camped on head waters of
grand round   plenty feed and pine to burn.

Oct. 6   made 18 miles   passed over one difficult stony
mountain   came down into grand round   O if grand
round was west of the Cascade mountains how soon
it would be taken up   it is level and covered with
grass and watered with brooks and springs   it has a
river flowing through it   no timber except on the river
but the mountains which surround it are promisquisly
covered with pine and fur   we camped on grand
round.

Oct 7   ascended a mountain a mile and a half long
covered with pine and grass   when we came to the
top we found a pretty open place level and a good soil
coverd with grass   rolled 5 miles over level land
decended the mountain which was steep   a[nd] diffi-

cult the men havin to stiddy the waggons down while we women carried and led our children camped on a branch of grand round river here the men made tar out of pine here we are surrounded with mountains covered with tall pines.

Oct. 8 ascended a steep mountain travled through thick pine woods came to another mountain had to double teems to some wagons they put 9 yoke of oxon all of those mountains has a good soil covered with grass camped without water rained last night.

Oct 9 doubled teems up another mountain made 15 miles camped at pine camp good feed and water me and my husband are both sick with the summer complaint.

Oct 10 [Sunday] layed by to hunt some lost cattle. Oct 11 made 12 miles camped near a branch of the Youtilla [Umatilla] river.

Oct 12 went 3 miles here our company seperated some went to Whitmans Mision to winter and they were masacreed in the jeneral massacree of which I suppose you have al ready heard the masacree is atributed to the Catholicks [12] and circumstances proves it true here my husband bought a beef of the indians it was 18 months old it weighed 400 and 30 pounds he payed them a cow and a calf and a new shirt

Oct 13 made 20 miles camped without feed. Oct 14 made 10 miles camped on Utilla river dusty roads scarce feed very hard and cold winds.

---

[12] Dr. Clifford Merrill Drury in his various writings about the Whitmans and the Henry Spaldings has put this idea to rest. Mrs. Smith must have added this to her diary before she sent the copy east on May 25, 1848.

Oct 15 made 15 miles on sandy roads camped on a branch good feed disagreeable cold.

Oct 16 hilly and dusty roads travled untill after dark made 18 miles camped without wood or water went to bed cold.

Oct 17 [Sunday] cold and windy we made a fire of a little wood that we carried all day yesterday made a bite to eat our cattle ran off in search of water which hindered us till late made 4 miles camped without wood except a small shrub called greece wood it burns like greeced weeds I used to wonder why it was said man must be dressed in buckskin to come to this country but now I know. evry thing we travle through is thorny and rough there is no chance of saving your cloths here we found a great hole of water 12 or 15 feet a croos had to water a hundred and fifty head of cattle with pails had to stand out all night in the rain to keep the cattle from drownding each other after water in this hole.

Oct 18 made 15 miles found wood water and good feed.

Oct 19 layed by to rest our cattle.
Oct 20 made 18 miles camped at a spring had ceder to burn midling feed.

Oct 21 made 12 miles camped on John Days river scarce feed willows to burn here we put a guard for fear of indians which we have not done for 3 months before.

Oct 22 travled up a long steep ascent between 2 mountains the road was so narrow that a wagon could scarcely squeze a long and very at that. made

12 miles   camped without wood or water   dry grass
it was told to us before we left the states that the
dry grass was better than the green   be it so or not
always when we have had a dry feed the first green
grass we come too we stop to let the cattle feed.

Oct 23   made 12 miles   camped on the Columbia
river   scarce feed no wood nor shrubs   we had to
burn little green weeds

Oct 24 [Sunday]   crossed falls or Shutes [Deschutes]
river   it was high rapid and dangerous   the water
came clear to the top of the waggon beds   me and my
children with as many more women and children as
could stow them selves in to a canoe was taken over
by two indians which cost a good many shirts   the
indians are thick as hops here and not very friendly
   any body in preparing to come to this country should
make up some calico shirts to trade to the indians
in cases of necesity you will have to hire them pilot
you a cross rivers   a gainst we got here my folks were
a bout striped of shirts trousers jackets and wamases.[13]

Oct 25   ascended   a   mountain   made   10   miles
camped on a creek   plenty feed and willows   bought
a beef of the indians and killed it.

[October] 26   made 10 miles over mountains all
the way saw oak trees for the first in oregon   camped
on the Columbia

Oct 27   passed what is called the Dalls mision [14]

---

13 "Wamases" is her word for "Wamus," a kind of cardigan or tough
outer jacket.

14 The Dalles Methodist Mission was sold by the Methodists in 1847
to Dr. Marcus Whitman. The Whitman "massacre" of November of that
year led to its abandonment. The two white mission families were the Rev.
and Mrs. Daniel Lee and the Rev. and Mrs. H. K. W. Perkins.

where two white families live a mong the indians
it looks like starveation   made 10 miles   camped on
the Columbia where we expect to take water.

Oct. 28   here is a great many emegrants encamped
men making rafts others going down in boats which
have been sent up by speculators.

Oct 29   rain most all day   cold wether
Oct 30   rainy day   making rafts   women cooking
and washing   children crying   indians bartering potatoes for shirts   they must have a good shirt for a
half a peck of potatoes.

Oct 31 [Sunday]   cold and rainy   snow close by on
the mountain   we should have went over the mountains with our wagons but they are covered with snow
consequently we must go down by water and drive
our cattle over the mountains.

Nov 1 [Monday]   we are lying by waiting for the
wind to blow down stream in order that we may
embark on our raft.

Nov 2   we took off our wagon wheels layed them on
the raft placed the wagon beds on them and started
there are 3 families of us Adam Polk, Russel Welch
and our selves on 12 logs 18 inches through and 40 ft
long   the water runs 3 inches over our raft.

Nov 3   we are floating down the Columbia   cold
and disagreeable weather.

Nov 4   rain all day   layed by for the water to calm
we clamberdered a side hill a mong the rocks and
build a fire and tryed to cook and warm our selves
and children while the wind blew and the waves rolled
beneath.

Nov. 5   still lying by wating for calm weather   Mr Polk is very sick.

Nov. 6   layed by till noon wating for the waves to quit rolling but finely put out in rough water   made 6 miles and landed safe.

Nov 7 [Sunday]   put out in rough water   moved a few miles   the water became so rough that we were forced to land   no one to man the raft but my husband and oldest son of 16 years   Russell Welch and our youngest boys were driving our cattle over the mountains   here we ly smoking our eyes burning our cloths and trying to keep warm   we have plenty of wood but the wind takes away the warmth.

Nov. 8   finds us still lying at anchor wating for the wind to fall   we have but one dayes provision a head of us   here we can see snow on the top of the mountains whose rocky hights reaches to the clouds   by times a few indians calls on us and steals something from us but we are not afraid of them   cold weather my hands are so numb that I can scarcely write.

Nov 9   finds us still in trouble   waves dashing over our raft and we al ready stinting our selves in provisions   my husband started this morning to hunt provisions   left no man with us except our oldest boy

it is very cold   the icesickles are hanging from our wagon beds to the water   to night a bout dusk Adam Polk expired no one with him but his wife and my self   we sat up all night with him while the waves was dashing below.

Nov 10   finds us still wating for calm weather   my husband returned at 2 oclock   brought 50 pounds of beef on his back 12 miles which he had bought from

another company   by this time the water became calm
and we started once more but the wind soon began to
blow and we were forced to land   my husband and
boy was an hour and a half after dark a geting the raft
landed and made fast while the water run knee deep
over our raft   the wind blew and was freezeing cold
us women and children did not atempt to get out
of our wagons tonight.

Nov 11   layed by most all day   started this evening
ran a bout 3 miles and landed after dark   here we
found Welch and our boys with our cattle for they
could be drove no farther on this side for mountains
here was a ferry keped for the purpose of ferrying
emegrants cattle

Nov 12   ferried our cattle over the river and buried
Mr Polk. rain all day   we are living entirely on beef.

November 13   we got the ferry men to shift our load
on to thir boat and take us down to the falls where
we found quite a town of people wating for their cattle to pull them round the falls   rain all day

Nov 14 [Sunday]   unloaded the boat   put our wagons together   drizly wether.

Nov 15   rainy day
Nov 16   rain all day
Nov 17   rainy weather
Nov 18   my husband is sick   it rains and snows
we start this morning round the falls with our waggons
we have 5 miles to go   I carry my babe and lead or
rather carry another through snow and mud and water
al most to my knees   it is the worst road that a team
could possibly travel   I went a head with my children and I was affraid to look behind me for fear of

seeing the wagon turn over in to the mud and water
with evry thing in them   my children give out with
cold and fatigue and could not travle and the boys
had to unhitch the oxon and bring them and carry the
children on to camp I was so cold and numb that I
could not tell by feeling that I had any feet at all
we started this morning at sunrise and did not get to
camp untill after dark and there was not one dry thread
on one of us not even my babe   I had carryed my babe
and I was so fatigued that I could scarcely speak or
step   when I got here I found my husband lying in
Welches wagon very sick   he had brought Mrs. Polk
down the day before and was taken sick here   we had
to stay up all night to night for our wagons is left
half way back   I have not told half we suffered.
I am inadiquate to the task   here was some hundreds
camped wating for boats to come and take them down
the columbia to vancouver or Portland or Origon City.

Nov 19   my husband is sick and can have but little
care   rain all day.

Nov 20   rain all day   it is allmost an imposibility
to cook and quite so to keep warm or dry   I froze
or chilled my feet so that I cannot wear a shoe so I
have to go round in the cold water bearfooted.

Nov 21 [Sunday]   rain all day   the whole care of
evry thing now falls upon my shoulders   I cannot
write any more at present
              [Here she misses several days.]
[Nov] 27   embarked once more on the Columbia on
a flat boat   ran all day though the waves threatened
hard to sink us   passed fort vancouver in the night
landed a mile below   my husband never has left his
bed since he was taken sick.

Nov 28   still moving on the water.

Nov 29   landed at Portland on the Willamette 12 miles a bove the mouth at eleven oclock at night.

Nov 30   raining this morning   I ran a bout trying to get a house to get into with my sick husband   at last I found a small leeky concern with 2 families already in it   Mrs Polk had got down be fore us She and another widow was in this house   my family and Welches went in with them and you could have stird us with a stick   Welch and my oldest son was driving the cattle round. me and my children carried up a bed   the distance was nearly a quarter of a mile made it down on the floor in the mud   I got some men to carry my husband up through the rain and lay him on it and he never was out of that shed untill he was carried out in his coffin   here lay 5 of us bed fast at one time and we had no money and what few things we had left that would bring money I had to sell I had to give 10 cents a pound for fresh pork 75 cents per bushel for potatoes 4 cents a pound for fish. there are so many of us sick that I cannot write any more at present — I have not time to write much but I thought it would be interesting to know what kind of weather we have in the winter.

[Here she skips over several weeks.]

january 14 [1848]   rain this morning   warm weather   we suppose it has rained half of the time that I have neglected writing.

jan 15   my husband is still alive but very sick   there is no medicine here except at fort Vancouver and they will not sell one bit not even a bottle of wine.

jan 16 [Sunday]   warm and dry   we are stil living

in the old leeky shed in Portland   it is 6 miles below vancouver down the Columbia and 12 miles up the Willamette   Portland has two white houses and one brick and 3 wood colored framed houses and a few cabins

jan 17, 18, 19   warm and dry.

j 20   cool and dry   soldiers are collecting here from evry part of Oregon to go and fight the Indians in midle oregon in concequence of the masacree at Whitmans mision   I think there were 17 men killed at the masacree but no women nor children except Whitmans wife   they killed every white man there except one and he was an engleshman   they took all the young women for wives robed them of their clothing and evry thing.   the oregon government bought the prisoners at a dear rate and then gave them indians fight but one white man I believe was killed in the war and not many indians   the murderers escaped.

jan 21   warm and dry
jan 22   cool and cloudy   a little rain at night
jan 23 [Sunday]   warm and dry
jan 24   dry but rain at night
jan 25   misty
jan 26   misty   rain at night
jan 27   misty
jan 28   rain all day
jan 29   snow an inch deep but when the sun a rose the snow disapeared and it was clear all day

jan 30 [Sunday]   rainy.
jan 31   rain all day.   if I could tell you how we suffer you would not believe it   our house or rather a shed joined to a house leeks all over   the roof de-

sends in such a manner as to make the rain right down in to the fire I have diped as mutch as 6 pails of water off of our dirt hirth in one night here I sit up night after night with my poor sick husband all a lone and expecting him evry day to dye I neglected to tell you that Welches and all the rest moved off and left us he has not been moved off his bed for 6 weeks only by lifting him by each corner of the sheet and I had hard work to get help enough for that let alone watchers I have not undressed to lie down for 6 weeks besides all our sickness I had a cross little babe to take care of in deed I cannot tell you half.

feb 1 [Tuesday] rain all day this day my Dear husband my last remaining friend died.

feb 2 to day we buried my earthly companion, now I know what none but widows know that is how comfortless is that of a widows life espesily when left in a strange land without money or friends and the care of seven children – cloudy

feb 3, 4, 5 clear and warm
feb 6 [Sunday] clear and cool
feb 7 clear and warm
feb 8 cloudy some rain
feb 9 clear and cool perhaps you will want to know how cool I will tell you we have lived all winter in a shed constructed by seting up studs 5 ft high on the lowest side the other side joins a cabin it is boarded up with clabboards and several of them are torn off in places and there is no shutter too our door and if it was not for the rain puting out our fire and leeking down all over the house we would be comfortable.

feb 10, 11   clear and warm.

feb 12   cool and cloudy.

feb 13 [Sunday]   rainy.

feb 14   cloudy   rain in the afternoon.

feb 15   rain all day.

feb 16   rain and snow all day.

feb 17, 18, 19   rain all day.

feb 20 [Sunday]   rain and hail all day.

feb 21   clear and cool   you will think strange that we do not leave this starved place   the reason is this the road from here to the country is impasible in the winter the distance being 12 miles and besides our cattle are but two weak.

feb 22, 23   clear and cool.

feb 24   clear and warm.   to day we left Portland at sunrise no one to assist us   we had to leave one wag-gon and part of our things for the want of a teem we travled 4 or 5 miles all the way up hill and through the thickest woods I ever saw all furr from 2 to 4 ftt through with now and then a scattering cedar and an intolerable bad road   we all had to walk   some times I had to sit down my babe and help to keep the wagon from turning over   when we got to the top of the mountain we descended through mud up to wagon hubs and over logs 2 feet through and log bridges torn to pieces in the mud   sometimes I would be behind out of sight of the wagon carrying and tuging my little ones along   sometimes the boys would stop the teams and come back after us   made 9 miles encamped in thick woods   found some grass   unhitched the oxon   let them feed 2 hours then chained them to trees   these woods are infested with wild cats pan-thers bears and wolves   a man told me that he had

killed 7 tigers but they are a species of wolves. we
made us a fire and made a bed down on the wet ground
and layed down as happy as circumstances would ad
mit   glad to think we had escaped from Portland a
sick game place.[15]

TWO LETTERS FROM OREGON

                                            Bute ville [16]
Sept 2 1850, oregon Ty yam hill county [17]
Dear and estemaable friends Mrs. Paulina Foster and
Mrs. Cintha Ames

---

[15] The last few words are very difficult to read with the manuscript in
its present condition. We have not used the interpretation given by George
Himes, who was the transcriber for the published version in the Oregon
Pioneer Association *Transactions,* (Portland, 1908), 179. His transcription
was wrong when compared with the original. It read, "Portland, such a
game place."

[16] Butteville, sometimes spelled "Buteville" by the pioneers. This was a
small river town in Marion County, not Yamhill County. The Geers lived
right across the river in Yamhill County. Life in early Oregon in the Willamette Valley was tied securely to the river. It was first a highway of
humanly powered boats: canoes, keelboats, flatboats and rafts, all carrying
wheat which would be shipped from Oregon City, Fort Vancouver, and
Astoria to Alaska to the Russians or to California, or to Hawaii. Butteville
was one of these wheat exporting towns. The California gold rush came
on, and, suddenly the demand for wheat and flour expanded beyond what
anyone would possibly have expected. A chronicler of this scene, Randall V.
Mills, wrote in 1947, just 100 years after Mrs. Smith's journey, that "A
river of wheat rode on the river itself." Mills goes on in his fine book,
Stern-Wheelers up Columbia (Palo Alto, Calif., 1947), to tell how the
hand operated boats were supplanted by steam boats in the early 1850's.
Another Oregon writer, Howard McKinley Corning, dealt with the small
river towns that grew up, lived for a short time, and then died — or went
to sleep — as the boat traffic waxed and waned. His book, *Willamette Landings* (Portland, Ore., 1947) has become a little classic.

[17] This is her way of writing "Oregon Territory, Yamhill County." This
county was one of the original four districts of the Oregon Territory under
the Provisional Government. Though reduced in size, it is still a Willamette
Valley county.

I promised when I saw you last to write to you when I got to Oregon and I done it faithfully but as I never have received an answer I do not know whether you got it or not concequently I do not know what to write I wrote four sheets full and sent it to you but now I have not time to write I write now to know whether you got my letter but I will try to state a few things my husband was taken sick before we got to any settlement and never was able to walk afterwards he died at Portland on the Willamett river after an illness of two months I will not attempt to describe my troubles since I saw you suffice it to say that I was left a widow with the care of seven children in a foreign land with out one solitary friend as one might say in the land of the living but this time I will only indever to hold up the bright side of the picture I lived a widow one year and four months my three boys started for the gold mines and it was doubtful to me wether I ever saw them again perhaps you will think strange that I let such young boys go but I was willing and helped them off in as good stile as I could they packed through by land Russel Welch went by water the boys never saw Russel in the mines

well after the boys was gone it is true I had plenty of cows and hogs and plenty of wheat to feed them on and to make my bread in deed I was well off if I had only knew it but I lived in a remote place where my strength was of little use to me I could get nothing to do and you know I could not live without work
I imployed myself in teaching my children yet that did not fill my mind I became as poor as a snake yet I was in good health and never was so nimble since I was a child I could run a half a mile without stop-

ing to breath   well I thought perhaps I had better try
my fortune again so on the 24 of June 1849 I was
married to a Mr Joseph Geer 14 years older than
myself though young enough for me   he is the father
of ten children   they are all married but two boys
and two girls   he is a yankee from Connecticut and
he is a yankee in evry sense of the word as I told you
he would be if it ever proved my lot to marry a gain
though I did not get all, I did not marry rich but
my husband is very industrious and is as kind to me
as I can ask indeed he sometimes provokes me for trying to humor me so much   he is a stout healthy man
for one of his age.   the boys made out poor at the
mines   they started in April and returned in sept
I think they was sick part of the time and hapned to
be in poor digings all the while.   they only got home
with two hundred dollars a piece   they suffered very
much while they were gone. when they came home
they were less than when they started   Perley did not
get there   he started with a man in partnership, the
man was to provide for and bring him back and he
was to give the man half he dug but when they got
as far as the umpqua river they heard it was so very
sickly there that the man turned back but Perley would
not come back   there were two white men keeping
ferry on the umpqua so Perley stayed with them all
summer and in the fall he riged out on his own hook
and started a gain but on his way met his brothers
comeing home and they advised him for his life not
to go and so he came back with them   at this time
we are all well but Perley I can not answer for him
he is gone to the umpqua for some money due him
the other two is working for four dollars a day

the two oldest boys has got three town lots in quite a
string   a place called Lafayette in yam hill County
Perley has four horses   a good indian horse is worth
one hundred dollars a good american cow is worth
60 dollars   my boys lives about 25 miles from me so
that I cannot act in the capasity of a mother to them
so you will guess it is not all sunshine with me for you
know my boys is not old enough to do with out a mother   Russel Welch done very well in the mines   he
made a bout 20 hundred dollars   he lives 30 miles
below me in a little town called Portland on the Willamette river   Sarah has got her third son   it has been
one a year since I saw her.   Adam Polk's two youngest
boys lives a bout where ever they see fit   the oldest
if he is a live is in California.   there is some ague in
this country this season but me nor my children except
those that went to california has had a days sickness
since we came to Oregon   I believe I will say no more
untill I hear from you   write as soon as possible and
tell me evry thing.   my husband will close this epistle

                           Elizabeth Geer

                      Buteville Sept. 9. 1850
Dear Ladies,   As Mrs Geer has introduced me to you,
as her old Yanky husband, I will say a few words, In
the hope of becoming more acquainted hereafter, She
so often speaks of you, that you seem like old neighbors, she has neglected to tell you that she was once
the wife of Cornelius Smith. She has told you how
poor she became while a widow, but has not said one
word about how fat she has become since she has been
living with her yanky husband, this is probably reserved for the next epistle so I will say nothing about

it. Of her I will only say she makes me a first rate wife, industrious, and kind almost to a fault to me, a fault however that I can cheerfuly overlook, you know. We are not rich but independant and live agreeably together. which is enough. We are located on the west bank of the Willamette river about 20 miles above Oregon City about 40 yards from the water, a very pleasant situation, intend puting out a large orchard as soon as I can prepare the ground have about ten thousand apple trees, & about 200 pear trees on hand, trees for sale of the best kinds of fruit. apple trees worth one dollar & pears $1.50 apiece, I have not room to give you a description of this best country in the world, so I will not attempt it, but if you will answer this I will give a more particular accont next time. I will give a brief account of my self. I left my native home Windham, Conn. Sept. 10, 1818 for Ohio, lived in Ohio till Sept. 9, 1840. When I left for Ill. left Illinois April 4. 1847. for Oregon arrived here Oct. 18. same year. buried my first wife Dec. 6th, 47. Now I wish you or some of your folks to write to us and let us know all about the neighbors as Mrs Geer is very anxious to here from you all. Direct to Joseph C. Geer Sen. Buteville, Marion County Oregon Territory. My best respects to Mr Ames, and if there is a good universalist preacher there tell him he would meet with a cordial welcome here as there is not one in this Territory. I must close for want of room

Yours respectfully
Joseph C Geer sen

Mrs P. Foster & Mrs C. Ames
        sent to Laport, Laport County Indiana

EPILOGUE   Three poems by Mrs. Elizabeth Markham as they appeared in the *Oregon Spectator,* pioneer newspaper of Oregon City:

I
A Contrast on Matrimony

1   The man must lead a happy life,
2   Free from matrimonial chains,
3   Who is directed by a wife
4   Is sure to suffer for his pains.

1   Adam could find no solid peace,
2   When Eve was given for a mate,
3   Until he saw a woman's face
4   Adam was in a happy state.

1   In all the female face, appear
2   Hypocrisy, deceit and pride;
3   Truth, darling of a heart sincere,
4   Ne'er known in woman to reside.

1   What tongue is able to unfold
2   The falsehoods that in woman dwell;
3   The worth in woman we behold,
4   Is almost imperceptible.

1   Cursed be the foolish man, I say,
2   Who changes from his singleness;
3   Who will not yield to woman's sway
4   Is sure of perfect blessedness.

To advocate the ladies' cause, you will read the first and third, and second and fourth lines together. E. M.   *Oregon Spectator,* June 15, 1848.

II
Road to Oregon

We left our friends in foreign lands—
    Our native country dear;
In sorrow, took the parting hand
    And shed the falling tear.

For Oregon, three cheers they gave,
   From us to disengage—
Fearing that we might find our graves
   Amidst the sand and sage;

Or met by cruel savage bands,
   And slaughtered on the way—
Their spectred visions, hand in hand,
   Would round our pathway play.

To the Pacific's temperate clime
   Our journey soon began—
Traversing through the desert sands
   Towards the setting sun.

On Platte the rocks like battlements,
   Were towering tall and high;
The frightened elk and antelope
   Before our trains would fly.

And herds of buffalo appear—
   On either side they stand;
Far as our telescope could reach,
   One thick and clustering band.

O'er sinking sands and barren plains,
   Our frantic teams would bound—
While some were wounded, others slain,
   Mid wild terrific sound.

And in these lone and silent dells
   The winds were whispering low;
And moaning to the Pilgrims, tell
   Their by-gone tales of woe.

Deserted on those mountains wild,
   No ear to hear his cry—
Near by a spring, on a rude bluff,
   They laid poor Scott to die.

Unaided grief and blighted hope,
   Midst savage beasts of prey—
The fate of poor deserted Scott
   Is wrapped in mystery!

Our toils are done, our perils o'er—
  The weary pilgrims' band
Have reached Columbia's fertile shore—
  That far-famed happy land.

O'er mountains high and burning plains,
  Three thousand miles or more—
We are here; but who can e'er explain
  Or count the trials o'er?

Such clouds of mist hang round the scene,
  O'er which we have no control;
It's like a half-remembered dream,
  Or tale that's long been told.

                                        E. M.

Oregon City, December, 1850.   *Oregon Spectator,* Jan. 9, 1851

III

Lines

Composed whilst the Lot Whitcomb made her first ascent of
the Rapids.

Lot Whitcomb is coming!
Her banners are flying—
She walks up the rapids with speed;
  She ploughs through the water,
  Her steps never falter—
Oh! that's independence, indeed.
  Old and young rush to meet her,
  Male and female, to greet her,
And the waves lash the shore as they pass.
  Oh! she's welcome, thrice welcome,
  To Oregon City;
Lot Whitcomb is with us at last.
  Success to the Steamer,
  Her Captain and crew;
She has our best wishes attained.
  Oh! that she may never
  While running this river
Fall back on the sand bar again.

Oregon Spectator, June 5, 1851.   E. M.

A Pioneer Mormon Diary § Patty Sessions

INTRODUCTION

There is a series of small notebooks in the Historical Department of the Church of Jesus Christ of Latter-Day Saints in Salt Lake City, Utah, whose value is beyond the price of gold. They are the diaries of Patty Sessions, "Mother of Mormon Midwifery," from February 10, 1846, for some forty years following, off and on.

Her first entry reads as follows:

A Day Book
given to me
Patty Sessions
by Sylvia Lyon
this 10th day of Feb.
1846
Patty Sessions
her Book

I am now fifty one years six days old. Feb. 10, 1846 City of Joseph [another name for Nauvoo] Hancock Co Ill . . . My things are now packed ready for the west have been and put Richards wife to bed with a daughter. in the afternoon put sister Harriet Young to bed with a son.

It is with the permission of the Historical Department that the part of Patty Sessions' "Day Book" that tells of her overland covered wagon journey in 1847 from the Winter Quarters in eastern Nebraska to Salt Lake City is here published.

She is reputed over a career of many years to have

delivered 3,977 babies and to have lost very few of them.[1]
Her own birth had been in Bethel, Maine, on February 4,
1795, to Enoch and Anna Bartlett. Her father was a shoemaker and her mother a weaver. She was seventeen years
old[2] when she was married to David Sessions in Newry,
Maine, on June 28, 1812. In her diaries she constantly
refers to her husband as "Mr. Sessions."

Another entry in the 1840's diary, that of April 22, 1847,
tells something of her family:

> David came   I was almost overcome again   my children all
> that were living were soon seated around the table with their
> Father and Mother   we rejoiced together and thanked the Lord

The children were oldest son, Perrigrine;[3] daughter Sylvia
Lyon, wife of Dr. Winsor P. Lyon;[4] and David, the
youngest, who would be 23 years old soon on May 9, 1847.[5]
Five other children had died in early life in the several
epidemics that had swept through the family.

Having long been Methodists, the Sessions became Mormons: Patty in 1833, and David in 1834. In 1837 they
moved to Kirtland, Ohio, then to Missouri, then to Nauvoo,
Illinois, only to be driven out once more to move on to the
Mormon "Winter Quarters," now part of Omaha, Nebraska, immediately after the above February 10, 1846, diary

---

[1] The best modern source for the life of Patty Sessions is Susan Sessions
Rugh, "Patty Sessions," a chapter in the book edited by Vicky Burgess-Olson,
Sister Saints (Provo, Utah, 1978), 304-22. Mrs. Rugh now lives in Chicago
and has been most helpful by means of several long distance telephone
calls. Some other key sources have been Chris Rigby Arrington, "Pioneer
Midwives," in *Mormon Sisters,* edited by Claudia L. Bushman, and Maureen
Ursenbach Beecher, "Women's Work on the Mormon Frontier," *Utah Hist.
Qtly,* XLIX, no. 3 (Summer 1981), 276-90.

[2] Claire Noall, "Mormon Midwives," *Utah Hist. Qtly,* X, (1942), 84-144.

[3] Patty and David Sessions, Sr., traveled with Perrigrine Sessions' wagon
train. She often refers to him as P. G.

[4] Patty refers to Sylvia's husband as "Windsor" or "W. P." This was
Winsor Palmer Lyon, an army doctor who had become a Mormon.

[5] Patty gives this information about David, Jr., in her diary entry for
May 9, 1847.

entry. At Winter Quarters she faithfully kept the record of day to day events in her Day Book. She told of numbers of deliveries of babies and of an otherwise busy life. It was in June 1847, that they started farther west in earnest aiming for the Mormon "Promised Land," Salt Lake City, and it is then that we pick up the story in Patty Sessions' own words, with spelling just as she wrote it, and with the almost total lack of punctuation that was her style as she tells of each day of the covered wagon journey. She drove a four-ox team herself most of the way. She mended wagon covers. She delivered babies. She also thanked God over and over for being so good to her. Leonard J. Arrington has classified her as "a remarkable blend of things temporal and spiritual." [6] and that is true of her Day Book also.

Dr. Arrington finds that this combination of the temporal and the spiritual is nowhere better illustrated than in the entry she made on her fifty-second birthday, February 4, 1847:

> in the camp of Isriel Winter Quarters we had brandy and drank a toast to each other desiring and wishing the blessings of God to be with us all and that we might live and do all that we came here into this world to do   Eliza Snow came here after me to go to a little party in the evening   I was glad to see her told her it was my birthday and she must bless me   she said if I would go to the party they all would bless me   I then went and put James Bullock wife to bed then went to the party   had a good time singing praying and speaking in tongues before we broke up   I was called away to sister Morse then to sister Whitney then back to sister Morse   put her to bed 2 oclock.

The Mormon overland party was systematically divided

[6] Leonard J. Arrington, "Persons for All Seasons: Women in Mormon History," *Brigham Young Univ. Studies*, XX, no. 1 (Fall, 1979), 39-58, especially pages 44-45. See also his "The Economic Role of Pioneer Mormon Women," *Western Humanities Review*, IX, no. 2 (Spring 1955), 145ff. Dr. Arringon has also been most helpful with words of wisdom and encouragement.

into "Hundreds, Fifties and Tens." This was a count, not of wagons, nor of individuals or families, but of able-bodied men. There may have been as many as forty or fifty individuals in a "Ten." There were four Hundreds in the total migration. The Sessions clan was in the First Hundred, Captain Daniel Spencer. Perrigrine Sessions was Captain of the First Fifty, and Ira Eldredge was Captain of the Second Fifty.[7]

The Day Book has a number of references to the "Pioneers." This has always been the name of the party that had preceded this migration. Led by Brigham Young, himself, this party had left Winter Quarters on April 14, 1847, and would arrive at Salt Lake City on July 24. It was made up of 73 wagons, 143 men, three women, and two children. Patty Sessions often tells of returning members of the Pioneer party, as well as the coming back of certain individuals to give them help.

Patty Sessions lived many years after the trip to the Salt Lake Basin. On Sunday, August 11, 1850, she wrote telling of the serious illness of her husband, David: "grows worse has not spoke since Friday but I think he knows what we say Ten oclock he died very easy." She thought he had died of "numb palsey."

Time and time again she told in her diary of her lonesomeness after the loss of David. On December 14, 1851, after spending several days cutting her own fire wood, she recorded that she had married John Parry and that now she had someone to cut wood for her. Her biographer, Susan Sessions Rugh, writes that it was a "marriage of convenience" and that it "lacked romantic love, but Patty

---

[7] The best treatment of the subject of the systematic arrangement of the Mormon party is to be found in a note appended by LeRoi C. Snow to one of the episodes of his "Pioneer Diary of Eliza R. Snow," which ran serially in the Mormon publication, *The Improvement Era*, from March, 1943, to April, 1944. The pertinent reference to be found in the September, 1943, issue, on page 310. Eliza R. Snow was a close friend of Patty Sessions and one of the most eminent of Mormon women.

was content with her new husband." [8] John Parry was an immigrant from that land of music, Wales, and he became the first conductor of the now world famous Mormon Tabernacle Choir. Patty had to experience life in a polygamous family, as a second wife, Harriet, was added on March 28, 1854. Her expert midwifery was even used to deliver Harriet's babies.

John Parry lived until 1868. Patty lived many, many more years, most of them in Bountiful, Utah, where she moved to be near her son. She gave a great deal of time to gardening, and she became an expert horticulturist. Her main contribution in that field was the Sessions Plum, which is still grown in Utah.

On December 14, 1892, she died at age 97. The *Deseret Evening News* echoed the general feeling when it declared, "She has gone to her grave ripe in years, loved and respected by all who knew her." [9]

In order to avoid a veritable host of footnotes due to her mentioning of so many persons by name, more than fifty of them in her diary, a *"Dramatis Personae"* follows, in which we have made brief identifications. There is also appended her record of the mothers she "put to bed" and the babies they bore as Patty Sessions wrote them down in chronological order on two pages in the Day Book set aside for that purpose, for the latter half of 1847.

DRAMATIS PERSONAE

Dr. Bartlett, a trader, has not been identified.
Rufus and Harriet Cordelia Beach. Patty Sessions refers to "Dealia" Beach in her diary entry for September 21.
Ezra Taft Benson was one of the Pioneers.
John Wesley Binley was one of the Pioneers.

---

[8] Rugh, "Sessions," p. 316.
[9] December 22, 1892, quoted in Rugh, p. 318.

Brown and Sister Brown were two of a plenitude of Browns. It is difficult to sort them out when there is no given name. There were several among the 1847 overlanders.

Carlos. See Carlos Sessions.

Haden Wells Church was a returning member of the Mormon Battalion.

Elizabeth Covington's giving birth to a baby is reported by midwife Sessions as follows: "I also delivered Elizabeth wife of Robert D Covington of a son named Robert L born August the 1 – 15 minutes past 8 oclock P M."

Jesse Wentworth Crosby's story is told in "The History and Journal of the Life and Travels of Jesse W. Crosby," *Annals of Wyoming,* XI (July, 1939), especially pages 171-181.

James Davenport was one of the party of Pioneers who was detailed by Brigham Young to stay at a bad spot on the Platte River and to operate a ferry for the later wagon trains. See Dale L. Morgan, "The Mormon Ferry on the North Platte," *Annals of Wyoming,* XXI (July-October, 1949), 14-167.

Marten Dewit is listed in the 1860 Federal Census of Utah as living with his family in the Provo area.

Sister Elbrige was probably Patty Sessions' way of spelling Eldredge. Which of them this sister might be is difficult to ascertain. There are 56 Eldredges listed in the 1860 Federal Census for Utah.

Edmund Ellsworth was a member of the Pioneer Company.

Elijah K. Fuller would go on to California in November, 1847, to obtain livestock.

Jedediah M. Grant was Captain of the Third Hundred of the 1847 company. The Grants lost a babe of eight months on September 2, and Mrs. Caroline Grant, herself, died on September 26. Captain Grant moved ahead of the company with all deliberate speed to carry the body of his wife to their Utah destination for burial.

John Green was John Young Greene. He was one of the Pioneers, had driven Brigham Young's team into the Salt Lake Valley.

Amos and Catherine Gustin became pioneer settlers in Nephi, Utah.

John S. Higbee was a member of the Pioneer Company.

Hiram S. and Sarah Melissa Kimball were friends back at Winter Quarters.

James Lawson was a Scotsman born in Kinross who had worked in the shipyards of his native land. He was an expert at repairing and maintaining wagons, an indispensible member of the 1847 overland company.

William Leffingwell and his wife, Eunice, were traveling with a large family in the 1847 migration.

Lovlin was probably Chauncey Loveland, a member of the Pioneer Company.

Sylvia Lyon was Patty Sessions' own daughter, referred to as "Sylvia" several times. She did not accompany the 1847 overland company. Her husband was Winsor P. Lyon. Sylvia had been born on July 31, 1818, and she died on April 13, 1882.

Mary. See Mary Sessions.

Martha. See Martha Ann Sessions.

Mathews has not been identified. We don't even know if it is a given name or a surname.

Miller has not been identified.

Thomas and Mahala Moor and five children traveled to Utah with the overlanders of 1847. He later operated a ferry on Green River.

P. G, or as Patty Sessions wrote it, "P G," was her nickname for her son, Perrigrine Sessions.

Parley. See Parley P. Pratt.

Lyman Wight Porter was a member of the Pioneer Company.

Parley Parker Pratt was a major leader in the Mormon community. Patty Sessions knew him well enough to write of him as "Parley." See Reva Stanley, *Archer of Paradise, A Biography of Parley P. Pratt* (Caldwell, Idaho, 1937).

Jonathan Pugmire was a private in Company E of the Mormon Battalion. He had been released because of illness and was on his way back to Winter Quarters.

Charles Coulson Rich was another major figure among the migrating Mormons. See Leonard J. Arrington, *Charles C. Rich: Mormon General and Western Frontiersman* (Provo, Utah, 1974).

Shadrach Roundy was a member of the Pioneer Company.

Carlos Sessions was her grandson, son of Perrigrine and Julia Sessions. Born July 16, 1842, in Nauvoo, he was now 5 years old.

Martha Ann Sessions was Patty Sessions' granddaughter, the daughter of Perrigrine and Mary Sessions.

Mary was the wife of Perrigrine Sessions.

Perrigrine Sessions was Patty Sessions' oldest son. He was Captain of the First Fifty of the First Hundred of this highly organized traveling community.

Laura Shaw gave birth to a baby delivered by Patty Sessions. The midwife's record of the birth reads as follows: "I also delivered Laura A wife of James B. Shaw of a daughter name Laura Almira born June 29 9 oclock A M."

Elijah Funk Sheets' "Journals" are to be found in the Historical Department of the Church of Jesus Christ of Latter-Day Saints in Salt Lake City. Susanna Musser Sheets, a wife, also kept a diary of the 1847 journey which is in the same depository.

Henry G. Sherwood was one of the Pioneer Company members. He made the first survey drawing of Salt Lake City. Due to a shortage of paper it was drawn on a sheep's skin. His later life would much of it be spent in San Bernardino, California.

Br Singley is not identified.

Abraham Owen Smoot was a Mormon leader who later became Mayor of Salt Lake City.

Eliza R. Snow is the best-known of the women of Mormondom. Her manuscript diary is in the Huntington Library, San Marino, California. It is being edited for publication, along with her other writings, by Maureen Ursenbach Beecher of Brigham Young University. Eliza R. Snow and Patty Sessions were close friends.

Daniel Spencer was Captain of the First Hundred. He was experienced in wilderness travel and had already explored the region.

John Streater Gleason was a member of the Pioneer Company.

Sister Ann Standley Hunter was the wife of Edward Hunter, Captain of the Second Hundred.

Sylvia. See Sylvia Lyon.

John Taylor was later to become Third President of the Church.

Mercy Rachel Fielding Thompson was a widow, her husband, Robert Blashel Thompson, having died on August 27, 1841. Her nine-year-old daughter, Mary Jane, was with her.

Sylvira Turnbow. Patty Sessions' record of a birth in the Turnbow family reads as follows: "I Patty Sessions delivered Sylvira wife of Samuel Turnbow of a daughter name Margarett Ann born June 25, 9 oclock P M."

Sister Van Cott was Lucy, the wife of John Van Cott. Midwife Sessions' birth record tells of the event as follows: "I also delivered

Lucy L wife of John Van Cott of a son name Losee born August 23 half past 12 oclock P M."

Martha Van Cott was the nine-year-old daughter of John and Lucy Van Cott.

Edson Whipple was a member of the Pioneer Company.

Jeremiah Willey was a returning member of the Morman Battalion.

Harriet Young, wife of Lorenzo Young, had been one of the three women who had entered the Salt Lake Valley as members of the Pioneer Company. Midwife Sessions' own record of the birth reads as follows: "I also delivered Harriet Page wife of Lorenzo Dow Young of a son born Sept 26 7 oclock P M the first male born in this valley."

Joseph Young was the grown son of Lorenzo and Persis Young. According to Eliza R. Snow he had been out looking for lost cattle.

Phineas Young was Brigham Young's brother. He was a member of the Pioneer Company.

THE DIARY OF PATTY SESSIONS, 1847

Monday [June] 21 we wash the cannon and temple bell has come and sciff [1] we are all ready now to go in the morning we have been waiting almost two weeks for the cannon

Tuesday 22 on the banks of the platt river ready packed to move on start 8 oclock A M we are organised to move five a breast the two cannons sciff and temple bell heading the midle line go 15 miles camp near the platt river

---

[1] The "Artillery Company" was under the command of Charles C. Rich, for whom John Scott directly handled the large guns. There was also a long, narrow rowboat, the "sciff" mentioned here. Leonard Arrington has the best discussion of the "military phase" of the 1847 overland Mormon migration in his *Charles C. Rich: Mormon General and Western Frontiersman* (Provo, Utah, 1974), in his chapter, "The Trek West," pages 111-21. He says that the bell was "probably the one from the Nauvoo Temple," p. 114.

Wednesday 23   start 9 oclock   travel two a breast cannons heading one line sciff and the temple bell the other   travel 15 miles   camp on the prairi 2 miles from the river on a place looking some like our old place in Maine

Thursday 24   start 8 oclock A M   go 10 miles   stop 1 oclock waiting for the rest of the co to come up as some of the camp had feelings they caled a meeting made all things right   received good instruction and had good feelings

Friday 25   10 oclock   move on   go 10 miles   camp a company of traders came along   Dr. Bartlett was one   had been to Pawnee   I then was sent for to [go] back 3 or 4 miles   I went back put sister Turnbow to bed   she had a daughter   come home 12 oclock at night

Saturday 26   start 8 oclock   go 20 miles camp on beaver creek   I have got the tooth ache bad   it rains to night

Sunday [June] 27   cloudy   I feel bad   my face sweled bad   can hardly set up   its quite hard on me to drive the team all the way but the Lord will give me strength according to my day   11 oclock I feel impresed upon to go and see sister Snow   I went and found her sick we had a little meetting   she and I were both healed by the power of God   I then went to a publick meeting   it was good   I then went to visit Sister Elbrige   she was lame   I laid hands on her she blesed me and I blesed her   I then came home had a litle meeting in our waggon   it was good   my granddaughter Martha Ann had the gift of tongues but through fear did not speak. after the sisters had

gone she asked me to let her and Martha Van Cott
have a litle meetting and wished me to attend we
went into our waggon she spoke in toungues and
prayed I gave the interpretation and then told them
to spend their time in that way and they would be
blessed she is eleven years old

Monday 28 we wash the men are caled out to drill
we have prayers night and morning at the ringing
of the bell we start 1 oclock go 6 miles camp. The
cannons go in the rear of our co we are still at the
front of Parleys division his division goes in the rear
this week 12 oclock at night I was sent for to go on
two miles to put sister Shaw to bed she had a daughter born 9 oclock A M she traveled on when our
co came up 10 oclock we traveled 10 miles camp on
the loop fork of Plat river we pass the Pawnee vilage to day it has been burnt by the Sues [Sioux]
we then crosed a creek chalk in the bottom so that it
stuck to the waggon wheels we camp on the bank of
the loop [Loup] drove our cattle all together into
the river to drink it was a prety sight

Wednesday 30 start 8 oclock wait for Smoots co
to start along and get out of our way one hour go
10 miles came up with the whole camp the men
go to find a place to cross we have pased another
Indian vilage today we do not cross to night camp

Thursday [July 1] Br Taylors Co cross first P G [2]
and some few others have gone hunting returned
saw some antalopes got nothing this afternoon we
cross the Loop camp on the bank our co have all
got over safe go 1 mile to day

---

[2] P. G. stands for Perrigrine Sessions, for which it is a nickname.

Friday July 2   we start half past 7 oclock   go 20
miles   camp on the prairia without wood or watter
only what rain fell from the clouds   we had a heavy
shower of wind and rain   it beat into the waggons
a good deal

Saturday 3   start 7 oclock   go 16 miles   strike the
Pioneer trail near the Platt river camp   P G shot an
Antalope today   we crosed the sleiugh on a bridge
made of grass where we watered at non   Br Sheets
cals this creek Muskeetoe bend   here we took out our
stove   found old indian wickeups to burn in it

Sunday 4   I took some of the things out of the waggons   found some wet a litle   it rains a litle. a man
broke his arm last night in our Co rasling   his name
is Martin DeWitt   the sun comes out   we go to meeting   have good instruction   I had a meeting in at
sister Tomsons tent at 6 oclock P M   we had a good
time

Monday 5   we have made a bridge to cross the creek
last night there was an indian seen creeping up to
the camp   when hailed he ran through the creek and
fled   we have to get more teams to put onto the cannon at ten oclock they fire both cannons and start
go 15 miles   they held a counsel last night   Parleys
Co was to go in the front   we have traveled all day
on the Pioneers track   camp on their camp ground
find a guide board 2:17 [217] miles from winter
quarters   the way we have come 1:90 [190] miles

Tuesday 6   start 8 oclock   go 18 miles   camp on the
bank of a stream from the platt river where the Indians had camped   we burnt their wickeups for wood
some waided the river to get wood   brought it over

on their backs   the camp did not all get up last night
neither have they to night   Smoots co have not been
heard from since Monday   Grants co did not get up
to night

Wednesday 7   Start 8 oclock   go 15 miles   camp
where the Pioneers did   found another guide board
it said they had kiled 11 buffaloe the 2 of May   PG
had the waggon wheel run over his foot   lamed him
so that he cannot drive his team   The Dr boy [3] drives
for him   we have passed a great many of these litle
dogs that live in the ground in holes

Thursday 8   start half past 8 oclock   cross a sleiugh
go 2 miles come to where the Pioneers camped 3
days   found another guide board   then we went up
the creek 3 miles   found two horses   PG was the
first that saw them   Br Pratt was with him   Pratt
and Taylor caught them and kept them   we make a
bridge   cross over   go 2 miles   make another bridge
cross   go 5 miles   camp   see some buffaloe

Friday 9   some of the men have gone to kill the buffaloe   we start half past 7   the men return   see no
buffaloe   past the Pioneers campground when we
first start but the sleiughs are so high we cannot follow
their trail   go up   make a bridge of grass   cross
go 12 miles to day   strike their trail   camp on the
bank of the platt river   Br Crosby waided it   the
girls wash   it is very warm   we find a pine tree floated
down the river

Saturday 10   start 8 oclock go 5 miles   camp 11
oclock   we are now 252 miles from Winter Quarters

---

[3] There seems no way to identify the "Dr boy" who drove for Perrigrine
Sessions.

to burn coal and fix waggons wash, &c &c six men
went out to hunt went horse back they do not return to night

Sunday [July] 11 the hunters have sent for a waggon to bring their game I have meeting in our waggon with the litle girls sister Tomson was with us &
then went to a public meeting then to sister Snows
she sent for me we had a meeting there I then went
to a public meeting I then went had a meeting to
sister Tomsons the hunters came in got 18-00 cwt
of buffaloe meat

Monday 12 divide it out among the 50 the men
went out of our co P G went they went out of other
co but did not get so much meat any of them as our 50
that sent out six men there was one dead buffaloe in
the willows where we camped we start 9 oclock
pass buffaloe s[pr]ings where they lay it looks like
our camp ground we go 12 miles camp on the river
they smoke the meat waid on to the island to get
wood Br Spencer capt over the first hundred

Tuesday 13 start 2 oclock go 15 miles camp on
the river waid to the island to get wood it has been
a complete pasture for buffaloe the grass is fed short
  some men went out hunting this afternoon kiled
4 bufaloe left the meat for co to bring in their herd
broke out of the yard last night and broke waggons
kiled a cow broke of[f] several horns one horses leg
and they have got to stop and repair waggons

Wednesday 14 go 6 miles stop for the rest of the
camp to come up see two herd of buffaloe near the
camp ground find a guide board with a letter in it
stating it to be 3-60 [360] miles from winter quarters

we call it 284 it is very warm   some men have
gone out to kill a buffaloe   kiled 1   divide it out in
our 50

Thursday 15   start 8 oclock   go 5 miles   camp at a
spring   we put our milk in it to cool   P Gs black ox
was sick to day   Br Singley let him have a pair

Friday 16   he is a going to yoke the well ox and put
it on forward   we start 8 oclock   go 18 miles   get
along first rate   see thousands of buffaloe   camp on
the North Fork of Platt river 14 miles from the mouth
    after we had camped a herd of buffaloe ran in among
our cattle   we shot one wounded three more   took
oxen and drew him in to camp before he was dresed
he was kiled in full vieu of the camp   went after
the others but did not get them

Saturday 17   start 8 oclock   go 16   at noon kill another buffaloe and draw it into camp   dress it while
the team are baiting   hear that letters have come from
pioneers   I gather a few dry weeds   build a little
fire on a buffaloe dung   broiled some meet for my
diner   drank sweeten[ed] ginger and water   I have
seen many thousands of buffaloe today   one crosed our
track just forward of us   we had a fair view of him
    camp on the river   no wood   get news that Br
Grants co had lost 75 head of catle by their breaking
out of the yard   we take out our stove   burn buffaloe
dung

Sunday [July] 18   bake mince pies bread and meat
over buffaloe dung   11 oclock go to public meeting
hear that Grants Co had not found their catle   some
of our men went this morning to look for them
    4 oclock caled together to hear leters read from the

pioneers   they were from some individuals that were
left at the ferry which they had made   they had ferried over four hundred Oregon waggons   they had
heard from the rest of the pioneers the 28 of June
they were well and in the south pass of the mountains
    I then had a meeting at sister Tomsons   P G is not
well   I gave him some medicine

Monday 19   he is some better   he has met for counsel   sent men of each co to hunt for Grants catle
he is 20 miles back   we cannot go on untill he comes
up with his co   we must get them along some way
    10 oclock I meet with the little girls in my waggon
have a good time   the Lord is pouring his spirit
out on the youth   they spoke in toungues and rejoiced
in God   my heart was made glad   2 oclock had a
meeting at sister Tomsons   we had a good time   I
blesed and was blesed   the men that went to hunt for
Br Grants catle   some of them have come in   found
3 three oxen of the Oregon co.s loosing the rest   kiled
a buffaloe   they kiled an Antalope   P G is worse

Tuesday 20   he is no better   start 8 oclock   go 10
miles   camp on the river   find some flood wood to
wash with   they have sent word from Br Grants co
that they have found none of their catle   20 yoke of
oxen gone   we have caled a meeting saying 4 hundred must make out 5 yoke out of each hundred
we have made out the 5 yoke

Wednesday 21   sent Br Gusten back with them   we
start 8 oclock   go 15 miles   where we watered at
noon they kiled 6 buffalo   gave Br Taylors Co 3 of
them   divided the other 3 in our co   we did not camp
untill dark   the catle was very uneasy   I went into

the waggon looked out saw them go round and round like a whirlpool the men saying they would break and run away I knelt down and prayed for the Lord to quiet them I arose they were quite still we went to bed heard no more from them

Thursday 22 heard this morning that the Indians killed 13 buffaloe close by us yesterday but none seen by us only the carcases of the buffaloe found warm the men are commanded to sleep with one hand on the lock of his gun last night we saw more than two thousand buffaloe at one time yesterday we go on 10 miles pass many dead buffaloe saw an encampment of Indians and as soon as we were camped there was more than 100 came to our camp it is the first I have seen since we left Winter quarters we have fired the cannon and one six shooter for them to see and hear gave them some bread and they feasted rode round the camp and then we rang the bell our men paraded and motioned to them to go a way · they went we sent word back to Br Taylors and Smoots co that were back to come up they have not come we made safe guard P G is better so he got out of the waggon walked round gave some orders

Friday 23 it rains and has all night the Indians have come in sight this morning the guard is caled orders gave to let them come near the waggons but they went on their way 10 oclock they begin to come we stay here today many Squaws came today they appear friendly they sing dance and ride around we dance and have music fire two cannons Parley and Taylor feast and smoke with the Cheif. Br Grants co came in sight to night Mr Sessions stands on guard

Saturday 24 we are at Ceder Bluffs start go 10 miles pass see and trade with many Indians pass their lodges on the other side of the river P G went over and many others camp on the river. Grants Co came up this morning but do not get up to night

Sunday [July] 25 7 oclock some of the Pioneers came into the camp we have stoped to repair waggons and wash and have a meeting I go hear leters read from the Pioneers I send a leter to Sylvia by Pugmire as he is from the Pioneers and going back to Winter Quarters

Monday 26 start 7 oclock go 20 miles at noon water and bait[4] a grove of ceder on the other side saw the Indians on the other side they stoped unloaded their ponys in the cedars we pased over the hardest sand hill we have found I drove my team was not well went a foot untill I could scarce stand crosed many small creeks camp on large one two rods wide Br Spencer is a head he started last night went five miles Br Rich came up

Tuesday 27 start 7 oclock go 18 miles in the forenoon Indians came some we have not seen before a big chief among them when we stoped to bait they came like bees their loges were across the river I drove into a mudhole got stuck put on more team came out camp near the river kill a ratlesnake close to the waggon thunders and lightens hard rains some

Wednesday 28 go 18 miles cross many water places mudy holes pased over ground that was over flowed

---

4 "Bait" is an old word for feeding animals during a break in a journey.

by the rain last night but litle rain where we were at noon baited on the last grass we found till night   in the afternoon came up a dreadful wind thunder lightning   a very litle rain where we were   on the other side of the river the ground was all aflood   we pased over sand bluffs in the wind   the sand and gravel flew in our eyes so we could not see at times   we had to hold our waggon covers to keep them from bloing off this is ruin bluffs   we camp on the Pioneers camp ground

Thursday 29   go 20 miles   at noon bait and water at the river   good feed   we are in sight of chimney rock bluff of sand looking like a tower on the other side the river or an old courthouse   go over the blufs camp on the river   go and lay hands on Mary Jane Tomson   we have traveled to day behind Br Spencer we came up with him last night

Friday 30   go 20 miles   pass the chimney rock many places that looked like ancient buildings   camp on the river   find good feed   kill a ratle snake   save the gall and greace

Saturday 31   go 15 miles   camp on the river   no wood and poor feed   the bluff on the other side looks like the temple   last night Brown & others went over the river on to the bluff   kiled 3 antalopes   a very curious looking place   the bluffs look like ancient edifices   some have gone over to night   we met Br Devenport this morning from the Pioneers   it gladened my heart to see him   he was in co with men that had been to Oregon   two women with them

Sunday August 1   I was caled to sister Covington I went back 5 miles   she came back with me   I put

her to bed this evening with a daughter   P G Mary
& Martha went over on the Bluffs   got 6 quarts of
black curants   two catle died to day by eating a unfit
substance that lay on the ground

Monday 2   go 22 miles   travel over dry prairia
no feed only one place   come to that 1 oclock but a
small place there   do not get to feed to camp till dark
leave the catle out   but litle feed here   two catle
died in Spencers co

Tuesday 3   go 12   meet men from the Army   Br
Willey came here at night half mile from the river
poor feed

Wednesday 4   wrote a letter to sister Kimble   sent
it by Willey this morning about 8 oclock go 12 miles
find black currants   get 6 quarts   camp   the Indians came into the camp spread their flag   we fed
them   they went off   plenty of wood here   we pased
some yesterday   15 days since we have had any wood
except a very litle flood wood   we have picked that
up and carried it along

Thursday 5   go 7 miles   pass fort Larrimee   see
many Indians   feed them   but litle feed yesterday and
today   I have fixed my waggon cover   the girls baked
currant pies

Friday 6   go 5 miles   pick more currants about 12
quarts and chouk cherrys a plenty   we stop to burn
coal and fix waggons and make yokes   we have come
over a very bad hill especialy to come down   camp
near the foot of it

Saturday 7   the men set waggon tires   women wash
we bake pies   hull corn

Sunday [August] 8   we wash iron &c   start 2 oclock
go 3 miles   camp

Monday 9   go 15 miles   we have had bad hills
come over one where we first started very rough went
a mile turned to the left went a mile turned back went
up a hard rough hill over a high prairia one dry river
no feed   broke two axeltrees some spokes out   we
camp where there is but litle feed

Tuesday 10   get the waggons fixed all ready to start
one of Mores oxen were gone   we went on and left
him   he found it come up at night   we go 17 miles
pass no feed and find but little at night   go over a
high hill and low beds of gravel   camp at a good
spring

Wednesday 11   go 3 miles over the worst hills we
have found   broke some waggons   stop to repair
but litle feed   have to go back down the hill to a spring
to get water   buffaloe seen here

Thursday 12   go 19 miles over hills and valeys   all
the way hard   dry big timber   cross creek   go a peice
through a deep gulley   camp on the bank   but litle
feed

Friday 13   go 18 miles   pass over the red Butes
Br Beach got a wild horse   broke to [two] waggons
crosing [blank space] creek   do not get camped untill
after dark   today is the first day since last friday that
I have been able to drive   yet I have drove with Martha to help me   I have been sick   tooth ache and fever
no appetite to eat

Saturday 14   stop to mend waggons   good feed
3/1 [1/3] of a mile to the south kill 4 buffaloe   some

of the hunters did not get into camp till after dark
they could not find the camp   we hallow and P G and
others went to them and piloted them in   sister Brown
got lost when she went to milk   she hallowed and was
piloted in

Sunday [August] 15   I jerk the buffaloe meat   one
of the Pioneers came in to the camp with news from
the twelve   say we are 458 miles from salt lake where
they have located   we had a confession meeting
partook of the sacrament &c

Monday 16   Brs Benson Porter & Bindley came into
camp   Porter eat breakfast with us   bring good news
from the Pioneers and their location   they go back to
meet the other Cos   we go 13 miles   camp on the
platt river   Br Church met us camped with us   Br
Parleys litle waggon broke down   the back chain
broke on my waggon as we came down the hill to camp
good feed over the river   stove coal in the bend of
the riverbank ten rods from the road east

Tuesday 17   go 15 miles   camp on the river   crosed
dear creek this forenoon   met John Higbee Joseph
Young Phineous Young and E Elsworths   come to
us   eat with us

Wednesday 18   wrote a letter to Br Kimbal   go 18
miles   camp at the old fery   but litle feed   have
come down and up some bad places

Thursday 19   it rains   some of the catle are mising
   I have wrote a leter to Sylvia to send by Phineas
Young   start and go 5 miles   P G had his waggon
turned over with Carlos in it into the water   got his
things wet   Carlos not hurt although he was under
water all but his face and sacks of grain and trunks

a top of him he cut the cover and got him out and all the rest of the things loaded up again forded river camped opened the things it rained we could not dry them

Friday 20 go 12 miles a big bull came down the hill in the road to us we caught him yoked him turned out one of my team that had a sore neck put him in we then went on kiled two buffaloe camped on a flatt the water poison 2 catle died there after we crosed the river last night Mathews little girl went down to the river found a ten dollar gold piece at the edge of the water

Saturday 21 go 13 miles killed 3 buffaloe camp on a spring willow stream Br Benson Porter & Bindley left us to go back to the Pioneers we found another bull he is lame

Sunday [August] 22 go 13 Br Pratt kiled a buffaloe Brown kiled an antalope camp on a small stream that runs into the sweet water good feed and water

Monday 23 we stop to recruit our teams I put sister Van Cott to bed with a son it has been a good day to day dry our things that got wet when the waggon turned over we have got them all dry up till late giving the catle new milk they had eat or drank something that made them sick two died

Tuesday 24 go 10 miles start before breakfast camp on sweet water at Independence Rock I went up on the Rock got a peice off of the top to carry along we have got sallaratus [5] plenty just before we

---

[5] Saleratus is another name for sodium bicarbonate, or baking soda. See also her entry for August 30, where she says, "hull corn with some of the saleratus." This means that she used the soda for soaking corn to make hominy, which when dried became "grits."

came to this Rock   the lake that had the best was at the left when we came

Wednesday 25   go 15 miles   camp a mile from water we are in the pass   very cold   I wanted mitens to drive with

Thurday 26   kiled an indian dog last night in the camp   good feed here   frost here this morning   have a very warm day   go 10 miles   camp on the sweet water   Parley went after the catle   good feed

Friday 27   frost again but a warm day   go 10 miles camp where we left Carlos

Saturday 28   go 11 miles   cross sweet water 4 times once in the mountains where they shut close together camp on it   Br Gustins last cow died here

Sunday [August] 29   go 16 miles   camp on the river again   meet some more Pioneers going back to meet their families

Monday 30   go 10 miles   camp on the river   hull corn with some of the saleratus   Br Pratt went upon the mountain   cut black birch stick

Tuesday 31   go 7 miles and camp   had up hill and rocky roads   the worst we have found   here we meet more Pioneers Br Rounday Lovlin Gleason & others they bring us good news from the valley

Wednesday Sept 1   go 12 miles   camp on sweet water in sight of table Rock

Thursday 2   go 14 miles   camp on the Pacific spring see indians here   trade some with them   get some skins

Friday 3   go 25 miles   camp on little Sandy   drive till after dark before we get to feed

Saturday 4   go 1 mile   stop   good feed here   the
Pioneers came to us   it made our hearts glad to see
them   they staid all nght with us eat and drank with
us   had a good meeting

Sunday [Sept.] 5   they bid us good by with their
blessing and left us to go to their families   they give
a good report of the valley   said it was the place for
us   we start 12 oclock   go 8 miles   camp on the big
sandy   but litle feed

Monday 6   go 16 miles   camp on big sandy with
traders   lent one of them some sugar & coffee   Miller
it rained in the night and snowed

Tuesday 7   snow on the ground this morning   go
16 miles   cross green river   hail and rained   go down
the river   camp   very cold   gather a peck of black
currants

Wednesday 8   lay still & rest   warm and pleasant
to day   we hull corn   Sister Tomson and I went down
on the river bank   had prayer alone

Thursday 9   go 13 miles   then had to go 1 mile out
of the road to camp and find feed   camp on mudy fork

Friday 10   go 7 miles   camp on hams fork   on a
branch of green river get a peck of currants   last night
spread them to dry   today Fuller and Leffingwell had
a meeting to setle difficulty   al[1] go a berying this
afternoon   get one bushel of currants and bull berys

Saturday 11   go 15 miles   camp on blacks fork
spread our berys   pass rocks very high on the left close
to the road   looks like some old monument   clay
coular [color]   the bull lay down as we went into
camp

Sunday [Sept.] 12 go 9 miles camp on blacks fork picked berys put them to soak this morning cook them this afternoon go to meeting Parley told us some items of the law of the valey [6]

Monday 13 go 10 miles camp at fort Bridger
Tuesday 14 go 13 miles over mountains and down steep places on the new road round and down the valley camped where the water stood but did not run
Br Pratt did not get into camp till near dark Br Lawson broke his waggon coming down the hill in the valey

Wednesday 15 stop mend the waggon start 11 oclock go 19 miles camp on a mountain see a big bear track near where we camped drove the catle into the valey we drove on a mountain 4 miles new road cut of 3 miles

Thursday 16 go 10 miles camp on Bear river pass the tar spring 30 miles from fort Bridger between the tar spring and the river a bad hill doubled teams to come up steep to come down droped the tea-kettle led [lid] coming down to get some strawberys vines to cary on we have some curant bushes also Br Sherwood came from the valey to us here

Friday 17 bad finding catle this morning get them start 11 oclock go 5 miles camp good feed but no wood had a meeting to setle a quaral cut 3 off from the church

---

[6] This "law of the valey" was a letter of instructions for governing the new settlement. It had been issued by Brigham Young and the Twelve three days earlier on September 9th. Undoubtedly that is what Parley Pratt was relating to the overlanders. It would be read officially in Salt Lake City on September 26, 1847. See Patty Sessions diary entry for "Sunday 26" at the end of this journey.

Saturday 18   has a fuss with Sister Hunter and family
this morning   go 10 miles   camp at cave Rock   them
that were cut off would not come along with us   Sister
Hunter would not come   we took the children along
she has come up to night very much enraged   sais
she will have revenge and Perrigrine shall be kiled
for she has backers to back her up   he and Br Pratt
took her had her bound with a cord and put under
guard   Porter and John Green came into camp in the
night

Sunday [Sept.] 19   those that were cut off came up
this morning while the men were hunting catle   went
on   she went on with them   we have found the catle
    go 10 miles   camp   a good spring came out of the
hill ran by the head of our corall   sister Hunter stoped
camped with us   met Joseph Young with teams going back to help on the rear of the camp   Porter and
Green has gone back to the valey   left this morning
    I gave them some crackers lent them two tin cups
    the mountains here are very high on each side
some small pines on the north side of us

Monday 20   go 12 miles   camp on weaver [Weber]
river   we have pased through one canion   I drove
through safe   red majestic rocks on the right all the
way   P G caught two trout

[Tuesday] 21   Br shelton pased with two yoke of
oxen   stay here till noon to mend Parleys waggon
made a new box   Br Losson [Lawson] did not get up
last night   come this forenoon   start 1 oclock go 8
miles   camp on a willow stream   set the waggons any
way   John Smith turned his waggon over down hill
    sister hunters axaltree broke   we put a pole under

drove into camp   there was more broke   I was caled
to Dealia Beach in the night

Wednesday 22   divide the co   each ten go by themselves   we go 10 miles   camp on a fork of weaver
river   our waggons stand in the road   I have took
up some goosbery bushes   the Doctor broke his waggon twice   P G shot a duck   saw where grisly Bear
pased   Dewitt saw him

Thursday 23   Br Wipple pased us   we lost the bull
here   P G found him   overtook us after we got almost
over the mountain   I drove up and down till he come
had to leave one of my oxen   he was lame   go 10
miles   camp on willow spring

Friday 24   go 14 miles   P G went back and got the
ox   we drove him into the cannion   left him   got
into the valley   it is a beautiful place   my heart flow's
with gratitude to God that we have got home all safe
lost nothing   have been blesed with life and health
I rejoice all the time

Saturday 25   P G went back to help up the rear of
his camp   they have all got here safe   some broken
waggons but no broken bones   I have drove my waggon all the way but part of the two last mts P G drove
a litle   I broke nothing nor turned over   had good
luck   I have cleaned my waggon and my self and
visited some old friends

Sunday [Sept.] 26   go to meeting   hear the epistle
read from the twelve then went put Lorenzo Youngs
wife Harriet to bed with a son the first male born in
this valley [7]   it was said to me more than 5 months ago
that my hands should be the first to handle the first

born son in the place of rest for the saints even in the city of our God   I have come more than one thousand miles to do it since it was spoken

EPILOGUE: RECORD OF BIRTHS

Patty Sessions' Record of Births, June 25 to December 14, 1847. She had left two pages of the diary blank immediately preceding the section we have reproduced. She filled these pages in gradually as the births took place.

I Patty Session delivered Sylvira wife of Samuel Turnbow of a daughter name Margarett Ann born June 25 9 oclock P M

I also delivered Laura A wife of James B Shaw of a daughter name Laura Almira born June 29 9 oclock A M

I also delivered Elizabeth wife of Robert D Covington of a son name Robert L born August the 1---15 minutes past 8 oclock P M

I also delivered Lucy L wife of John Van Cott of a son name Losee born August 23 half past 12 oclock P M

I also delivered Harriet Page wife of Lorenzo Dow Young of a son born Sept 26 7 oclock P M the first male born in this valley

I Patty Sessions delivered Sally Ann wife of James Brinkerhoff of a son name Levi born Nov 5 8 oclock A M 1847

I also delivered Elizabeth M wife of Simeon T Huffacre of a son name David L born Nov 6 half past 12 oclock P M 1847

I also delivered Ann wife of Daniel M Thomas of a daughter name Nancy C born Nov 6 half past 1 oclock P M 1847

I also delivered of a daughter Mary wife of James Brown name Mary Eliza born Nov 8 half past 12 A M 1847

I also delivered Lydia Ordelia C Elen wife of Gilbert Hunt of a daughter name Mary Elen born Nov 17 2 oclock A M 1847

I also delivered Dorcas A wife of Joseph C Kingsbery of a daughter name Bathsheba born Nov 19 7 oclock A M 1847

---

[7] This baby was named after his father, Lorenzo Dow Young. The newcomer lived only six months, however, dying on March 22, 1848.

I also delivered Emily wife of A O Smoot of a son name Albert born Nov 22 7 oclock A M 1847

I also delivered Rhoda wife of Albert Carrington of a son name Young Brigham born Dec 13 ¼ 11 A M

I also delivered Sophia wife of John Taylor of a daughter name Hariet Ann born Dec 14 6 oclock A M 1847

BIBLIOGRAPHY

Although it is planned that the final volume of this series will contain a comprehensive bibliography, it was thought that it would not be amiss to include here some basic references to fundamental books and articles on early Mormon experiences, especially that of women.

Arrington, Chris Rigby, "Pioneer Midwives," in Vicky Burgess-Olson, *Mormon Sisters* (Salt Lake City, 1976), 42-65.

Arrington, Leonard J., and Davis Bitton, *The Mormon Experience* (New York, 1979).

Arrington, Leonard J., "Persons for All Seasons: Women in Mormon History," *Brigham Young Univ. Studies,* xx (Fall, 1979), 39-58.

Arrington, Leonard J., "The Economic Role of Pioneer Mormon Women," *Western Humanities Rev.,* ix (Spring, 1955), 145ff

Bancroft, Hubert Howe, *History of Utah* (San Francisco, 1890).

Beecher, Maureen Ursenbach, "Women's Work on the Mormon Frontier," *Utah Hist. Qtly.,* xxxix (Summer, 1981), 276-90.

Beeton, Beverly, "Woman Suffrage in Territorial Utah," *Utah Hist. Qtly.,* xxxvi (Spring, 1978), 100-113.

Bitton, Davis, *Guide to Mormon Diaries & Autobiographies* (Provo, Utah, 1977).

Brooks, Juanita, *John Doyle Lee, Zealot-Pioneer Builder-Scapegoat* (Glendale, California, 1962).

Clayton, William, *William Clayton's Journal* (Salt Lake City, 1921.)

Derr, Jill Mulvay, "Woman's Place in Brigham Young's World," *Brigham Young Univ. Studies,* xviii (Spring, 1978), 377-95.

Froiseth, Jennie A., *Women of Mormonism* (Detroit, 1882).

Jenson, Andrew, *Latter-Day Saint Biographical Encyclopedia* (Salt Lake City, 1901), 4 volumes.

Noall, Claire, *Guardians of the Hearth, Utah's Pioneer Midwives and Women Doctors* (Bountiful, Utah, 1974).

Noall, Claire, "Mormon Midwives," *Utah Hist. Qtly.*, x (1942), 84-144.

Rugh, Susan Sessions, "Patty B. Sessions," in Vicky Burgess-Olson, *Sister Saints* (Provo, Utah, 1978), 304-22.

Tullidge, Edward W., *Women of Mormondom* (Salt Lake City, 1877).

The Commentaries of ⸸ Keturah Belknap

INTRODUCTION

No pei sons who told their story of the overland journey to Oregon used such an ingenious method as did Keturah Belknap. Beginning with her marriage date, October 3, 1839, in Allen County, Ohio, she kept not a diary, but what she termed a "memorandum," in which she periodically recorded what had happened in the period since her last entry. Evidently later in life she added notes to the original and recorded other memories. It is even difficult, therefore, to separate out added material from her "memorandum." She records events in the past tense for several entries; then all of a sudden the present tense makes an appearance, such as, "Now we're skirting the timber on the DeMoines River and its tributaries." Then she reverts to the past tense again.

The question arises for the editor whether such a "memorandum" ought to be included in a volume of contemporary records such as diaries and letters. The answer is that the nub of her running commentary in her story is built so closely around the day-by-day or week-by-week records that they dominate and the "memorandum," therefore, has an immediacy which no reminiscence written years later can capture. This is especially true of the overland part of her record, which seems to have been written on the spot while in the wagon.

The early pages have to do with the life of the George Belknaps before they left for Oregon. She goes into minute detail about events in such a way as to paint a picture of day-to-day life in Van Buren County, Iowa, during the

1840's. She tells of the births of their first four children — and the deaths of three of them. She describes the activities of devoted frontier Methodists, who often used the Belknap home, meager though it might be, as a meeting house.

On May 15, 1847, she writes, "Husband and I and two children start for Ohio to visit my father and mother." They made the journey while other Belknaps and their friends were starting for Oregon. George and Keturah and their children began their return trip from Ohio to their Iowa home in June, 1847, and she writes a vivid description of the several methods of travel, including the train. During the next autumn she made another entry that read, "My dear little girl, Martha, was sick all summer and the 30th of October she died, one year and one month old. Now we have one little baby boy left." Jesse Walker Belknap was the child's name, born December 23, 1844, and now three years old.

Sometime during 1847 she and her husband decided to follow others of the family to Oregon during the next overland season, 1848. George's parents, Jesse and Jane Belknap, also decided to go with them. Keturah's description of the details of preparation for the long overland trek is classic, one of the best of such records that have come to light.

Her story of the journey begins with the words, "Tuesday, April 10, 1848. Daylight dawned with none awake but me." The little Jesse is "in his place with his whip starting for Oregon." From that day on she goes into great and descriptive detail about every facet of the covered wagon journey. Here again, sometimes she makes day-by-day entries, at other times making an entry after several days, or an update covering a week or more. Her last lines are two undated ones reading, "Some of the men went thru to Fort Hall on horse back and returned to meet

us and say we can make it by noon." The context makes
it appear that this would have been in mid-July. Her baby
boy was very ill, and evidently she had no time for writing.
Just before the above two last lines she had told of hold-
ing her little son on her lap on a pillow and of tending
him all night long. She had written, "I thot in the night
we would have to leave him here and I thot if we did I
would be likely to stay with him but as the daylight, we
seemed to get fresh courage."

That tender little Jesse Belknap did finish the journey
to Oregon. He lived on for many years after 1848. The
Pacific Christian Advocate, the west's Methodist newspaper, later reported that he and his wife, Florence, both
died in December, 1871, leaving a two-year-old son.

There was another reason Keturah quit writing: In
addition to having a sickly tiny boy child to care for, she
was pregnant. She gave birth to another son, named Lorenzo, on August 10, 1848, somewhere in eastern Oregon.
The family tradition says it was about where Vale, Oregon
is today. Lorenzo also survived the journey to live a long
life. He died on February 28, 1926.

Keturah's own vital dates are elusive. In another "memorandum," published in the September 1937 *Oregon Historical Quarterly,* she jotted down the words, "And now
I am going to Make out A report and we will write August
the 15, 1847, this is my 27 birthday." This would mean
that she was born on August 15, 1820, and celebrated her
28th birthday in eastern Oregon not long after Lorenzo's
birth. She lived many, many years. Her obituary appeared
in the Portland *Oregonian* newspaper on August 24, 1913,
with a story out of Coquille, in southwestern Oregon, dated
August 23, and saying, "With the passing of Mrs. George
Belknap, of this city yesterday at the age of 93 years
another of the earliest pioneers of the Oregon country
has departed." So her vital dates are August 15, 1820 -
August 22, 1913.

In addition to the one telling of her overland journey, there are several other Keturah Belknap "running commentaries." The Oregon Trail record, transcribed from a typescript in possession of the Washington State University Libraries, Pullman, Washington, has a long title which reads, "History of the Life of My Grandmother, Kitturah Penton Belknap. Copied from the Original Loaned Me by My Cousin, Walter Belknap, son of Jessie Spoken of in This Manuscript." The typist mis-spells Keturah, Benton, and Jesse. Another commentary telling of the later life of Belknap family was published in the *Oregon Historical Quarterly* for September, 1937, and is entitled, "Ketturah Belknap's Chronicle of the Bellfountain Settlement," edited by the late Robert Moulton Gatke of Willamette University, Salem, Oregon. The spelling reproduced by Professor Gatke reveals a manuscript not so sophisticated in its orthography as the typescript we have used. Evidently the copier of our overland commentary "straightened out" Keturah Belknap's spelling, punctuation and capitalization.

We are indebted to Mrs. Frances Milne of Pullman, Washington, for informing us of two other Keturah Belknap commentaries: One of them is a typescript labeled "Part III," which continues the Belknap story after the arrival in Oregon. In this one she says she has lost her "memorandum" and "cannot give dates, have to write from memory."

The second manuscript is labeled "Part IV," and it was written by Katherine Barrett, a granddaughter, with the help of her mother, Lovina Belknap Christian. Mrs. Barrett says near the beginning of this reminiscence that her grandmother "is now 85 but . . . is in good health and mentally alert." These two women sum up the remainder of the overland journey of 1848, according to family traditions. The key paragraphs in this reminiscence are as follows:

We have no recollections of any thing unusual in their trip across the plains after they left Fort Hall until they reached Fort Boise. There we remember grandmother telling about camping there for several days, resting and washing their clothes in the hot springs. . .

The next event was the birth of a baby boy [Lorenzo] who was born near the present town of Vale, Oregon. They stopped a day or two and then went on, grandmother and baby quite comfortable in the bed she speaks of earlier that they had fixed up in the covered wagon.

They crossed the Blue Mountains and on down the Columbia River to the Dalles. There the men took the stock and oxen by trail and Indians took the women, children, and household goods in canoes and wagon beds down the river to Portland. They had to portage around the rapids at Cascade. At Portland there were only a few houses and a trading store. They didn't like the dense timber there so went on to what is now Benton County, 20 miles from Corvallis, near Monroe, Oregon, where they established a settlement which was known as "The Belknap Settlement."

It was October when they arrived and most of them were able to build log houses for shelter before winter came which was very mild in comparison with Iowa winters. Grandfather got his little family settled during the winter of '48 and in '49 he, with most of the young able bodied men, went to California to the gold fields. I think he did pretty well and was able to buy stock and necessary equipment for his farm. They took up a Government donation claim of 640 acres of land. In those days, many boys married young girls just in order to get the 320 acres of land which they could claim.

The Belknaps were all Methodists and very soon had a church in the making. At first they met at each other's as they had done in Iowa. In 1854 Bishop [Matthew] Simpson came to hold the first conference in the log school house. The church known as Simpson's Chapel today, stands near the spot where this first conference was held.

KETURAH BELKNAP'S
RUNNING COMMENTARY

George Belknap and Keturah [1] Penton were married October 3, 1839, both of Allen County, Ohio.

On October 17th we gathered up our earthly possessions and put them in a two horse wagon and started to find us a home in the far west. We had heard of the prairie land of Illinois but we had never seen anything but heavy timber land so we set our faces westward. (There were no railroads then).[2] We traveled thru part of Ohio and across Indiana and Illinois and crossed the Mississippi at Fort Madison into Iowa; was four weeks on the way and saw prairie to our hearts content, and verily we thought the half had never been told.

We camped out every night, took our flour and meat with us and were at home; every night cooked our suppers and slept in our wagon. We had a dutch oven and skilet, teakettle and coffee pot, and when I made

---

[1] Her given name is spelled in several ways by family and in the published literature, a common rendering being "Kitturah." She, herself, spelled is "Ketturah" in her "Chronicle of the Bellfountain Settlement," *Oregon Hist. Qtly*, XXXVIII, no. 3 (Sept. 1937), 271. The name is spelled "Keturah" in the 1870 federal census records.

The name is a biblical one. In the King James Bible, the version used by the pioneer Methodists, it appears as "Keturah" whenever used. "Keturah" was one of Abraham's wives and is mentioned in Genesis 25:1-4 and in I Chronicles 1:23-33. It is hard to believe that the parents would have named their newborn daughter for one dubbed by the biblical writer as a "concubine," nevertheless that is what happened. The meaning of the Hebrew word is "fragrance."

According to Robert Moulton Gatke, who edited the above "Chronicle," the family could not agree as to whether there should be double "t" or one. Our conclusion is to use "Keturah," under the assumption that such a devout family would have followed the Bible in usage.

[2] The statement in parentheses was added later, either by the writer or by some copier or editor.

bread I made "salt rising." When we camped I made rising and set it on the warm ground and it would be up about midnight. I'd get up and put it to sponge and in the morning the first thing I did was to mix the dough and put it in the oven and by the time we had breakfast it would be ready to bake; then we had nice coals and by the time I got things washed up and packed up and the horses were ready the bread would be done and we would go on our way rejoicing.

When we wanted vegetables or horse feed we would begin to look for some farm house along towards evening and get a head of cabbage, potatoes, a dozen eggs or a pound of butter, some hay and a sack of oats. There were not many large towns on the way and there was no canned goods to get then. Where there were farms old enough to raise anything to spare, they were glad to exchange their produce for a few dimes.

We stopped at Rushville, Illinois and stayed four weeks; expected to winter there but we heard of a purchase of land from the Indians west of the Mississippi and again we hitched up and mid-winter as it was we started, never thinking of the danger of being caught on the prairie in a snow storm. The second day we had to cross an eighteen mile prairie and in the afternoon it turned cold and the wind from the Northwest struck us square in the face and we had bought some cows at Rushville, had some boys driving them, and they would not face the storm so I had to take the lines and drive the team while my husband helped with the stock. I thought my hands and nose would freeze; when I got to the fire it made me so sick I almost fainted. We came to a little house with a big family of children and they had plenty of wood for

there was a point of timber run down into the prairie
and in after years there was a town there called West-
point. We got there about 4 o'clock in the afternoon,
had our provisions cooked up for the trip so we thawed
it out a little and made some coffee and the kind lady
put a skillet in the corner and made us a nice corn
cake. We had bread, butter, good boiled ham and
doughnuts and with good appetites we ate and were
thankful.

When we had cleared up the woman hunted up the
children and said, "Now children you get off to bed
so these folks can have a show to make down their
beds for if they cross that 20 mile prairie tomorrow
they will have to start early and that little woman
looks all pegged out now and now 'Honey' the best
thing for you to do is to get good and warm and get
to sleep". But, the "little woman" had the toothache
so she was not sleepy. There was another family with
us; four of them and us two and eight of the household. We furnished our own beds and made them down
on the floor. Tomorrow we cross the Mississippi into
Iowa.

Up at 4 o'clock in the morning, got our breakfast
before the family was up; crossed the river just afternoon, traveled till about 4 o'clock then came to another
18 mile prairie, put up for the night; the next day
started as soon as it was light, had to drive the team
again today and face the wind. It commenced snowing
before we struck the timber; it was hard round snow
and it seemed every ball that hit my face would cut
to the quick. That night we had plenty of wood and
a room to ourselves and the next day we went thru
patches of timber and, Oh my! but it was cold.

Now we're skirting the timber on the DeMoines River and its tributaries; thot we could make it to our destination that day but the snow made it such heavy traveling that we could not quite make it so we camped again. The next day we got to the place about noon; found the family living in the house yet to hold the claim and it was too cold for them to get out and their feed was there for their stock. The house was a double, hued log house; they let us have one room, and the two families of us lived in one room and we unloaded and commenced business.

The folks we bought the claim of went back to Missouri so we made trades with them and got ploughs, foder, chickens and hogs, made us some homemade furniture and went to keeping house. We had a quarter section of land. We thought that sounded pretty big but it was not paid for yet. The land had just been bought of the Indians and had not been surveyed yet so it was not in the market yet. We could settle on it and hold our claim and make improvements, but we must have the cash to pay when it was surveyed and came in to market or some land shark was ready to buy it from under us; then we would lose improvements and all so we had to get in and dig to have the money ready. The first thing was to get some land fenced and broke.

Our timberland was 2 miles from the prairie. I would get up and get breakfast so as to have my husband off before it was fairly light and he would cut rail timber all day in the snow and bring a load home at night; would take his dinner and feed for horses, come in at night with his boots froze as hard as bones, strange to say he never had his feet frozen.

Now, we must save every dollar to pay for our land; we had clothes to last the first year, and we got a dollars worth of coffee and the same of sugar that lasted all winter and till corn was planted. We did not know anything about spring wheat then so our crop was all corn. Then while the corn was growing, husband made some rails for a man and got some more groceries. He had hauled the rail cuts and scattered them along where he wanted the fence and split the rails odd spells and laid up the fence when the frost was coming out of the ground. We had 20 acres of broke land fenced to plant to corn the first spring; then we hired a man with a prairie team to break ten acres that was put into sod corn for foder, it was not tended any, did not get very big, was cut up in fall and fed out ears and all. The breaking team was five yoke of oxen with a man to hold the plough and a good sized boy with a long whip to drive the oxen.

Now it is spring and we have got a few sheep on the shares and they are sheared. All this winter I have been spinning flax and tow to make some summer clothes; have not spent an idle minute and now the wool must be taken from the sheep's back, washed and picked and sent to the carding machine and made into rolls, then spun, colored and wove ready for next winter. I can't weave so I spin for my mother-in-law and she does my weaving. Our part of the land had no house on it so we still live in the little kitchen and Father Belknaps[3] live in the other room.

Now its harvest time. George is off swinging the cradle to try to save a little something, while I am

---

[3] The "Father Belknaps" were Jesse and Jane, parents of George Belknap, Keturah's husband.

tending the chickens and pigs and make a little butter (we have two cows). Butter is 12½¢ a pound and eggs 6¢ a dozen. I think I can manage to lay up a little this year.

This year is about out. We sold some meat and some corn: fresh pork 5¢ per pound, corn twelve and a half cents per bushel in the ear; did not have to buy any clothes this year so we have skimped along and have $20.00 to put in the box (all silver). We will put the old ground into wheat this fall and break some more land for corn. Will have twenty acres of wheat in and now its spring of 1840.

The work of this year will be about the same. I have been spinning flax all my spare time thru the winter, made a piece of linen to sell, got me a new calico dress for Sunday and a pair of fine shoes and made me one home-made dress for everyday. It was cotton warp colored blue and copper and filled with pale blue tow filling so it was striped one way and was almost as nice as gingham. It is now May and the sheep are sheared and the wool must be washed and picked and got off to the carding machine.

So my summer's work is before me. It is corn planting time now so the men have their work planned till harvest and now the corn is layed by George and I are going to take a vacation and go about 10 miles away to a camp meeting. There are 4 young men and two girls going with us, but I made them promise there should be no sparking and they should all be in their proper places in time of service (for they were all members of the church), and if they did not set a good example before the world and show which side they were on they could not go with me and they behaved to the letter. Around the tent we were like one family but we were the head. This was the first camp meeting west of the Mississippi as far as I know. People came from far and near and I think there were about twenty clear conversions. Both the girls were married to two of the young men in the fall and lived to raise families who made good, useful men and women in church and state.

Samuel F. Starr married Cumie Belknap. Ausbery Beck married Nancy Marion. Cephas W. Starr and Noah Starr were the other two young men.[4]

Now we have had a rest and have got strengthened both soul and body we will go at it again. We have thot of trying to get things together this year to build a house next summer as we have about all the land fenced and broke that one man can handle. The crops are fine; our wheat is fine. Will have wheat bread new most of the time. The hogs did so well, can have our meat and quite a lot to sell. We more than make our living so we will have quite a lot to put in the box this year. We will get our wheat ground and get barrels to pack the flour in; then will have to haul it 60 miles to market and I think we got $3.00 a barrell. We took it to Keocuk on the Mississippi; then it was shipped off on steamboats.

It is now 1841 and we have most of the material together for the house. It will be a frame house, the only one in sight on this prairie and its miles across it. Now, the coming generations will wonder how we will build a frame house and no sawmill within 50 miles and will have to go that far for nails as we can-

---

4 None of these appear in the records of the 1850 federal census for Oregon.

not get any larger quantity at the little stores here. "Where there's a will there's a way". The timber is all hued out of oak trees that grew on Lick Creek 4 miles away; everything from sills to rafters are hued with the broad axe. The timber is very tall and fine oak and hickory trees making as many as three or four rail cuts and splits so straight we can make anything we want of it. We found a carpenter who had some tools and he got to work two days and layed out the work, then George and his father worked at it after the corn was layed by till harvest: got the frame up and the roof on; as there was one of our neighbors going to Burlington after goods for a man who was starting a store in a little town on the De Moines about 4 miles from us we got them to bring us some shingle nails and we had made shingles in the winter. While I spun flax George brought in the shaving horse and shaved shingles and we burnt the shavings and both worked by the same light. We now have the roof on and it can stand awhile.

August the 20th. Harvest is over and we have the sweetest little baby girl; call her Hannah.

We will now work some more on the house. While my husband is staying round he will be putting on the siding. He made that himself, cut the trees and sawed off cuts 6 ft. long, then split then out and shaved them with the drawing knife to the proper thickness, put it on like weather boarding and it looks very well. The house is 24 ft. long and 16 ft. wide. Will take off 10 ft and make two bed rooms. The balance is the living room with a nice stone chimney and fireplace with a crane in one end to hang the pots on to cook our food. The house is to be lathed and plastered will get the lath out this winter; there is plenty of lime stone and some men are burning lime kilns.

October 1st. At the house again; have it all enclosed and rocks on the ground for the chimney. Now it is time to gather the corn so when it is dry they will be husking corn as it is all cut and shocked. It will be husked out and stood up again and the foder fed to the hogs.

November 10th. Froze up and snowing; will have winter now till the 1st of April. We will spend another winter in the little log house.

December 1st. Cold and have had good sleding for 6 weeks and the upstairs drifted full of snow twice. The roof is put on with clapboards and weight poles. Father Belknaps live in the large room of the same house we do and have meeting there.

The 10th was quarterly Meeting and Saturday night it snowed and blowed so the upstairs was so full of snow Sunday morning that we had to shovel it out and build big fires to get it dryed out so it would not drip before meeting time. We took up some of the boards and shoveled snow down and carried it out in the washtubs (barrels of it). Our room was not so bad, loose floor and we had spread the wagon cover over it to keep out the cold so we rolled it up in a pile in the back corner and got breakfast in our room. The two families, the Presiding Elder, and two preachers all joined in prayers and then all took breakfast in that little room. I think it was 14 by 16 feet. No one seemed crowded or embarrassed and by the time breakfast was over the congregation began to gather. We opened the middle door and the preacher stood in the door and preached both ways for both rooms were crowded. It was a grand meeting. By night the roads were broke and both rooms were crowded till there was not standing room. Had meeting again Monday and Tuesday nights. It was a happy time.

Time passes on and now it is time for the Holidays. What will we have for Christmas dinner? For company, will have Father Belknaps and the Hawley family [5] and most likely the preacher – 12 in all – and now for the bill of fare.

Firstly; for bread, nice light rolls; cake, doughnuts; for pie, pumpkin; preserves, crab apples and wild plums; sauce, dried apples; meat first round: roast spare ribs with sausage and mashed potatoes and plain gravy; Second round: chicken stewed with the best of gravy; chicken stuffed and roasted in the dutch oven by the fire, for then I had never cooked a meal on a stove.

I think I can carry that out and have dinner by two o'clock if I get up early. I will cook in my room and set the table in the big room and with both of our dishes can make a good showing. Everything went off in good style. Some one heard the old folks say they had no idea Kit could do so well.

May 1st, VanBuren Co., Iowa, 1842   About the same routine of last year. Plant corn and tend it: we will be thru planting this month then by the first of June what was planted first will need to be tended for it wont do to let the weeds get a start so they will go thru it with the one horse plough, two furrows between every row and two or three boys with hoe to clean out the hills and pull out all weeds (quite a tedious job

---

[5] Chatman and Kesiah Hawley.

if you have 50 or 60 acres). But now it is all thru that
in suffering and now the sheep must be sheared.

Today the neighborhood all turns out to make a
sheep pen on the bank of the DeMoines River whither
they will drive their flocks to wash them before shear-
ing. And now the fun begins for all the men and boys
are there to help or see the fun. There were five men
with their sheep and their boys. George's was the first
ones in the pen (30). They were taken one at a time
out in the river where they could not touch bottom
with their feet, then hold their heads out of the water
with one hand and with the other rub and souse them
up and down till the water would look clean when
they squeezed it out of the wool. Then they took them
out to a clean apartment and when they got one man's
done they sent the boys home with them and put them
in a little clean pasture to dry and so on till all was
done. They all took their dinner and had a regular
picnic. Now it is the last of June. The men are back
in the corn except the sheep shearers. The sheep will
be sheared this week, then the wool will lay out a few
days to get the sheep smell off, then my work will
begin. I'm the first one to get the wool (25 fleeces);
will sort it over, take off the poor short wool and put
it by to card by hand for comforts, then sort out the
finest for flannels, and the courser for jeans for the
men's wear. I find the wool very nice and white but
I do hate to sit down alone to pick wool so I will
invite about a dozen old ladies in and in a day they
will do it all up.

June 20th. Have had my party; had 12 nice, old
ladies; they seemed to enjoy themselves fine. Had a
fine chicken dinner; for cake I made a regular old

fashioned pound cake like my mother used to make for weddings and now my name is out as a good cook so I am alright for good cooking makes good friends.

July 1st.   My wool came home today from the carding machine in nice rolls ready to spin. First, I will spin my stocking yarn. Can spin two skeins a day and in the evening will double and twist it while George reads the history of the U. S. Then we read some in the Bible together and have prayer and go to bed feeling that the sleep of the laboring man is sweet. My baby is so good she dont seem much in my way.

Time moves on and here it is September and the new house is about ready to live in this winter. Have been having meeting in it this summer so it's been dedicated and we will try to say "As for me and my house we will serve the Lord."

November. Everything is about done up and we have moved in our own house, have not got much to keep house with but it is real nice to have things all my own way. Have got my work for the winter pretty well in hand, have made me a new flannel dress colored blue and red; had it wove in small plaid. I am going to try and make me one dress every year then I can have one for nice and with a clean check apron I would be alright. I made some jeans enough for two pair of pants and a new *wames* [6] for George and have the knitting done so we have two good pair of stockings for all.

It seems real nice to have the whole control of my house; can say I am monarch of all I survey and there is none to dispute my right. I have curtained off a nice

---

[6] "Wames" is Keturah's spelling of "wamus," a kind of cardigan or tough outer jacket.

little room in one corner so we can entertain the preachers and they seem to enjoy it. Our house is right at the cross roads and they say it is such a handy place to stop; it is right on the road going any way so I try to keep a little something prepared.

March, 1843   The years have been much the same. This has been the most tedious winter I ever experienced.

April 1st and everything frozen solid yet. We have a nice little boy now and I dont see as two babies are any more trouble than one. I put them both in their little cradle and the little girl amuses the baby till he gets sleepy then I take them out, give the baby some attention while the little girl plays round the house and after they have exercised their muscles I fix up the little nest and lay the babe down to go to sleep; then the other comes running to be *"hept in to by by baby to seepens"* and they are both sound asleep. I fix one in each end of the cradle and shove it to one side and then I just make things hum for they are both babies – the oldest a year and a half old.

We have got fixed up very nice in our new home; have a good well close to the door; a nice little natural grove on the west (crab apples and wild plums). The crabs are large and fine for preserves and the plums are fine too. Back of the house north is a piece of very rich soil. It is called hazel ruff; it has hazel bushes all over it but when grubed out is very fine land. There we have prepared a place to raise melons and we have them in abundance and now I want to tell you how I make a substitute for fruit. Take a nice large water melon. cut them in two and scrape the inside fine to the hard rind and it will be mostly water and when

you get a lot prepared strain it thru a seive or thin
cloth, squeeze out all juice you can, then boil the juice
down to syrup. I then took some good melons and crab
apple about half and half and put them in the syrup
and cook them down till they were done, being careful not to mash them, put in a little sugar to take the
flat off and cook it down a little more and you have nice
preserves to last all winter (and they are fine when you
have nothing better and sugar 12½¢ a lb. and go 40
miles after it). On the east end of the house we have
a garden.

November, 1843. I have experienced the first real
trial of my life. After a few days of suffering our little
Hannah died of lung fever so we are left with one baby.
I expect to spend this winter mostly in the house but
as we have meeting here at our house I can see all the
neighbors twice a week for we have prayer meeting
Thursday evenings.

Have commenced to build a church on our land; it
will be brick. We are going to have Quarterly Meeting here about Christmas; if it gets very interesting
will protract it thru the holidays.

January 5, 1844. The Meeting is over and the
house cleaned up. We had a good time and the house
was packed every night; good sleighing, and everybody
seemed to be interested.

We had two beds in the house and a trundle bed
that we could shove under one bed, then in the evening
I would put both beds on one bedstead and take the
other outdoors till after meeting, then bring it in and
shift the beds and make it up for the preachers. The
one that was left in was used for a seat and to lay the
sleeping babies on while the sisters were helping carry

on the work and it was no uncommon thing for the
noise to become so great that it would rouse some of
the babes and a man would take it up and pass it along
to the fire place where there was always a warm corner
reserved for the sisters with little ones. The Meeting
lasted for 10 days; had over 20 conversions, and I thot
that was about the best time I ever had. I cooked by
the fire place and our one room served for church,
kitchen, dining-room, bed room, and study for the
preachers; sometimes we had three or four as they
came from adjoining circuits to help us thru the week.

January, 1845. We have another little boy baby
born Dec. 23, 1844. We call him Jesse Walker. The
first name for his grandfather Belknap, the second for
our family doctor who was also a local preacher and
a fast friend and good neighbor.

We are still taking up the subject of building a
church; have the lot on the west corner of our land
near the burying ground. We gave five acres for that
and two for the church; it is to be of brick; will do the
wind work this winter. Tonight we have company;
three neighbors and their wives have come to spend
the evening and while they are talking about the
amount of brick it will take to build the church I am
getting a fine supper in the same room by the same
fire. Took the chickens off the roost after they came
and will have it ready about 10 o'clock, have fried
cakes (had fresh bread), stewed chicken and sausage
and mashed potatoes. Had a fine time; had prayers
before they left 15 minutes till twelve.

June, 1845. Summer comes again with its busy
cares. They have got to work at the church and I am

boarding three men to get money to pay my subscription of $10.00 to the church.

I have had to pass thru another season of sorrow. Death has again entered our home; this time it claimed our dear little John for its victim. It was hard for me to give him up but dropsy on the brain ended its work in four short days. When our pastor was here a week before he said he thot that child was too good for this wicked world but he little expected to be called to preach his funeral in less than one week. We are left again with one baby and I feel that my health is giving way. A bad cough and pain in my side is telling me that disease is making its inroads on my system.

October 1st. We have got thru our summer work and now we are preparing for winter. Have raised a good crop but will have to feed it all out this winter; will have a lot of hogs to fatten.

November 10th. Have had a month of cold, frosty nights and now we expect a freeze up; cold northwest winds prevail. I'm going to stay at home this winter and see if I will take so much cold.

We have another baby; such a nice little girl, only 6 lbs. at first and though it is a month old is not much bigger than at first. It has never been well so we have two children for a while; neither of them are very strong.

The church is not finished but the roof is on so it will stand over winter and meeting will still be at our house. We are fixed nicely in our home now. Have had a very pleasant winter and now it is springtime (1847) again and they all think I had better go on a visit to Ohio. The past winter there has been a strange fever raging here (it is the Oregon fever) it seems to be contagious and it is raging terribly, nothing seems to stop it but to tear up and take a six months trip across the plains with ox teams to the Pacific Ocean.

May, 1847. Some of our friends have started for Oregon. L. D. Gilbert wife and six children; Oren Belknap, wife and four children; Ransom Belknap, wife and two children; S. F. Starr, wife and two children.[7] These were from our neighborhood. They will meet others at the crossing of the Missouri River and make laws and join together in a large company.

May 15th. Husband and I and two children start for Ohio to visit my father and mother. We go by wagon to Keocuck; there we take the steamer on the Mississippi to St. Louis thence to Cincinnati; there we get a team to take us out 6 miles to my sister's. Stayed there one week, then they took us out to Hamilton 30 miles to another sister's. Stayed here three days, then took the canal boat for St. Maries Got on the boat Monday evening, got off at the landing at three o'clock Tuesday morning. There was a little shack there and as there was no one on the stir we had to stay there till daylight. I took our wraps and made a bed for the children and we noded till people began to stir, then we hunted up the town and found the hotel and got breakfast. While we were eating we saw an old man eating, just on the other side of the table and we recognized Mr. Jones, one of our old neighbors so we kept our eyes on him and when he left the table we made ourselves known to him and he said "And this is little Kittie Penton that you carried off from us a few years ago. Well! Well! she has got to be quite a woman".

---

[7] Lorenzo and Harriet Gilbert; Owen and Nancy Belknap, and Samuel and Laura Starr.

He said he had just been in with a load of oats and was going home empty so he could take us to our journey's end. It was 12 miles to my father so we thot we were in luck.

We got to Mr. Jones at noon so we stopped and fed the team and got a good warm dinner; then had about 4 miles to go yet so the horses we hitched up again and about four o'clock we drove up to my father's gate. They were greatly surprised as we had not written them we were coming. We all seemed to enjoy the trip. The children seemed to be much better than when we left home but I was no better. Every one would say how changed I was till I really thot I was sick and going into consumption, but my baby seemed better.

I knew it would be the last visit I would make there whether I lived or not but I kept all these thots buried in my own breast and never told them that the folks at home were fixing to cross the plains while we were away but taking it all around we had a good time. We were there a month, then it came time to say good bye. The last few days the baby was growing weaker and I wanted to get home where it could be more quiet.

All the friends have visited us and Sunday we had a good social meeting and said Good bye to all the friends. It was hard for me to not break down but they all thot in about two years we would come again.

On Tuesday, June 1st, we were ready to start for home. We went by wagon 25 miles to Springfield and there we struck the railroad that was just being built from Cincinnati to Columbus, Ohio but was not finished any farther than Springfield so we stayed there all night and in the morning go on the car for Cincinnati. That was our first car ride and the first Railroad

we had ever seen. We got to ride 75 miles. Our little
boy was asleep when we got on and when he woke up
he looked all around surprised and said, "Where is the
horses?" At noon we were on the bank of the Ohio
River; if we had have went with a team it would have
taken 3 days. There we found the same old steam boat
that brought us down (The Victress) had made its
trip and just steaming up to leave the wharf so we got
on board again for home. Were on the water two days
and one night, then we were at the mouth of the Des
Moines River where we had arranged to get off and
meet a team to take us home (about 40 miles) but it
was a fine level road and by getting an early start we
could make it in a day. Now we had been gone a month
and traveled all kinds of ways.

Just as we landed Father Belknap drove up to meet
us We had friends there so we stayed all night with
them and the next day we went home. They thot I
looked better for the trip but the baby was failing
all the time.

We found the folks all excitement about Oregon.
Some had gone in the spring of '47; four families of
the connection and many of the neighbors but they
had not been heard from since crossing the Missouri
River. Everything was out of place and all was excitement and commotion. Our home was sold waiting our
return to make out the papers and it was all fixed up
for me to live with Father Belknaps as the man wanted
the house on our place. Ransom's [8] and Fathers had not
been sold yet. It did not suit me to live with them so
I told them it was out of the quesion so for the first

---

[8] Ransom or "Rant" Belknap was a younger brother of George. His
wife was Mahala.

time since our marriage I put my foot down and said "will and wont" so it was arranged for us to go on Rant's place and live in their home till it was sold. I knew it would use me and the little sick baby up so to be in such a tumult. There was nothing done or talked of but what had Oregon in it and the loom was banging and the wheel buzzing and trades being made from daylight till bed time so I was glad to get settled.

My dear little girl, Martha, was sick all summer and the 30th of October she died, one year and one month old. Now we have one little baby boy left.

So now I will spend what little strength I have left getting ready to cross the Rockies. Will cut out some sewing to have to pick up at all the odd moments for I will try to have clothes enough to last a year.

November 15, 1847. Have cut out four muslin shirts for George and two suits for the little boy (Jessie). With what he has that will last him (if he lives) until we will want a different pattern.

The material for the men's outer garments has to be woven yet. The neighbors are all very kind to come in to see me so I don't feel lonely like I would and they don't bring any work, but just pick up my sewing we think I will soon get a lot done. Then they are not the kind with long sad faces but always leave me with such a pleasant smiling faces that it does me good to think of them and I try not to think of the parting time but look forward to the time when we shall meet to part no more.

Now, I will begin to work and plan to make everything with an eye to starting out on a six month trip. The first thing is to lay plans and then work up to the program so the first thing is to make a piece of

linen for a wagon cover and some sacks; will spin
mostly evenings while my husband reads to me. The
little wheel in the corner don't make any noise. I spin
for Mother B. and Mrs. Hawley and they will weave;
now that it is in the loom I must work almost day and
night to get the filling ready to keep the loom busy.
The men are busy making ox yokes and bows for the
wagon covers and trading for oxen.

Now the New Year has come and I'll write (1848).
This is my program: will start out with the New Year.
My health is better and I don't spend much time with
house work. Will make a muslin cover for the wagon
as we will have to double cover so we can keep warm
and dry; put the muslin on first and then the heavy
linen one for strength. They both have to be sewed
real good and strong and I have to spin the thread and
sew all these long seams with my fingers, then I have
to make a new feather tick for my bed. I will put the
feathers of two beds into one tick and sleep on it.

February 1st, and the linen is ready to work on and
six two bushel bags all ready to sew up, that I will do
evenings by the light of a dip candle for I have made
enough to last all winter after we get to Oregon, and
now my work is all planned so I can go right along.
Have cut out two pairs of pants for George (Home
made jeans). A kind lady friend came in today and
sewed all day on one pair; then took them home with
her to finish. Another came and wanted to buy some
of my dishes and she took two shirts home to make
to pay for them.

And now it is March and we have our team all
ready and in good condition. Three good yoke of oxen
and a good wagon. The company have arranged to

start the 10th of April. I expect to load up the first wagon. George is practicing with the oxen. I dont want to leave my kind friends here but they all think it best so I am anxious to get off. I have worked almost day and night this winter, have the sewing about all done but a coat and vest for George. He got some nice material for a suit and had a taylor cut it out and Aunt Betsy Starr [9] helped me two days with them so I am about ready to load up. Will wash and begin to pack and start with some old clothes on and when we can't wear them any longer will leave them on the road.

I think we are fixed very comfortable for the trip. There is quite a train of connection. Father Belknap has one wagon and 4 yoke of oxen; Hayley has two wagons and 8 yoke of oxen; Newton [10] about the same; Uncle John Starr has two wagons and 4 yoke of oxen; G. W. Bethards [11] one wagon and 3 yoke of oxen; we have the same besides 3 horses and 10 cows. Now it is the 1st of April and the stock is all in our corn field to get them used to running together; in ten days more we will be on the road.

This week I will wash and pack away everything except what we want to wear on the trip. April 5th. This week I cook up something to last us a few days till we get used to camp fare. Bake bread, make a lot of crackers and fry doughnuts, cook a chicken, boil ham, and stew some dryed fruit. There is enough to last us over the first Sunday so now we will begin to gather up the scatterings. Tomorrow is Saturday and next Tuesday we start so will put in some things today.

---

[9] Betsy or Elizabeth Starr was the wife of John W. Starr.

[10] Abraham and Rachel Newton.

[11] George and Kesiah Bethards.

Only one more Sunday here; some of the folks will
walk to meeting. We have had our farwell meeting so
I wont go; don't think I could stand it so George stays
with me and we will take a rest for tomorrow will be
a busy day.

Monday, April 9th, 1848   I am the first one up;
breakfast is over; our wagon is backed up to the steps;
we will load at the hind end and shove the things in
front. The first thing is a big box that will just fit in
the wagon bed. That will have the bacon, salt and
various other things; then it will be covered with a
cover made of light boards nailed on two pieces of
inch plank about 3 inches wide. This will serve us for
a table, there is a hole in each corner and we have
sticks sharpened at one end so they will stick in the
ground; then we put the box cover on, slip the legs
in the holes and we have a nice table, then when it is
on the box George will sit on it and let his feet hang
over and drive the team. It is just as high as the wagon
bed. Now we will put in the old chest that is packed
with our clothes and things we will want to wear and
use on the way. The till is the medicine chest; then
there will be cleats fastened to the bottom of the
wagon bed to keep things from slipping out of place.
Now there is a vacant place clear across that will be
large enough to set a chair; will set it with the back
against the side of wagon bed; there I will ride. On
the other side will be a vacancy where little Jessie
can play. He has a few toys and some marbles and
some sticks for whip stocks, some blocks for oxen and
I tie a string on the stick and he uses my work basket
for a covered wagon and plays going to Oregon. He
never seems to get tired or cross (but here I am leaving

the wagon half packed and set off on the journey). The next thing is a box as high as the chest that is packed with a few dishes and things we wont need till we get thru. And now we will put in the long sacks of flour and other things. The sacks are made of home made linen and will hold 125 pounds; 4 sacks of flour and one of corn meal. Now comes the groceries. We will make a wall of smaller sacks stood on end; dried apples and peaches, beans, rice, sugar and coffee, the latter being in the green state. We will brown it in a skillet as we want to use it. Everything must be put in strong bags; no paper wrappings for the trip. There is a corner left for the wash-tub and the lunch basket will just fit in the tub. The dishes we want to use will all be in the basket. I am going to start with good earthen dishes and if they get broken have tin ones to take their place. Have made 4 nice little table cloths so am going to live just like I was at home. Now we will fill the other corner with pick-ups. The iron-ware that I will want to use every day will go in a box on the hind end of the wagon like a feed box. Now we are loaded all but the bed. I wanted to put it in and sleep out but George said I wouldn't rest any so I will level up the sacks with some extra bedding, then there is a side of sole leather that will go on first, then two comforts and we have a good enough bed for anyone to sleep on. At night I will turn my chair down and make the bed a little longer so now all we will have to do in the morning is put in the bed and make some coffee and roll out.

The wagon looks so nice, the nice white cover drawn down tight to the side boards with a good ridge to keep from saging. Its high enough for me to stand straight

under the roof with a curtain to put down in front and
one at the back end. Now it is all done and I get in
out of the tumult. And now everything is ready I will
rest a little, then we will eat a bite. Mother B. has
made a pot of mush and we are all going to eat mush
and milk to save the milk that otherwise would have
to be thrown out. Then we have prayers and then to bed.

Tuesday, April 10, 1848. Daylight dawned with
none awake but me. I try to keep quiet so as not to
wake anyone but pretty soon Father Belknap's voice
was heard with that well known sound "Wife, Wife,
rise and flutter" and there was no more quiet for anyone. Breakfast is soon over; my dishes and food for
lunch is packed away and put in its proper place, the
iron things are packed in some old pieces of old thick
rags. Now for the bed (feather); nicely folded the
two ends together, lay it on the sacks, then I fix it. The
covers are folded and the pillows laid smoothly on,
reserving one for the outside so if I or the little boy
get sleepy we have a good place to lie; the others are
covered with a heavy blanket and now my chair and
the churn and we will be all done.

Our wagon is ready to start; I get in the wagon and
in my chair busy with some unfinished work. Jessie is
in his place with his whip starting for Oregon. George
and the boys have gone out in the field for the cattle.
Dr. Walker calls at the wagon to see me and give me
some good advice and give me the parting hand for
neither of us could speak the word "Farewell". He
told me to keep up courage and said "dont fret, whatever happens don't fret and cry; courage will do more
for you then anything else". Then he took the little
boy in his arms and presented to him a nice bible with

his blessing and was off. The cattle have come and the rest of the train are lined up here in the lane and many of the neighbors are here to see us off. The oxen are yoked and chained together.

Uncle John Starr two are the last so they will be behind today. We will take them in after we get a mile on the road at their place. Now we roll out. Father B. is on the lead on old Nelly; Bart is driving the team; Cory [12] is on our old Lige driving the loose stock. Our wagon is No. 2. G. W. Bethers No. 3, J. W. Starr 4. Uncle Prather two wagons, Chatman Hawley two wagons and I think they all had one horse but Uncle John Starr. He had two yoke of oxen to each wagon; one wagon was a very shaky old thing. They had their provisions in it and when they get it lightened up they would put everything in one wagon and leave the old shack by the road side. They started with a family of eight and had to take in an old man to drive one team.

Now we are fairly on the road. It is one o'clock. We got started at 10; will stop for an hour and eat a lunch and let the oxen chew their cuds. We have just got out of the neighborhood; the friends that came a piece with us and we will travel on. Jessie and I have had a good nap and a good lunch and now we will ride some more. Evening we come to water and grass and plenty of wood. What hinders us from camping here? They say we have come 13 miles. Everyone seems hungry and we make fires and soon have supper fit for a king.

---

[12] Bart is so-far not identified, however, Corrington G. Belknap is listed in the 1850 census as working as a farmer, 20 years old, on the farm of Alvin F. Waller, a Methodist minister in Marion County, Oregon. "Uncle Prather" is so-far unidentified.

I will make the first call and am all the one that has a table and it has a clean white cloth on. I have my chair out. George piles in the ox yokes for him a seat and Jessie has the wash-tub turned up side down and will stand on his knees. Supper over and I fix the bed. The stock have all been looked after and are quietly chewing their quids. Some of the men take bedding and will sleep out to see that none of the stock will get up and scatter off.

April 11th. All astir bright and early; breakfast is soon over; some of the men have gone to relieve the night watch. My work is all done up, lunch prepared for noon and all put in its proper place. Here comes the oxen; our team is soon ready. We have two yoke of well trained oxen; all there is to do is to hold up the yoke and tell Old Buck and Bright to come under and they walk up and take their places as meek as kittens. But now comes Dick and Drab a fine pair of black matched four year olds steers; they have to be cornered. I am in the wagon sewing; Jessie is playing with his whips and now the word is "Roll out". The loose stock is started on ahead. Our wagon is in the lead today; will be behind tomorrow so now we are on the wing. It is a fine spring morning.

Noon. We stop an hour to let the teams rest and eat our lunch. We are in Missouri now; see once in a while a log hut and some half dressed children running away to hide. Every man to his team now. This afternoon we pass along a little creek with fine timber. The road is good and I am standing the ride fine. Now, we camp again. I think all days will be about the same now. Saturday evening. We have a fine start; everything seems to move along nicely.

Sunday morning. We hitch up and move on a few miles to better grass; then camp for the Sabbath. Ten o'clock we find a lovely spot; a fine little brook goes gurgling by with fine large trees and nice clean logs for seats and to spread out things on. We have cleaned up and put on clean clothes. There are some fine farms along the creek bottom; some of the ladies came out to visit us and brought some things along to sell to the immigrants but we had not been out long enough to get very hungry. I did get a nice dressed hen for 25 cents and 6 dozen eggs 6¢ a dozen. I started with quite a box of eggs and found them handy.

Now its Monday morning, April 17th. We start again; the next point is Missouri River; will cross at St. Joe. Have moved every day for a week; have had fine weather, good roads and all have been well. We have three good milch cows; milk them at night and strain the milk in little buckets and cover them up and set on ground under the wagon and in the morning I take off the nice thick cream and put it in the churn. I save the strippings from each cow in the morning milking and put in the churn also and after riding all day I have a nice roll of butter so long as we have plenty of grass and water.

The 22nd. Are nearing the Missouri River; will camp here over Sunday. Sunday. Breakfast over and the men come in from the stock and say there has been a band of sheep herded on the range for two days and they have spoiled the grass so the stock wont feed on it so some of the men get on their horses and go to look for a better place; 10 o'clock the word is "Move on". About 10 miles there is plenty of water and grass; some want to stay, others are getting their teams ready to move. Mr. Jackson's [13] voice is heard. He says if we stay it will break the Sabbath worse than if we go on so we all started but had only gone about 5 miles when a little boy was run over by the wagon and instantly killed. We then stopped and buried the child. We were near a settlement so it was not left there alone.

Monday we are on the trail again. every man at his post; made a big day's drive (20 miles they say).

Tuesday. Will get to the river tomorrow. Supper is over; we have a nice place to camp, some have gone to bed and others have gone out with the stock. They say there are some Mormons here that give us some trouble with our stock. They might want a good horse so we think it best to put a good guard out.

Wednesday. All are on the stir to get to the wharf before the other company gets here and now begins the scene of danger. The river is high and looks terrific; one wagon and two yoke of oxen are over first so as to have a team to take the wagons out of the way; it is just a rope ferry. All back safe. Now they take the wagons and the loose horses. They say it will take about all day to get us over. Next the loose cattle that go as they are in a dry lot without anything to eat. When they get the cattle on the boat they found one of our cows was sick; she had got poisoned by eating the Jimpson weeds. She staggered when she walked on the ferry and in the crowd she was knocked overboard and went under but when she came up the boat men had his rope ready and throwed it out and lassoed her and they hauled her to land but she was too far gone to travel so the boat man said he would take our wagon

---

[13] George Jackson, otherwise unidentified.

and stock over for the chance of her so they hauled her up to the house and the last we saw of her a woman had her wrapped in a warm blanket and had a fire and was bathing her and pouring milk and lard down her. She could stand alone the next morning so we bade farewell to the Missouri River and old Brock.

The Watts [14] company will stay here till the Jacksons get over the river and we will move on to fresh grass and water. Our next point will be the crossing of the Platte River near old Fort Larima; there is life there now.

This is the 4th week we have been on the road and now we are among the Pawnee Indians so we must get into larger company so we can guard ourselves and stock from the prowling tribes and renegade whites that are here to keep away from the law. They seem to have their eyes on a good horse and follow for days then if they are caught they will say they got him from the Indians and by paying them something they would give the horse up, then try to make us believe that they were sent out there to protect the emigrants.

Another week has past; have had nice road; will camp here till afternoon. At the Platte River; will stay here all day and get ready to cross the river and do some work on the wagons, get tires, mend chains & etc. We will now form a company and make some laws so all will have their part. Some of the oxen are getting tender-footed; they have been trying to shoe them but gave it up. I have washed and ironed and cooked nice skillet of corn bread (enough for two dinners for

---

14 Joseph Watt was the son of John and Mary Watt, who crossed the plains with this company with their other six children. They settled in Yamhill County, Oregon. They are recorded in the 1850 federal census.

George, Jessie and I). This morning the roll is called
and every one is expected to answer to his name. They
have quite a time with the election of officers. Every
man wants an office. George Jackson and Joe Watts
are pilots; they have both been over the road before
and have camping places noted down so now we take
the trail again. The order is for the first one hitched
up "roll out" so we are ahead on the lead today then
[15] are next but tomorrow we will be behind.

Now we are getting on the Pawnee Indians' hunting ground so we must make a big show. They are out
after Buffalo so we have to keep out an advance guard
to keep the herd from running into our teams. The
road runs between the bluff and the river and it is just
the time now when the buffalo are moving to the river
bottom for grass and water. A herd passed us a few
days ago; the guard turned them so they crossed the
road behind us; they killed a nice young heifer so we
have fresh meat. It is very coarse and dark meat but
when cooked right made a very good change. I cooked
some and made mince pies with dried apples which
was fine for lunch. During the hunt Dr. Baker [16] lost
his nice saddle horse and a fine saddle; he jumped off
and threw down the bridle to give his game another
shot and away went the horse with the buffalo; they
hunted for him but didn't find him or the buffalo but
in about two weeks the company that was behind sent
word to Dr. Baker that the horse had come to them
with the saddle still on but turned under his belly;
the head part of the bridle was on him yet so old Dock

---

[15] Unreadable word.

[16] This could be John and Elizabeth Baker who settled as neighbors to
the George Belknaps, according to the Oregon 1850 census.

got his horse and he never wanted to leave the train again. We have been on the route till its got to be June; all days about the same.

We will now go down the noted Ash Hollow and strike the Sweet River, then will rest awhile. We make the trip down the hollow all safe. Went as far as we could with the teams then took off some of the best teams and send down so they could move the wagons out of the way, then they would take one wagon as far as they could with the team, then unhitch and ruff-lock both hind wheels, then fasten a big rope to the axle of the wagon and men would hold to that to keep the wagon iron going end over end; some were at the tongue to steer it and others were lifting the wheels to ease them down the steps for it was solid rock steps from six inches to two feet apart so it took all day but we all got thru without accident.

We will stay here all night. I wash a little and cook some more, have a ham bone and beans. This is good sweet water; we have had alkali and nothing was good.

Just as we were ready to sit down to supper Joe Meek and his posse of men rode into camp. They were going to Washington, D. C. to get the government to send soldiers to protect the settlers in Oregon and they told us all about the Indian Massacre at Walla Walla called the "Whitman Massacre". They had traveled all winter and some of their men had died and they had got out of food and had to eat mule meat so we gave them all their supper and breakfast. The captain divided them up so all could help feed them. Father B. was captain so he and George took three so they made way with most all my stuff I had cooked up; on the whole

we are having quite a time; some want to turn back
and others are telling what they would do in case of
an attack. I sit in the wagon and write a letter as these
men say if we want to send any word back they will
take it and drop it in the first Post Office they come to
so I'm writing a scratch to a lady friend. While I'm
writing I have an exciting experience. George is out
on guard and in the next wagon behind ours a man and
woman are quarreling. She wants to turn back and he
wont go so she says she will go and leave him with the
children and he will have a good time with that crying
baby, then he used some very bad words and said he
would put it out of the way. Just then I heard a muf-
fled cry and a heavy thud as tho something was thrown
against the wagon box and she said "Oh you've killed
it" and he swore some more and told her to keep her
mouth shut or he would give her some of the same.
Just then the word came, change guards. George came
in and Mr. Kitridge [17] went out so he and his wife
were parted for the night. The baby was not killed.
I write this to show how easy we can be deceived.
We have a rest and breakfast is over. Meek and his
men are gathering their horses and packing, but he
said he would have to transact a little business with his
men so they all lined up and he courtmartialed them
and found three guilty and made them think they
would be shot for disobeying orders but it was only
a scare "Now every man to his post and double quick
till they reach the Hollow". The woman was out by
the road side with a little buget [buggy?] and her baby

---

[17] George and Maria Kitrich are listed in the 1850 census as living in
Washington County with their children, the youngest of whom was Eliza, 2,
the one here supposedly threatened with death.

asleep in the wagon under a strong opiate. After that we had trouble with those folks as long as they were with us; they would take things from those that did the most for them and there was others of the same stripe. They seemed to think when they got on the plains they were out of reach of the law of God or man.

It is afternoon; we will hitch up and drive till night. Here we are; it is almost sundown. We will have a cold lunch for supper, then shake up the beds and rest after the excitement of the day is over. We will leave the sweet water in the morning and have a long dry drive. Will fill our kegs and everything that will hold water so we will not suffer of thirst. We stop at noon for an hour's rest. It's very warm; the oxen all have their tongues out panting. George took the wash pan and a bucket of water and let all our team wet their tongues and he washed the dust off their noses; some laughed at him but the oxen seemed very grateful. George lays down to catch a little nap; if they start before he wakes the team will start up in their places. Time is up, the word along the line is "Move up" (George sleeps on). That means 10 miles of dry hot dirt. I have a little water left yet; will have to let the thirsty ox drivers wet their parched lips. It will be hot till the sun goes down, then it will be dusk. That night we got to plenty of water. I think old Bright's feet hurt; he is standing in the water. We eat a bite and go to bed.

We are coming near to the Green River; will have to ferry it with the wagons. The cattle will be unyoked and swim over; some Mormons are here. They have fixed up a ferry and will take us over for a dollar a

wagon. It will take all day to get over; it is the 4th
of July. While some are getting over they have got
Hawley's wagon over and have got out the anvils and
are celebrating The Fourth. The Jacksons are doing
their best to entertain the crowd; there is three of them.
Now we are on to the Pawnee Indians. They say they
are a bad set. We must pass right thru their villages;
they come out by the thousands and want pay for crossing their country. They spread down some skins and
wanted every wagon to give them something so they
all gave them a little something and they went to divid-
ing it amongst themselves and got into a fight. We
rushed on to get as near Fort Hall as we could. There
was a company of soldiers there to protect the immigrants. The scouts had been out and reported what the
Indians were doing and the troops soon settled them
and made them leave the road so we had no more
trouble; for us it was all for the best so that was all
the time we had any trouble with the Indians tho it
did look a little scary for a while. The General at the
Fort told us to make as big a show as possible.

For want of space I must cut these notes down; will
pass over some interesting things. Watts and the sheep
pulled out and fell behind. I got the blame for the
split. The old Mother Watts said after they got thru
"Yes, Geo. Belknaps' wife is a little woman but she
wore the pants on that train" so I came into noteriety
before I knew it but to return to the trail, they say we
are on the last half of the journey now.

My little boy is very sick with Mountain Fever and
tomorrow we will have to make a long dry drive. We
will stay here at this nice water and grass till about
4 o'clock. Will cook up a lot of provisions, then will

take what is known as "Green woods cut off" and travel all night. Must fill everything with water. We are on the brink of Snake River but it is such a rocky canyon we could not get to it if ones life depended on it.

It's morning. I have been awake all night watching with the little boy. He seems a little better; has dropped off to sleep. The sun is just rising and it shows a lot of the dirtiest humanity every was seen since the Creation. We just stop for an hour and eat a bite and let the teams breath again. We divide the water with the oxen. George has sat on his seat on the front of the wagon all night and I have held the little boy on my lap on a pillow and tended him as best I could. I thot in the night we would have to leave him here and I thot if we did I would be likely to stay with him but as the daylight, we seemed to get fresh courage.

Some of the men went thru to Fort Hall on horse back and returned to meet us and say we can make it by noon.

[The record ends here. The baby boy, Jesse Walker Belknap, recovered under her dilligent care and lived to a ripe old age. In her record of the journey at no point has Keturah revealed that she was pregnant. A baby boy, Lorenzo Belknap, was born on August 10, 1848, evidently somewhere in what is now called eastern Oregon. Keturah was too busy to continue to record the concluding days of their cross-country journey.]

The Diary of a Pioneer Girl ❦ Sallie Hester

INTRODUCTION

It was an engaging title, "The Diary of a Pioneer Girl," and the sub-title, "The Adventures of Sallie Hester, Aged Twelve, in a Trip Overland in 1849." This title appeared at the head of each of seven serialized episodes in the California weekly periodical, *The Argonaut,* from September 1 through October 24, 1925. The first episode opens with Sallie and her family leaving their hometown, Bloomington, Indiana, for California on August 25, 1849. The last episode closes with her marriage to James K. Maddock of Eureka, Nevada, on October 5, 1871.[1]

The very title is in error: Sallie was not "Aged Twelve," but was a mature 14-year-old at the time of the overland journey. She tells us her birthday and age in her diary. She indicated on "October 27 [1852]. — My birthday."[2] She had already told her age in an earlier entry, that on May 6, [1851], "I am only sixteen and engaged to be married."[3] Her tender age led to calling off the engagement. These two entries, however, do tell us that she would have been born on October 31, 1835. So at the time of the beginning of the diary and the departure for the long overland journey she was fourteen, not twelve.

The second sentence of the first entry in her diary, March 20, 1849, also makes the following statement: "Our family, consisting of father, mother, two brothers and one sister, left this morning for that far and much talked of country,

[1] *Argonaut,* Oct. 24, 1925, p. 4. [2] *Argonaut,* Oct. 3, 1925, p. 3.
[3] *Argonaut,* Sept. 26, 1925, p. 3.

California." One is naturally led to a consideration of these family members one by one:

Her father, Craven P. Hester, was a successful lawyer of Bloomington, Indiana. He had grown up in that state and studied law at Charleston, Indiana, under a Judge Scott of the Supreme Court of Indiana. Born on May 17, 1796, he was 52 when the family began their far western trek in March, 1849, and he turned 53 on May 17, a day on which Sallie made no diary entry. Craven Hester was elected District Attorney of the Third Judicial District in San Jose, California, on October 7, 1850. The following May (1851) he was appointed Judge of the Third Judicial District, which position he held for many years.[4] Judge Hester died on February 15, 1874, at the age of 78 years.[5]

Sallie's mother was Martha (Thompson) Hester,[6] a woman about whom precious little is known except what Sallie has to say in her diary. Martha Hester was listed in the 1860 census as being 60 years old at that time. (August, 1860),[7] so she must have been born in 1800, and she was 49 when she began the long overland journey in 1849. She died on June 19, 1877.

Craven and Martha Hester were married on August 25, 1819, for on that date in 1869 Sallie wrote in her diary, "My father and mother celebrated their golden wedding. The elite of San Jose were present and friends from different parts of the state." [8]

William F. Hester was Sallie's older brother, 18 years old in 1849.[9] Just after her diary entry telling of the fiftieth

---

[4] Frederic Hall, "The Hon. Craven P. Hester," *History of San José and Surroundings* (San Francisco, 1871), 378-83.

[5] San Jose *News,* June 9, 1972, "Hester St. Namesake Dull," p. 43; San Jose *Mercury-News,* Jan. 13, 1952, p. 5.

[6] *Argonaut,* Introduction to Sallie's "Diary," Sept. 12, 1925, p. 3.

[7] U. S. Federal Census, Santa Clara Co., Calif., 1960, Santa Clara Precinct, p. 491.   [8] *Argonaut,* Oct. 24, 1925, p. 4.

[9] Listed as W. F. Hester, 1860 Census, *op. cit.,* 29 years old, a "Stock-farmer."

anniversary of her parents marriage, there is an undated sentence telling that "Brother Will and Flora Burnett were married."[10] Flora was the widow of Armstead L. Burnett, second son of Peter H. and Harriet Burnett. Armstead had died on May 26, 1862. Flora's maiden name had been Johnson.[11]

Sallie has much to say in her diary about her sister, Lottie, who was three years younger than she.[12] Lottie married S. M. Thompson on Tuesday, September 13, 1855.[13] Their first child, Louis Hester Thompson, was born on August 25, 1856.[14] However, it was with sad words that Sallie told of the boy's death on February 2, 1869.[15]

There was another brother, John, whose age we don't learn from the diary or from the 1860 census. Evidently he was not living with the family at that time. Sallie says on June 14, 1855, that they went to Stockton and heard John give a speech at the Archonian Society of Pacific University, where he was a student.[16] Two weeks later, on June 28, she says, "John is going back to college at Asbury University, Greencastle, Indiana.[17] On April 14, 1859, she writes, "My father has gone east for John's graduation." John returned to California with his father.[18]

We are only publishing the part of Sallie Hester's diary that tells of the overland journey. The rest of the journal, though fascinating and filled with colorful descriptions of the social life in San Jose for many years, is not relevant to our purpose.

On October 5, 1871, Sallie Hester was married to James K. Maddock,[19] who was listed in business directories for

---

[10] *Argonaut*, Oct. 24, 1925, p. 4.

[11] Peter H. Burnett, *Recollecions and Opinions of an Old Pioneer* (New York, 1880), p. 6.   [12] 1860 Census, *op. cit.*, lists her as being 21.

[13] *Argonaut*, Oct. 3, 1925, p. 3.   [14] *Argonaut*, Oct. 10, 1925, p. 3.

[15] *Argonaut*, Oct. 24, 1925, p. 4.   [16] *Argonaut*, Oct. 3, 1925, p. 3.

[17] *Ibid.*   [18] *Argonaut*, Oct. 17, 1925, p. 3.

[19] *Argonaut*, Oct. 24, 1925, p. 4.

1871 and 1872 as being an assayer in Eureka, Nevada.[20]
Her last entry in her diary tells of her marriage:

I was married to James K. Maddock of Eureka, Nevada. A
quiet home wedding, only a few intimate friends present, Mrs.
Wakeman and Minnie Ludlum of San Francisco, Judge and
Mrs. Moore. Mr. Peake [21] of the Episcopal Church officiated.
Refreshments were served and we left soon after for Eureka.
Spent a few days in Sacramento. After a tedious trip by stage
and rail we reached this place. Eureka is a small mining town,
and the hotel where we are stopping is one only in name. I am
once more a stranger in a strange land, and now, Dear Journal,
I give thee up. No more jottings down of gay and festive scenes
– the past is gone and the future is before me. "So mote it be."

SALLIE HESTER'S DIARY

Bloomington, Indiana, Tuesday, March 20, 1849. –
Our family, consisting of father, mother, two brothers
and one sister, left this morning for that far and much
talked of country, California. My father started our
wagons one month in advance, to St. Joseph, Missouri,
our starting point. We take the steamboat at New Albany, going by water to St. Joe. The train leaving
Bloomington on that memorable occasion was called
the Missionary Train, from the fact that the Rev.
Isaac Owens [1] of the Methodist Church and a number

---

[20] *Pacific Coast Business Directory* (San Francisco, 1871), p. 352; *Gazet-
teer and Directory* (San Francisco, 1872), p. 536.

[21] The Rev. E. S. Peake, Rector of Trinity Church, San Jose. There is a
copy of the marriage license in the San Jose Museum.

[1] The Rev. Isaac Owen, a Methodist minister who traveled with the same
wagon train from Indiana as the Hesters. He became a pioneer of California
Methodism. He and his wife, Elizabeth, and four children, three boys and a
girl, are listed in the 1860 Federal Census, as neighbors of the Hesters in
Santa Clara Precinct.

of ministers of the same denomination were sent as missionaries to California. Our train numbered fifty wagons. The last hours were spent in bidding good bye to old friends. My mother is heartbroken over this separation of relatives and friends. Giving up old associations for what? Good health, perhaps. My father is going in search of health, not gold. The last good bye has been said – the last glimpse of our old home on the hill, and wave of hand at the old Academy, with a good bye to kind teachers and schoolmates, and we are off. We have been several days reaching New Albany [Indiana] on account of the terrible condition of the roads. Our carriage upset at one place. All were thrown out, but no one was hurt. We were detained several hours on account of this accident. My mother thought it a bad omen and wanted to return and give up the trip.

New Albany, March 24. This is my first experience of a big city and my first glimpse of a river and steamboats.

March 26. Took the steamboat *Meteor* this evening for St. Joe Now sailing on the broad Ohio, floating toward the far West.

St. Louis, April 2. Spent the day here, enjoyed everything.

April 3. On the Missouri River, the worst in the world,[2] sticking on sand bars most of the time.

Jefferson City, April 6. Stopped here for one hour, visited the State House, enjoyed everything.

---

[2] There is a classic saying among Missouri valley old-timers that "The crookedness you can see ain't half the crookedness there is."

April 14. Our boat struck another sand bar and was obliged to land passengers ten miles below St. Joe. Having our carriage with us, we were more fortunate than others. We reached the first day an old log hut, five miles from town, where we camped for the night. Next day an old friend of my father heard of our arrival, came to see us and insisted that we stay at his home until we hear from our wagons.

St. Joe, April 27. Here we are at last, safe and sound. We expect to remain here several days, laying in supplies for the trip and waiting our turn to be ferried across the river. As far as eye can reach, so great is the emigration, you see nothing but wagons. This town presents a striking appearance – a vast army on wheels – crowds of men, women and lots of children and last but not least the cattle and horses upon which our lives depend.

May 1 [Sunday]. Crossed the river. Camped six miles from town. Remained here several days, getting things shipshape for our long trip.

May 13 [Sunday]. This is a small Indian village. There is a mission at this place, about thirty pupils, converts to the Christian faith. Left camp May 6, and have been travelling all week. We make it a point to rest over Sunday. Have a sermon in camp every Sunday morning and evening. I take advantage of this stopover to jot down our wanderings during the week.

May 21, Sunday. Camped on the beautiful Blue River, 215 miles from St. Joe, with plenty of wood and water and good grazing for our cattle. Our family all in good health. When we left St. Joe my mother had to be lifted in and out of our wagons; now she walks a mile or two without stopping, and gets in and out of the wagons as spry as a young girl. She is perfectly well. We had two deaths in our train within the past week of cholera – young men going West to seek their fortunes. We buried them on the banks of the Blue River, far from home and friends. This is a beautiful spot. The Plains are covered with flowers. We are now in the Pawnee Nation – a dangerous and hostile tribe. We are obliged to watch them closely and double our guards at night. They never make their appearance during the day, but skulk around at night, steal cattle and do all the mischief they can. When we camp at night, we form a corral with our wagons and pitch our tents on the outside, and inside of this corral we drive our cattle, with guards stationed on the outside of tents. We have a cooking stove made of sheet iron, a portable table, tin plates and cups, cheap knives and forks (best ones packed away), camp stools, etc. We sleep in our wagons on feather beds; the men who drive for us in the tent. We live on bacon, ham, rice, dried fruits, molasses, packed butter, bread, coffee, tea and milk as we have our own cows. Occasionally some of the men kill an antelope and then we have a feast; and sometimes we have fish on Sunday.

Fort Kearney, May 24. This fort is built of adobe with walls of same.

Sunday, June 3. Our tent is now pitched on the beautiful Platte River, 315 miles from St. Joe. The cholera is raging. A great many deaths; graves everywhere. We as a company are all in good health. Game is scarce; a few antelope in sight. Roads bad.

Goose Creek, June 17 [Sunday]. This is our day of

rest. There are several encampments in sight, making one feel not quite out of civilization. So many thousands all en route for the land of gold and Italian skies! Passed this week Court House Rock. Twelve miles from this point is Chimney Rock, 230 feet in height.

Fort Laramie, June 19. This fort is of adobe, enclosed with a high wall of the same. The entrance is a hole in the wall just large enough for a person to crawl through. The impression you have on entering is that you are in a small town. Men were engaged in all kinds of business from blacksmith up. We stayed here some time looking at everything that was to be seen and enjoying it to the fullest extent after our long tramp. We camped one mile from the fort, where we remained a few days to wash and lighten up.

June 21. Left camp and started over the Black Hills, sixty miles over the worst road in the world. Have again struck the Platte and followed it until we came to the ferry. Here we had a great deal of trouble swimming our cattle across, taking our wagons to pieces, unloading and replacing our traps. A number of accidents happened here. A lady and four children were drowned through the carelessness of those in charge of the ferry.

Bear River, June 1 [Sunday]. Lots of Indians in sight, mostly naked, disgusting and dirty looking.

July 2. Passed Independence Rock. This rock is covered with names. With great difficulty I found a place to cut mine. Twelve miles from this is Devil's Gate. It's an opening in the mountain through which the Sweetwater River flows. Several of us climbed this mountain – somewhat perilous for youngsters not over fourteen. We made our way to the very edge of the cliff and looked down. We could hear the water dashing, splashing and roaring as if angry at the small space through which it was forced to pass. We were gone so long that the train was stopped and men sent out in search of us. We made all sorts of promises to remain in sight in the future. John Owens, a son of the minister, my brother John, sister Lottie and myself were the quartet. During the week we passed the South Pass and the summit of the Rocky Mountains. Four miles from here are the Pacific Springs.

Lee Springs, July 4 [Wednesday]. Had the pleasure of eating ice. At this point saw lots of dead cattle left by the emigrants to starve and die. Took a cutoff; had neither wood nor water for fifty-two miles. Traveled in the night. Arrived at Green River next day at two o'clock in the afternoon. Lay by two days to rest man and beast after our long and weary journey.

July 29 [Sunday]. Passed Soda Springs. Two miles further on are the Steamboat Springs. They puff and blow and throw the water high in the air. The springs are in the midst of a grove of trees, a beautiful and romantic spot.

August 3. Took another cutoff this week called Sublets. Struck Raft River; from thence to Swamp Creek. Passed some beautiful scenery, high cliffs of rocks resembling old ruins or dilapidated buildings.

Hot Springs, August 18. Camped on a branch of Mary's River, a very disagreeable and unpleasant place on account of the water being so hot. This week some of our company left us, all young men. They were jolly, merry fellows and gave life to our lonely evenings. We all miss them very much. Some had violins, others guitars, and some had fine voices, and they always had a good audience. They were anxious to hurry on without the Sunday stops. Roads are rocky and trying to our wagons, and the dust is horrible. The men wear veils tied over their hats as a protection. When we reach camp at night they are covered with dust from head to heels.

Humboldt River, August 20. We are now 348 miles from the mines. We expect to travel that distance in three weeks and a half. Water and grass scarce.

St. Mary's River, August 25. Still traveling down the Humboldt. Grass has been scarce until today. Though the water is not fit to drink – slough water – we are obliged to use it, for it's all we have.

St. Mary's, September 2 [Sunday]. After coming through a dreary region of country for two or three days, we arrived Saturday night. We had good grass but the water was bad. Remained over Sunday. Had preaching in camp.

September 4. Left the place where we camped last Sunday. Traveled six miles. Stopped and cut grass for cattle and supplied ourselves with water for the desert. Had a trying time crossing. Several of our cattle gave out, and we left one. Our journey through the desert was from Monday, three o'clock in the afternoon, until Thursday morning at sunrise, September 6. The weary journey last night, the mooing of the cattle for water, their exhausted condition, with the cry of "Another ox down," the stopping of train to unyoke the poor dying brute, to let him follow at will or stop by the wayside and die, and the weary, weary tramp of men and beasts, worn out with heat and famished for water, will never be erased from my memory. Just at dawn, in the distance, we had a glimpse of Truckee River, and with it the feeling: Saved at last! Poor cattle; they kept on mooing, even when they stood knee deep in water. The long dreaded desert has been crossed and we are all safe and well. Here we rested Thursday and Friday – grass green and beautiful, and the cattle are up to their eyes in it.

September 8. Traveled fourteen miles; crossed Truckee twelve times.

September 9. Sunday, our day of rest.
Monday, September 10. Traveled four miles down to the end of the valley.

Tuesday, September 11. Made eighteen miles. Crossed Truckee River ten times. Came near being drowned at one of the crossings. Got frightened and jumped out of the carriage into the water. The current was very swift and carried me some distance down the stream.

Thursday, September 14. We arrived at the place where the Donner Party perished, having lost their way and being snowed in. Most of them suffered and died from want of food. This was in 1846. Two log cabins, bones of human beings and animals, tops of the trees being cut off the depth of snow, was all that was left to tell the tale of that ill-fated party, their sufferings and sorrow. A few of their number made made their way out, and after days of agony and hunger finally reached Sutter's Fort. We crossed the summit of the Sierra Nevada. It was night when we reached the top, and never shall I forget our descent to the place where we are now encamped – our tedious march with pine knots blazing in the darkness and the tall, majestic pines towering above our heads. The scene was grand and gloomy beyond description. We could not ride – roads too narrow and rocky – so we trudged along, keeping pace with the wagons as best we could. This is another picture engraven upon the tablets of memory. It was a footsore and weary crowd that reached that night our present camping place.

Yuba Valley, Sunday, September 16. We are now 108 miles from Sutter's Fort.

September 17. Left camp this morning. Traveled down to the lower end of the valley. Lay by two days. Had preaching out under the pines at night. The men built a fire and we all gathered around it in camp-meeting style.

September 19. Started once more. Roads bad, almost impassable. After traveling for twenty-five miles we halted for one day. Good grass three miles from camp.

September 21. Reached Bear Valley by descending a tremendous hill. We let the wagons down with ropes. Stopped over Sunday. At Sleepy Hollow we again let our wagons down the mountain with ropes. Rested in the hollow, ate our dinner and then commenced our weary march over the mountain. Left one of our wagons and the springs of our carriage. Cut down trees for our cattle to browse on. Thanks to a kind Providence we are nearing the end of our long and perilous journey. Came on to Grass Valley and rested four or five days.

October 1 [Monday]. Arrived at Johnson's Fort. Thence we went to Nicholson's ranch.

Vernon, California, October 6. Well, after a five month's trip from St. Joe, Missouri, our party of fifty wagons, now only thirteen, has at last reached this haven of rest. Strangers in a strange land – what will the future be? This town is situated at the junction of the Feather and Sacramento Rivers.

Fremont, October 10. This is a small town on the opposite side of the river from Vernon. My father has decided to remain here for the winter, as the rains have set in and we are worn out. We have had a small house put up of two rooms made of boards with puncheon floor. On this mother has a carpet which she brought with us and we feel quite fine, as our neighbors have the ground for a floor. The rooms are lined with heavy blue cloth. Our beds are put up in bunk style on one side of the room and curtained off. Back of these rooms we have pitched our tent, which answers as a store room, and the back of the lot is enclosed with a brush fence. My father has gone to Sacramento to lay in provisions for the winter.

Fremont, December 20 [Thursday]. Have not written or confided in thee, dear journal, for some time. Now I must write up. My father returned from Sacramento with a supply of provisions. Everything is enormously high. Carpenter's wages sixteen dollars per day; vegetables scarce and high; potatoes the principal vegetable; onions, fifty cents each; eggs, one dollar apiece; melons, five dollars, and apples, one dollar each. The rain is pouring down. River very high.

Christmas, 1849 [Tuesday]. Still raining. This has

been a sad Christmas for mother. She is homesick, longs for her old home and friends. It's hard for old folks to give up old ties and go so far away to live in a strange land among strange people. Young people can easily form new ties and make new friends and soon conform to circumstances, but it's hard for the old ones to forget. Was invited to a candy pull and had a nice time. Rather a number of young folks camped here. This is a funny looking town anyway. Most of the houses are built of brush. Now that the rains have set in, people are beginning to think of something more substantial. Some have log cabins, others have clapboards like ours.

New Years, January 1, 1850 [Tuesday]. It's gloomy old New Year's for us all. What will this year bring forth?

January 11. Raining. The river is very high. Six inches will bring it over the whole town.

January 12. Water over the banks of the river, all over town except in a few places. Our house has escaped, though it's all around us. Mother has planted a garden in the rear of lot and that has been swept away. Nearly everybody is up to their knees in mud and water. Some have boots. As far as the eye can reach you see nothing but water. It's horrible. Wish I was back in Indiana. Snakes are plenty. They come down the river, crawl under our beds and everywhere.

January 20 [Sunday]. Water receding.

Fremont, February 27 [Wednesday]. It's raining very hard. A little snow by way of variety. Horrible weather. Received several letters from schoolmates at home.

Saturday, March 30. Nothing of importance has transpired worth putting down. I am invited out so much that I am beginning to feel quite like a young lady. Girls are scarce; I presume that is the reason. Young men are plenty. There was a wedding here a few days ago. Had one of those old-fashioned serenades – tin pans, gongs, horns and everything else that could be drummed up to make a noise. It was dreadful. Weather windy and cold.

April 1 [Tuesday]. Quite a number of our old friends who crossed the Plains with us have stopped here for the winter, which makes it pleasant for mother. My father has gone to San Jose, the capital, to look for a permanent home.

April 27 [Sunday]. My father has returned from San Jose. He gives glowing accounts of the place and lovely climate. We have not seen very much as yet of the mild and delightful climate of California so much talked about. We leave next month for San Jose. We are all glad that we are going to have a home somewhere at last. Have met a number of nice young men here – George W. Crane,[3] of Baltimore, a young lawyer, and William Allen,[4] who has been in California for some time. I am too young for beaux, but the young men don't seem to think so.

Pueblo de San Jose, June 3, 1850 [Tuesday]. Left

[3] Hubert Howe Bancroft, *Works: History of California,* Vol. II (San Francisco, 1885), p. 771, "Pioneer Register," says that George W. Crane traveled to California in 1846. He was a Virginian "said to have arr. in May; served in the Cal. Bat. . . . miner in '48; became a lawyer; member of legisl. from Yolo '50. and from Mont. '57; d. at S. Juan B. '68, age 41, leaving a widow and several children."

[4] There were too many William Allens in California in 1850 to identify this one.

Fremont the first of May. We traveled by land in our
wagons. The first night out was unpleasant. Mosquitoes
nearly devoured us. The second days we arrived at Cash
[Cache] Creek. Wednesday were at Wolfscales [Wolf-
skill's].[5] Friday we reached Benicia. We were detained
here three days crossing the straits. Continued our journey and arrived here on Tuesday. Rev. Owens, who
crossed the Plains with us, is living here, and we have
pitched our tent near his house, with adobe ell, built
only as a temporary home for the present. Started
school. Have met Mrs. Reed's family. They crossed
the Plains in 1846. They were of the Donner Party.
Two of the Donner girls are living with Mrs. Reed,
Mary and Frankie.[6] Mattie Reed is a lovely girl with
big brown eyes. She is near my own age. She has a
piano, and Mrs. Reed has kindly asked me to come
there and practice. I go every day. There was a race
here a few days ago – a $15,000 bet.

---

[5] Wolfskill's was the *Rio de los Putos* ranch of John Wolfskill, brother
of the trapper, William Wolfskill. It was on Putah Creek, in Solano County,
some miles west of Sacramento. Iris Higbie Wilson, *William Wolfskill, 1798-
1866* (Glendale, Calif.), see Chap. 5, "The Sacramento Valley," pp. 115-42.

[6] Letters of two members of the Donner Party, Mrs. Tamsen Donner, and
Virginia Reed, are printed in this volume, pages 68-82.

A Letter from California, 1849

ℒ Louisiana Strentzel

INTRODUCTION

Louisiana Strentzel — the name is sheer poetry all by itself. Of course, her maiden name had been Louisiana Erwin, not so poetic — or is it poetic in a different way?

She was born to the Samuel Erwins in Lawrence County, Tennessee, on October 31, 1821. Her own mother died, however, when Louisiana was three years old, and she gained a step-mother when her father married Sallie Rogers Crisp. The family migrated to Honey Grove, Texas, where she spent her growing up years.

In the Bancroft Library in Berkeley, California, among the Strentzel papers, is a marriage license dated December 31, 1843, declaring that Louisiana Erwin and John Strentzel were married in Fannin County, Texas, by Judge R. M. Lee. John Theophil Strentzel was a 30-year-old expatriate medical doctor from Poland. He had been among those Poles who took part in a revolution in 1830 against Russia, and, because of this activity, he and his brother, Henry, four years younger than John, fled to the New World rather than be inducted into the Russian army.

The Strentzels, Louisiana, John, and Henry, lived in Lamar County, Texas, for several years, and then, with two small children, two-year-old Louisa (Louie), also nicknamed "Little Pussy," and baby John, they started on March 22, 1849, on a long westward wagon journey for California. They traveled the southwestern route that led them across Texas, through present New Mexico and Arizona, and across the deserts of southern California.

Dr. Strentzel remembered later, "We had not even a guide to direct us the way. Nothing except a map and compas to go by. The country was entirely unknown to us, not one of the party ever having been through it." They saw California as offering "unexpected opportunity" because of the "rapid emigration from every part of the world." Louisiana's letter here published was based in part upon a journal kept along the way and tells the story of their seemingly endless journey.

Certainly the land of gold proved to be a secure and profitable haven for Louisiana and John. They moved in their wagons north from San Diego and settled in the valley of the Tuolumne River near LaGrange, a mining camp, where they "established a ferry, hotel and a store of general merchandise for trade with the miners, put up large tents or canvas houses for all needs." Here they remained for two years.

As part of the mobile California population of that day — and of every day since — they then moved to the Merced River, on the banks of which they purchased 600 acres of choice land. However, that very next winter the Merced overflowed its banks and washed out their holdings.

During this period Louisiana's health was not good, and the doctor wished to get her to as suitable a climate as possible. Santa Cruz was recommended by a friend, but they decided to try Benicia, the new mobile capital city of California on the north shore of the Carquinez Straits, where the merged San Joaquin and Sacramento flow into San Francisco Bay. There they found a neighbor from back home in Texas who was living just south of the Straits in Martinez. They decided to settle near that town in "a lovely fertile valley protected by high hills, from the cold winds and foggs of San Francisco." The valley was known as *Canada del Hambre,* or "Hungry Valley." Louisiana detested the name, and she declared it would in future be the "Alhambra Valley," which it has remained.

In their newly-named Alhambra Valley they purchased twenty acres at $50 per acre and set out fruit trees of all kinds. Over the next 37 years their orchards grew both in numbers of trees and in acreage, as they pioneered as horticulturists and even became the first to grow successfully orange trees in northern California.

Their family was struck with tragedy in 1857 when little nine-year-old Johnny died of diphtheria, and all the skill of his doctor father could not save him. Henry, John's brother, continued with them until 1865 when he, too, died, a "kind hearted benevolent man."

Louie, the remaining daughter, was educated at the "Atkins Seminary for Young Ladies" in Benicia and became a lover of art, literature, music, and nature. On April 14, 1880, there was added another John to the family, filling the void of the loss of early years of their only son. It was on that day that Louie was married to the already famous naturalist and writer, John Muir. In his correspondence this young man had only glowing words for the "trinity" of the Strentzel family: mother, father, and daughter. The parents gave the young people the original house they had built long before, and for a period John Muir even ran the ranch for all of them. Financially it did very well, and, at the urging of his new family, John was able to devote all of his time to his first love, pioneering as a new type of naturalist in his beloved western mountains.

The parents grew older, and on Louisiana's 69th birthday, October 31, 1890, Dr. Strentzel died. The writer of our letter, Louisiana, lived on for seven more years, and in the autumn of 1897 she died.

The Strentzel papers are deposited in the Bancroft Library at the University of California, which has been most generous in making them available for our *Covered Wagon*

Women project. Much of the above introduction is based on Dr. Strentzel's "Biography," a typescript of the original written out for Hubert Howe Bancroft by the doctor himself. Louisiana's own letter is also a typescript copied by Mrs. Lizzie Galbraith of Galveston, Texas, August 5, 1912. It is used here with the gracious permission of its present owner, Mrs. L. M. Pettis of Bonham, Texas.

Sources on the life of John Muir are also sources on the Strentzel family: William F. Bade, *Life and Letters of John Muir,* 2 volumes (Boston, 1924); Linnie Marsh Wolfe, Ed., *John of the Mountains: The Unpublished Journals of John Muir* (Boston, 1938); Stephen Russell Fox, *John Muir and His Legacy* (Boston, 1981).

THE LETTER OF LOUISIANA STRENTZEL

California, Mission of San Diego,
December 10th, 1849.

Dear Father and Mother, Brothers and Sisters:

After an absence of eight long months I at last have an opportunity of writing to let you know that we are alive and have reached in safety the borders of the promised land. We have made our way through a wilderness of eighteen hundred miles; underwent many hardships and privations; passed through many dangers and difficulties; crossed garden and desert; landed safely in California and are enjoying very best health at present.

We have not heard one word from home [1] since we

---

[1] "Home" for Louisiana Strentzel was Honey Grove, Fannin County, northwest Texas. After her marriage to Dr. Strentzel, the couple moved to Lamar County, the next one to the west, but her parents to whom she was writing

left and suppose you have heard nothing from us. We wrote several letters on the way but met with no certain chance to send one until after we came to this place   leaving for   on the third inst., and we wrote a brief letter informing you of our arrival here and promising the particulars of our journey by the next vessel.

We have kept a journal of everything of interest that transpired on the way and will give you extracts as we think will be of interest to you. After leaving the upper cross-timbers [2] we had a very good road from there on to the Brazos River, a distance of two hundred and thirty miles from home; fine grass and water all the way. We reached this river an the 22nd of April and forded it without much difficulty. From here we traveled too much west and struck the river again in about sixty miles. While a band of Tonkoway [3] Indians came into camp in daylight and stampeded and drove off seven head of horses. A company of sixty men immediately followed after them and the next day returned with all the horses. We had several false alarms after this but saw no more Indians from here to El Paso.

---

this letter were still in Honey Grove. There is an interesting story about a reunion fifty years later that appeared in the Honey Grove *Signal* for August 25, 1892. Mrs. Strentzel attended, gave a short speech to the gathering, and talked to the *Signal* reporter about her girlhood. The clipping is among the Strentzel papers in the Bancroft Library, Berkeley.

[2] The "Cross Timbers" stretched from the Arkansas Valley to the Brazos River in southern Oklahoma and northern Texas. The "pole" oaks stood far enough apart for wagons to pass through without difficulty in any direction. This was the place where axles, axle-trees, and broken spokes could be replaced. Guide books suggested that travelers take advantage of the oak and black walnut timber to repair wagons. Ralph H. Brown, *Historical Geography of the United States* (New York, 1948), 377.

[3] The Tonkawa Indians were a small nomadic tribe in central Texas. They were later moved to Oklahoma, where 40-50 individuals live today.

From this place on a distance of 200 miles we had a good road and plenty of grass and water.

On the 16th of May we came to a large spring of excellent water and lay by several days to cut wagon tires. While at this place Mr. Sims of Blossome Prairie [4] died of liver disease The morning we left here I was taken very sick with diarhea and severe fever and continued very sick for about two weeks.[5] After recovering from this I have enjoyed excellent health ever since. From this spring the next water was 25 miles and was strong sulphur and salt, so that we would have been better off without it. After leaving this water we struck a level plain and traveled 70 miles without water. The first we found was large pools of pure cold water in a ridge of sand hills. We were three days and nights crossing the plains. The animals gave out so that we had to stop the wagons and send them on about ten miles to the water, and after resting and recruiting them returned for the wagons. A great many of the company believe if we had traveled more south we would have found water plenty, but I don't know, for we sent water hunters many miles in every direc-

---

[4] Mr. Sims, the man who died, was mentioned many years later in a letter published in the *Pacific Rural Press* of San Francisco, Nov. 15, 1890. A letter-to-the-editor published under the headline, "Dr. and Mrs. Strentzel on the Plains," was written soon after the doctor's death. The writer was another member of the Strentzel wagon train, J. L. P. Smith, a resident of Adelaide, San Luis Obispo County. "My messmate, Mr. R. Simms, was in poor health before he started and the doctor treated him all the time until he died on the headwaers of the Colorado of Texas, and if my friend had been a brother of the doctor, he could not have been more kind and attentive to him. . . . I wanted to pay him for his services, but he would not take one cent."

[5] Her medical doctor husband later remembered her malady as "gastric fever" in a manuscript autobiography he wrote out for Hubert Howe Bancroft, (page 4), a typescript of which is now in the Bancroft Library, Berkeley. The manuscript is entitled, "Biography of John Theophil Strentzel."

tion. We remained at this place one week and then went on about 80 miles and came to the Puerco river, a narrow, deep, muddy stream. We made boats of wagon beds and ferried across the loading; pulled the wagons across with ropes and swam the animals. We crossed the river on the 3rd of June. On the 4th we went on and within two miles of the crossing fell into a plain wagon road which had been made by a company of fifty wagons from San Antonio. We now had a firm level road for 60 miles up the river, but the grass and water not good. After leaving the river we had about 80 miles of mountainous country, some places bad – good grasses and fine spring water all the way. While in the mountains we came up with San Antonio company; eight families and one hundred men.[6]

The first water we came to after getting through the mountains was very salt and made the animals all sick to drink it.

The Indian guide who was with the San Antonio company said it was yet 90 miles or better to El Paso, and little or no water and we had better travel in small companies. Some rushed their teams clear through to the Rio Grande; some stopped and dug wells; some went twenty or thirty miles and sent their teams back to the salt springs, and others left their wagons on the way, drove their animals on to water and then returned for the wagons. We and a few others stayed behind waiting for rain, and the same evening we left salt water there fell a tremendous heavy rain so that the road was a flood of water and the branches and ravines all running. The road was level and good, and the way

---

[6] The seemingly excessive number of men characterized the wagon trains to California during the gold rush years.

except one place about three miles through a range of mountains was very rocky and bad; grass was tolerably good. A great many animals died on the way, and a great many so broke down that they were fit for nothing any more.

We traveled slowly, stopping at every good patch of grass, saving our animals as much as possible, and arrived at El Paso the 1st of July. We expected to send letters back from this place but met with no opportunity. Colonel Bryant from Trinity,[7] who returned home, left El Paso the morning before we came in. A great many sent letters home by him.

We remained in El Paso 12 days. The Mexicans were friendly to Americans. We bought peaches, pears, apples, grapes, onions, green corn, green beans, wheat and unbolted flour. There was no bacon to be had and very little beef or mutton, and that very indifferent. Mules and oxen were not to be had. The Indians were constantly making incursions on the inhabitants and driving off their stock. At this place the company divided, some went one way and some another; some left their wagons and went on with pack mules. While we remained here the emigrants were daily coming in but we could get no news later than 17th April. We left El Paso the 13th July and traveled slowly up the river, making camp every few days until the animals were rested enough to go on. We had a fine smooth road and plenty of grass all the way – of the river 80 miles above El Paso we had to take the wagons to pieces

---

[7] This "Colonel Bryant" was Lieutenant Francis T. Bryan of the Topographical Engineers. Bryan was an important figure in opening wagon routes through western Texas in late 1840's and early 1850's. A. B. Bender, "Opening Routes Across West Texas, 1848-1850," *Southwestern Hist. Qtly.*, XXXVII, no. 2 (Oct. 1933), 116-35.

and cross in a little canoe and spliced on each side –
empty kegs. We left the Rio Grande on the 28th July
and traveled about 20 miles and came into Cook's trail
a large plain wagon road. Hundreds of wagons had
already been before us to Guadaloupe Pass, a distance
of 220 miles. We had a beautiful level road with a few
exceptions, fine tender grass and plenty of good water
all the way. The Pass is about 16 miles through and
tremendous bad road. We had to back our wagons
seventy times in going six miles, but we came through
safe without breaking our wagons. From this place to
Santa Cruz is about 112 miles. Here is the range of
wild cattle, hundreds of them were killed by the emigrants. We killed one and barbecued as much as we
could haul. Along here was the best grass we had on
the whole route, a very good road and excellent water.
About ten miles before we came up to Santa Cruz we
had a very bad mountain to cross, but by doubling teams
we went through without much difficulty. Santa Cruz
is a little isolated Mexican village of about 300 inhabitants; unprotected and exposed to the mercy of the
Apache Indians who come in at times and drive off
all their stock; kill and take them prisoners. We bought
of them peaches, apples, quince, pomgranites, tender
green corn, onions and coarse unbolted flour. They had
no meat of any kind to sell. The articles that traded
best with them were calicos and white domestic. From
this place to Tucson is 108 miles of very good road,
good grass and good water. About 50 miles from Santa
Cruz we passed an old deserted village with orchard
hanging full of most delicious peaches and quince.
We laid us in a full supply. Tucson is a Mexican town
of about 500 inhabitants. They had to sell mules, oxen,

cows and calves, sheep, green corn, unbolted flour, cheese, grapes and dried beans. From Tucson to Pimose [Pima] village is 75 miles; beautiful level road all the way but grass and water scarce. About 12 miles from the village we came in sight of the long wished for Gila River. It is narrow at this place, runs swift, the water cool and good tasted. The Pimose are a tribe of friendly Indians settled along the river in villages. They raise fine corn, wheat and melons and supply the emigrants to feed their animals across the desert. The articles most in demand with them were blue blankets, white domestic and hard beans. At this place begins the desert. It is about 200 miles from the last of these villages to the crossing of the Colorado at the mouth of the Gila.

No other water but the river, and very little grass. We bought 12 bushel of corn and wheat, we could haul no more, and left the village the 22nd of September. After leaving the village we had about 45 miles without water or grass and the whole way very sandy. We hauled water in kegs, enough for the animals to drink, and the 2nd day reached the river, but found no grass. The first we came to was 20 miles further on, only a small patch and mighty eaten down by the stock before us. At this place we met a company of Mexicans returning from the gold mines. They gave awful accounts of the road before us, that the way was strewn with dead animals, and that wagons and property of every kind were left on the road all the way through the desert. This news created great alarm amongst all the emigrants. We immediately unpacked our wagons and threw out all heavy articles we could possibly dispense with to lighten the load. From here we traveled about five miles to a large patch of excellent grass. Here we lay by 8 days to recruit the teams. The emigrants all rested and recruited their animals on this grass. At this place we learned from a pack company that Ex President Polk was dead [8] and that the cholera was raging all over the United States. A great many of the emigrants put on mourning.

We found that the only way to get through was to travel slowly in the cool of the day, save the animals as much as possible and stop at every little grass we could find. We soaked corn in water and gave each a small ration every day. From here down to the mouth of the Gila we had alternately dust and sand nearly the whole way and very little grass; some places on the banks of the river little patches of green corn grew. The Gila and Colorado both overflow their whole valleys leaving a light ashy loam when the water recedes. The dust was almost insufferable; it was generally from six to twelve inches deep. It was almost impossible for our wagons to travel nearer than fifty yards to another.

We met caravans of Mexicans almost every day. They all gave bad news and we found their statements to be but too true.

A great many, when their teams began to fail, left their wagons and packed what they could; others left wagons and everything except enough to take them through. Boxes and trunks of clothing were thrown out, chests of costly medicine, chests of carpenters tools – many would throw their things into the river to pre-

---

[8] James K. Polk died on June 15, 1849. This is the one and only political remark made by any of our representative women of the 1840's in their diaries and letters.

vent the Indians and Mexicans from getting them; some sold – iron tools, cases of surgical instruments, cases of watch-makers instruments, chests of valuable books and bed-clothing – them in the sand, and other would dig them up. The most of the wagons were burned, – cooking utensils, cooking stoves, vessels of every description, guns, powder and lead, gold washers, shovels, axes, chains of all kinds, whole sacks of coffee, barrels of lard, bacon and other provisions; blacksmith tools; table-ware of every description; and in fact you can name nothing that was not lost on this road, yet, a great many who had good teams, traveled slowly and managed them with care, came through without much loss. A man came in from Houston, Texas, who threw his patent gold washer in the river; built a fire, burned up his wagon and everything else but enough provisions to bring him through.

The first emigrants reached the Colorado about the middle of August and they have been coming in one continuous line ever since. We arrived at the crossing of the Colorado the 15th October. We had dreaded this river the whole way for we had heard that several Americans had been killed by the Indians, and that it was dangerous crossing, but gratitude to our Government, a company of soldiers were here for the protection of the emigrants. One of the ferrymen told me that upward of two hundred wagons crossed the river during the month of November. Here we found plenty of grass, cane and muskite beans. While we lay by the river waiting to cross Captain Thorn, U. S. dragoon,[9] and three men fell off the boat and were drowned, it was caused by imprudence.

---

[9] This was Captain Herman Thorn, who had distinguished himself in

We crossed the river the 19th, and landed safely on California soil. From the crossing 15 miles down the river – We then left the river and traveled 15 miles to the emigrant wells, the whole way very sandy. Here we found plenty good water and muskite beans but no grass. These beans grow in clusters on the muskite trees. They are termed by the emigrants "bread fruit" because they grow in the desert, they are sweet and when ground make good cole-flour and mush. They are as good food for animals as corn or oats. We rested at the wells three days, gethered as many beans as we could haul, and at four o'clock in the evening filled all our vessels with water and started across the main desert. We now had 37 miles without water or grass, the whole way a heavy bed of sand. We started again at daybreak and traveled slowly, resting the animals at short intervals, and at 12 o'clock stopped and gave each a little water and rested there three hours; then traveled on till dark and encamped for the night and early next morning traveled on again, and about noon arrived at Camp Salvation on the Poca River. Here was a large lake of good water with a brook running off from it and plenty of good grass. Had it not been for this water, the muskite beans and the corn at the Pimose village, not one wagon could have come through. There are various opinions about this water; some think it comes from the Colorado, others that it is rain water accumulated; at any rate General

several battles of the Mexican War. John W. Audubon wrote in his journal on October 17, 1849, " . . . on the road we heard that Captain Thorn had been drowned. . . . So ends the life of an officer of distinction, whose quiet, gentlemanly manner won from me my admiration and good-fellowship during the few hours of intercourse we had enjoyed." Frank Heywood Hodder, Ed., *Audubon's Western Journal, 1849-1850* (Glorietta, N.M., 1969), 161, 165.

Kearney,[10] Captain Cook [11] and others went through without finding it. We remained here several days to rest and recruit our mules; cut hay to do them through the rest of the desert, and on the 30th, left Camp Salvation and traveled 13 miles to the next water, a large lake of excellent water, but no grass. This fifteen miles was fine road. From here to the next water was 25 miles; the way very sandy but not so bad as the previous road. The first we came to was a small creek, the water a little brackish and no grass. Our mules were so tired that we had to rest here one day. From this the next water was 16 miles along the bed of a dry creek and the worst sand of the desert. In going this 16 miles I counted 27 dead animals immediately by the road, besides those that wandered off in search of water and died. We left camp early and traveled about 9 miles, the whole way like pulling up a steep hill. The mules gave out so we encamped and rested until morning, then went on 7 miles and arrived at valley Uta, the end of the desert. Here we found good water and tolerable grass. From this place to Worner's [12] ranch is 35 miles, tolerably good road, plenty of water, but grass rather scarce. We rested at Valley Uta one day, then went on and reached Worner's the

---

10 General Stephen Watts Kearny.

11 Philip St. George Cooke. See Otis E. Young, *The West of Philip St. George Cooke, 1809-1895* (Glendale, California, 1955).

12 Jonathan Trumbull Warner, who went overland to California with Ewing Young in 1834, stayed on in southern California to become one of the earliest American settlers. The Mexicans called him Juan José Warner, and nicknamed him "Juan Largo" ("Long John") because he was six feet, three inches tall. His "Warner's Ranch," near Temecula, became a stopping place for Americans for many years. Kenneth L. Holmes, *Ewing Young, Master Trapper* (Portland, 1967), 92, and Lorrin L. Morrison, *Warner, The Man and the Ranch* (Los Angeles, 1962).

9th November. Here we lay by two weeks. We were advised by Colonel Worner and others to go either to San Diego or Los Angeles and remain over the winter, that on account of the rainy season it would be impossible to travel to San Francisco by land this winter, and that nothing could be done in the mines before spring. We concluded to go to San Diego, arriving here the 29th of November. From Worner's this place is 70 miles, some very bad road but good water and grass. It is a mountainous country, beautiful valleys, some large oak timber though scarce.

We at first thought to sell our wagons and mules and go up to San Francisco by water, but the emigrants had brought so many and sold that now there was no demand for them. There is no chance to get a house in town; every one is taken up and a great many living in tents; provisions scarce and very high; flour is 25 cents per pound and other things in proportion. Emigration to California I believe had no parallel in history. Every place we can hear from is full to overflowing and hundreds still coming in. The most of them go to Los Angeles and Monterey. Hundreds leave their train and come on foot to San Diego and go up by water. Of the country we know nothing as yet only what little we can hear from passengers. We understand there is a great deal of fatal sickness in San Francisco caused by being exposed at the mines.

The climate around San Diego is mild and pleasant and very healthy. As far as I can learn the emigrants have been remarkably healthy on the road and comparatively few deaths. A great many would have suffered for provisions but the Government sent aid to them. We had enough to bring us into the settlement.

We hear no certain account from those who went the Northern paths. The latest news from mines, is, that gold is found in 27 pound lumps, but I expect such pieces are few and far between.

We know not yet whether we shall settle in California or return to Texas, it is altogether owing to how we like the country when we see more of it. The doctor has [not] been sick a day since we left the cross-timbers and looks better than you have ever seen him. I have never enjoyed better health in my life than I have done since last May. Little Pussy [13] and Johny [14] have not been sick an hour since we left Bonham; they both look red and rosey and have grown so they cannot wear a garment that was made for them when we left home. They both rode in a carriage the whole way, never appeared to get tired but was always ready of a morning to start on. Puss would the whole way gather flowers and pretties for her Grand Ma, and still talks about her every day and says when she learns to write she will send her a letter. She can talk right plain now. John is a great big fat fellow, he has been running everywhere since July but cannot talk much. His whole delight is to drive the mules. Every evening when we would stop, the first thing, he would grab the whip, then run about and hollow at every thing in his way.

Well, I think my paper is about filled – or – Remember me to one and all, and may we all meet again is my prayer.   Affectionately,

Louisiana Strentzel.

---

[13] "Little Pussy" was a nickname for the Strentzel's daughter, Louise (Louie) Wanda, aged two years at this time.

[14] "Biography of John Theophil Strentzel," "But the greatest trial of our lives was the death of our only son, a bright promising boy of nine years, who died of diphtheria in Sept. 1857," (page 18).

[Written across other end of page:]

I intended to have gove you in this letter a full history of the way we were treated by Doustin,[15] Eliza, Y. Johnson and the old man Scott, but have not space to tell you, only that they all joined together against us and told everybody on the road that Doustin was well settled at home, had plenty of everything around him and good farm opened, good comfortable homes and plenty of stock and was doing well, that they were unwilling to move, and that the Doctor was going to California on speculation and persuaded them to break up and come for his own benefit; that Doustin had a good wagon and could have brought up and come for his own benefit; himself with everything but that we persuaded them to come with us and leave everything behind; that they had sold nothing, left everything behind standing just so, and that we would not even let them bring their clothing; that Thomas was going to school in Paris and that we persuaded him to quit school and come with us; that he had a good saddle and gun and could have furnished himself provisions and everything but that the Doctor would not let him bring anything; and finally they were only going for our benefit and that the Doctor must pay them for driving his teams. The old man Scott told every body on the road day by day that my sister was going to marry

---

[15] John Strentzel listed in his "Biography" for Bancroft the women of the overland party who showed great courage "in undertaking, against the entreaties and advice of friends, to go with their children on a tiresome journey of more than 2000 miles, over a trackless wilderness, through the midst of hostile Comanches and Apache Indians." One of these ladies in his list was "Mrs. Doustine," (page 3). Evidently this family stayed on in El Paso. There is simply not enough information given in Mrs. Strentzel's document to identify some persons she mentioned.

Charlie Schoot[16] and go with him to California but
the Dr. and Mrs. Strentzel interfered and would not
let her come and she cried to come every day before we
left, and that Charlie had promised to go back for her
next fall but that his mother was so much opposed to
it that she would try to persuade him not to come; that
she was a pretty girl and a smart one, and would have
come with Charlie had it not been for them. These
things were daily told to the company of course people
that did not know better would believe them. It would
fill a column to tell you all, and as soon as I can will
write you everything from first to last. But enough at
present, that we traveled together the sand hills every
day worse and worse; that the horses and mules were
neglected and when Doctor would give directions how
to manage them, the reply would be "you damn rascal
I'll manage the horses as I think proper". Here the
Dr. told Thomas he could take him no further he had
become so insulting, would do nothing and was constantly off gambling. Eliza was sick the whole way,
once we thought she would die. At the sand hills one
of the teams died and at the Puerco river two more
were drowned. We had to leave the wagon. Doustin
took out his things without Doctor telling him and
got Mr. Hackelford [Shackleford][17] to take him to

    16 In his "Pioneer Register," now published in one volume, Hubert Howe
Bancroft listed a Charles Shooter, Company D, New York Volunteers, as
living in San Joaquin County. *California Pioneer Register and Index, 1542-
1848* (Baltimore, 1964), p. 327. The 1850 Federal Census of California
listed Charles Shootur, 25 years old, born in Germany, living in San Joaquin
County. Alan P. Bowman, Comp., *Index to the 1850 Census of the State of
California* (Baltimore, 1972), 422.

    17 "Mr. Shackleford" is mentioned by another member of the wagon train
in a newspaper article in later years as "an old Texan," who was "pilot
in 1849." Letter to the editor by L. L. P. Smith, *op. cit.,* Nov. 15, 1890.

El Paso. Doctor hired another man to haul 230 pounds of bacon and before we got to El Paso (they all went on before and reached town several days before we did) Doustin went to the man who had the bacon, told him the bacon belonged to him; took it out, paid the man for hauling it and sold it to the emigrants at 25 cens a pound; amounting in all to $65.00; 16 fine middlings. With his money he dressed himself and his wife, went into El Paso and there met with an old acquaintance from Santa Fe; told him the old story of how he had left every thing and had no money. The man went and got him a house, assisted in getting him boarders and last we heard from them Eliza had entirely recovered and they were keeping boarding house and taking in from ten to fifteen dollars a day. When Thomas left us he went with Vice   of Paris, [Texas], and the last we heard from him he was in El Paso gambling.

[Written across second page:]

I know not what to say to you about coming, but I do not think that even if the counry should prove to be everything that it had been represented to be or that we anticipated, or even Eden itself, that it would be better for those who are well settled at home and doing well, to await until the storm has calmed and those already here settled or returned back home. From the best information the gold is inexhaustible and people can do as well to come after while as at present, but if you do come I advise you to come by water, it is far less expensive and you can come in half the time that you can by land. I cannot advise any family to come the overland route, but if they should let them

prepare well for the journey and travel in small con-
solidated companies, say about ten wagons and twenty
or twenty-five men, to each family I would say one
light strong carriage for women and children to ride
in (with two mules) and a woman can drive it anywhere; one strong wagon with six mules. If you have
more wagons you must have more teams and help to
manage them and consequently more provisions and
baggage. Put nothing in your wagon except provisions
and clothing and such articles as are indespensibly
[*sic*] necessary on the road. Bring vessels to haul about
fifty gallons of water; india-rubber sacks are the best.
Let each family have about five or six good milk cows
two boys can drive any number. I believe there would
would have been little or no sickness amongst the emigrants if they could have lived on a milk diet. The
most prevalent diseases were diarhea and gastric fever produced by bad water and irregular living. We
brought our own cow clear through. She has been
worth thousands of dollars to us, yes, I may say millions, for she has been the means of preserving the
lives of our children. A great many worked cows to
their wagons clear through and I believe they stood the
trip better than oxen.

You could bring a few good riding horses but they
will not do to work in a wagon. Do not corral your
animals but have good hobbles and keep herders constantly; unwind when you stop.

No company of Indians will attack twenty-five men
well armed and on their guard. There were some few
men killed by Indians but in every instant when they
were alone and without arms.

Each company should have the same kind of teams

so they can travel all alike, let them in no case separate. For this reason you should travel in small companies. You can get along a great deal faster and then there are many places with water and grass for a few animals but not enough for a large drove. Several women rode horse-back all the way but a carriage is best, especially in bad weather.

We have just heard from the emigrants who came the other route and from what we can learn they suffered a great deal more than those who came the Southern route.

The troops have now left the Colorado and the emigrants are still crossing. San Diego is crowded with emigrants awaiting to get passage up but the vessels are so crowded that a great many will have to turn and go by land. Ship arrived yesterday from Panama, she had on board three hundred passengers and could take none from here. She brought New York paper 7th November, containing the Hungarian news,[18] cholera,[19] etc. This is the first news received here since August.

Direct your letters to   and do write every chance.

Louisiana.

[Doctor Strentzel's letter written across front page:] You will find a true description of our journey so

---

[18] Dr. Strentzel was always interested in central European news. On August 13, 1849, the Russian armies crushed the Hungarians, who had been inspired by the patriot, Lajos Kossuth, their leader against the Austrian dynasty. Kossuth was forced to go into exile.

[19] The year, 1849, was notorious for being the time of a major cholera epidemic in the United States. Charles Rosenberg, *The Cholera Years: The United States in 1832 1849, and 1866* (Chicago, 1962).

far, compare our   you will find as much information about the subject as required.

We have concluded to travel on slowly along the
coast to Los Angeles and Monterey, camping at each
rainy spell. By this means we can live cheaper and do
something toward reaching the Eldorado.

Today the 27th, I did read the New York Herald
of the 7th November. Then no mail did come here for
the last four months. It appears that through the United
States an office is a sinecure to the holder, to do the
duty appertaining to it is out of question. Here civil
and military officers are only full of speculation how
to depreciate the value of the little property the emigrants save. They buy mules from five to twenty dollars. I wonder how much Uncle Sam has to pay for
these. Previous to, and when we arrived here, the
quartermaster would issue rations to emigrants at cost;
dry bread and pork, some had to pay, some got grat-
ituitously at different prices, now they refuse it, but
it requires two and three days before you get the
quartermaster's order, and another day or two to get
it from the issuing Sergeant. Consider that all that
time great many had to hunger because there was no
provisions to be had anywhere else and the quartermaster be on a visit and Mr. Sergeant drunk. We buy
now wheat at $6.00 a 2½ bushels; grist it on a coffee
mill and make very tasty pancakes by greasing the pan
with tallow. We have plenty of rabbits, quail, ground
squirrels and some ducks, and eat as hearty meals as
ever. We remember you at our Christmas dinner and
had as good as the country afforded.

In closed is a note for $14.00 on Ligon which I did
forget to leave for collection. Be particular about re-
peating business news.

Do not forget to pay our taxes. To Mr. Augustus my special compliments, and I hope he did collect on the notes. If you have any funds grease a little to obtain the patent for the 320 acres on South Sulphur of Mr. Keys certificate, etc., etc., etc.

You address to Monterey. Now for 1850, a jubilee year. May it to you my friends be a year of jubilee; be happy, improve your home, let it be a "Sweet home" and if you have enemies persuade them for a land journey to California.

The Lord bless and protect you.

Yours sincerely,
Wm. [not certain about signature.]

[At the bottom of third page and written across it:]

Colonel Jack Hayse [20] of Texas is expected here today. He had just landed through the desert and encamped at a ranch 12 miles back.

Our mules have recruited finely on the green tender grass; the weather is warm and pleasant like spring, and the road up the coast reported to be good. We shall start on in a few days. Will write every opportunity.

---

[20] Colonel John Coffee Hays had come to Texas as early as 1836 and become a dynamic leader of the Texas Rangers. Ralph P. Bieber, Ed., *Exploring Southwestern Trails, 1846-1854,* Vol. VII of *Southwest Historical Series* (Glendale, California, 1938), 258; also Maybelle Eppard Marten, "California Emigrant Roads Through Texas," *Southwestern Hist. Qtly.,* XXVIII, no. 4, (April 1925), 287-301.

Running a Boarding House in the Mines

INTRODUCTION

This volume has been filled with the primary written records of mainstream American women telling of an extraordinary experience. The records are personal, so much so that it is easy to imagine that any one of the women who wrote them would have been aghast to see how they are now being made so public — for every one to read — down to the minutest details. These were anonymous persons who will never again be anonymous. Alongside them traveled thousands who retained their anonymity. Such a one is the writer of the following short letter which appeared in an eastern newspaper not long after it was written.

It was published in the *California Historical Quarterly* of December, 1945, as an "Anonymous Letter from a Woman in the California Mining Country," and with that publication's permission, it is reprinted here.

———

We have now been keeping house three weeks. I have ten boarders, two of which we board for the rent. We have one hundred and eighty-nine dollars per week for the whole. We think we can make seventy-five of it clear of all expenses, but I assure you I have to work mighty hard – I have to do all my cooking by a very small fire place, no oven, bake all my pies and bread in a dutch oven, have one small room about 14 feet square, and a little back room we use for a store room about as large as a piece of chalk. Then we have an open chamber over the whole, divided off by cloth. The gentlemen occupy the one

end, Mrs. H – – – and daughter, your father and myself, the other. We have a curtain hung between our
beds, but we do not take pains to draw it, as it is no
use to be particular here.

The gentleman of whom we hire the house has been
at housekeeping; he loaned us some few things [for
furniture], but I assure you we do not go into luxuries.
We sleep on a cot without any bedding or pillow except
our extra clothing under our heads.

Tell Betty they have to pay twenty-five dollars for
making a dress. If there was anything pleasant here
I should like to have you all come immediately. But
there has been no rain for three months, nor won't be
for so long to come; not a green thing to be seen except
a few stunted trees, and so cold we have to keep a fire
to be comfortable. When you are eating corn and beans
think of your poor mother, who does not get any fruit
or vegetables excepting potatoes, and those eight dollars a bushel, and as soon as we are worth ten thousand
I shall come home, if I do not find some pleasanter
place than this. . . Mrs. H – – – took some ironing to do,
and what time I had I helped, and made seven dollars
in as many hours. I have not been in the street since
I began to keep house; I don't care to go into a house
until I get ready to go home; not that I am homesick,
but it is nothing but gold, gold – no social feelings –
and I want to get my part and go where my eyes can
rest upon some green things.

A Boarding House Keeper, formerly of
Portland, Maine, to her children
Portland *Advertizer,* quoted by Missouri
Republican, Oct. 6, 1849 [1]

---

[1] *California Hist. Qtly.,* "California Emigrant Letters," XXIV, No. 4,
Dec., 1945, p. 347.

Index